Christian Democracy

in

Italy and France

by
Mario Einaudi
and
François Goguel

Archon Books   1969

SBN: 208 00801 2
Library of Congress Catalog Card Number: 69-19224
Printed in the United States of America

PREFACE

Christian Democracy represents the most important concrete expression of Europe's effort to direct its postwar political life towards democracy and constitutionalism. As the strongest antagonist of Communism, Christian Democracy has in general been the pivot of government coalitions around which weaker Socialist, Radical Socialist, Liberal and Conservative groups have intermittently rallied. For developments since 1945, Christian Democracy must therefore take a large part of the credit or, conversely, assume a large part of the blame.

Nowhere has the significance of Christian Democracy, after the end of World War II, been greater than in France and in Italy. In France, the Mouvement Républicain Populaire moved suddenly to the forefront of political life, in a development that was as dramatic as it was novel, and sought to give to French governments that idealism and originality of program with which France was eager to herald the rebirth of democracy.

In postwar Italy which immediately had the singular good fortune (not shared by Germany) of being united politically and wholly self governing, Christian Democracy was reborn upon the earlier foundations of Luigi Sturzo's Popular Party. In its new form the Party has been thrust into a position of even greater responsibility and, since 1948, had had a practical monopoly of power.

Christian Democracy is therefore the best standard to use in measuring the hopes, the successes and the failures of those forces which in Europe have been trying to set up an alternative to Communism other than that of a dictatorship of the right. Furthermore, a study of Christian Democracy, as one of the basic political currents of the contemporary world, appears particularly desirable in the case of France and Italy since there it has developed in a predominantly Catholic climate as well as in direct competition with the two strongest Communist parties of Western society.[1]

---

[1] This volume is part of the "French-Italian Inquiry" started at Cornell University in 1949 with the support of the Rockefeller Foundation. A previous volume of the Inquiry is *Communism in Western Europe* by Mario Einaudi, Jean-Marie Domenach and Aldo Garosci (Cornell University Press,

This volume is divided into two parts, in the first of which the Italian Christian Democratic party is studied by the writer of this Preface. The historical origins, ideal program, concrete achievements, use of power and future outlook are reviewed, while some general considerations are added on the nature of Christian Democracy and on the problems posed by a party bearing this name.

The second part, on the M.R. P., is written by François Goguel. Those familiar with his previous work will recognize in these pages the same objective care and keen power of analysis that have made Goguel's name foremost among the younger generation of French political scientists.

I wish to thank the Committee on International Relations for its interest in the publication of this volume and for the opportunity given me to lecture in 1950 at the University of Notre Dame on some of the problems discussed here. My thanks are also due to the Editors of the *Review of Politics* for permission to use some excerpts from articles published in 1947 and 1948.

I am grateful to Eleanor Tananbaum for permission to include in this volume the bibliography which is part of her Cornell University doctoral dissertation on "Christian Democracy in Italy." For invaluable editorial assistance I am also much indebted to Ina Loewenberg, and to Roy Pierce of Smith College.

Mario Einaudi

Cornell University
December, 1951

1951), pp. ix-239. In its Foreword, I described the significance of the area covered by the Inquiry: "First of all, some of the more far-reaching political ideologies of today, such as Communism and Christian Democracy, have developed there in an especially characteristic way, at the same time that new constitutional experiments and wide structural economic reforms have been undertaken.

"Secondly, the parallel lines of many of the ideological and political developments of France and Italy offer an interesting opportunity, from a methodological point of view, to follow ideas and problems across national lines.

"Finally, the one hundred million inhabitants of the two countries occupy a decisive position in determining the relationship of Europe to the United States and to the Soviet Union. A clarification of the nature of their domestic problems is useful both in formulating American policies and in understanding the essence of the struggle against the Soviet conquest of the continent."

TABLE OF CONTENTS

Part II

Christian Democracy in France
by
François Goguel

Part I

CHRISTIAN DEMOCRACY IN ITALY

by Mario Einaudi

Chapter One

JUSTIFICATION AND ORIGINS OF ITALIAN CHRISTIAN DEMOCRACY

The decisive historical crisis which explains and justifies the growth of Christian Democracy is the conflict between Church and State. In countries which have been spared that conflict, no Christian Democratic movement as such has arisen, even though it is common for individuals and groups to entertain ideals of a democracy influenced by the principles of Christianity. As a rule, the governing classes of Great Britain and of the United States have always considered it desirable and proper to underline the need of divine guidance in human affairs. But no Christian Democratic party has ever developed, or is ever likely to develop, in Great Britain or in the United States.

The necessary prerequisite, then, of Christian Democracy as a positive organized political movement is the existence of a conflict between Church and State or between the religious and political spheres, as well as of a sentiment in the community that the time is at hand to overcome that conflict and to restore to the political sphere criteria of action and values that had been discarded because of the conflict.

The development of Christian Democracy in Italy and in France stems from the common historical root of the clash between the temporal and the spiritual world, brought about chiefly by the century of Enlightenment and by the French Revolution. While the influence of rationalism, of individualism, of political societies freed from the protective hand of ecclesiastical authorities, spread beyond the boundaries of Western Continental Europe, Italy and France had to face peculiar problems because in those two countries the Catholic Church survived as the dominant and almost exclusive religious organization, as well as a political power about which the State could legitimately express some concern.

1

I. *Church and State*

Historically, the conflict between Church and State in France and in Italy developed along essentially parallel lines, from the time when the Catholic Church began to be viewed as an institution which usurped powers properly belonging to lay political authorities. France after 1789 and Italy after 1848 approved legislative measures which, to an ever increasing degree, were designed to contain the power of the Church within narrowly defined religious limits. This meant taking away from the jurisdiction of the Church areas of social control, chief among them education, which the Church had always considered primary for the fulfillment of its mission.

Generally speaking, for most of the century which preceded the outbreak of World War I, political power was in the hands of a ruling class not only anxious to preserve the full autonomy of the State against the Church, but also convinced that only through the application of a rationalist and positivist philosophy to the problems of government could democracy and progress be secured. Accepted as part of the permanent order of political life was a duty to rule out any but pragmatic considerations from the realm of politics and a duty to organize a monopolistic state system of education which would firmly cut off the young generations from any sort of moral or religious inspiration. All political currents, liberal, radical, socialist, republican, democratic, were at one in attempting to safeguard the political community from any return of the Church's influence, an influence identified with principles which man, in his efforts to achieve scientific progress and untrammelled individual freedom, was bound to reject.

In France and Italy the relentless assertion of the lay spirit carried with it not only the building up of the strength and influence of the State but also an attitude of unfriendliness towards the Church whose social functions the state was taking over. It was not difficult for the average politician to justify this attitude since the Church, in reaction against attacks upon herself, was becoming extremely hostile to the liberalism and democracy which she viewed as responsible for her weakened position. A good many decades before Marxian socialism appeared to complicate the terms of the

2

conflict, the Church and liberalism were engaged in a struggle which has continued to this day.[1]

A paradoxical result of the conflict was that it did not even lead to the practice of separation of Church and State, unless we consider the refusal of public men to attend religious ceremonies as the substance of Separation. Unlike the President of the United States who feels that he can safely go to church on Sunday without imperiling the prevailing American principle of separation between Church and State, the average Italian or French politician traditionally would go to any length to avoid being seen in the vicinity of a religious building, convinced as he was that only by sustained and continuous denunciation of the Church could the political independence of the State be maintained. But this did not signify, especially in Italy, a neutral and hands-off policy towards the Church, for the State retained control over the whole machinery of ecclesiastical life through a complex network of laws, many of them indeed made necessary by the intricate web of ancient relationships.

Therefore, while in the United States a complete separation of State and Church at the organizational level has led to a higher reconciliation and solidarity of the ideals of the political and of the prevalent religious communities, in France and Italy the deep split of ideals between the two communities has been accompanied by their inextricable entanglement at the level of material interests.

As the Church reacted against the strange new surroundings of the nineteenth century world, she continued practices of political

---

[1] As the most careful and impartial historian of relations between Church and State in Italy, D. A. Binchy, observes, "The official attitude towards the Church at the peak of the *dissidio* was beyond all doubt unfriendly. A petty secularism dictated most of the government's policy: in the State schools, where teaching of religion was obstructed, in the public hospitals, from which Sisters of Charity were expelled, in the administration of public charitable trusts (*Opere pie*), in which clerics were no longer represented, although most of the funds were vested in religious societies. Further, the extreme anti-clericals were allowed to attack the Church and the Christian faith not merely in speech and writing but also in action: violent interference with processions and blasphemous parodies on Catholic ritual took place in Rome itself, although the police usually dispersed the more provocative displays." Binchy, *Church and State in Fascist Italy* (Oxford, 1941), pp. 45-46.

3

administration which were incompatible with the climate of the times. This was especially true in Italy, where until well past the middle of the last century the Church controlled vast territorial domains cutting through the heart of the peninsula from the Tyrrhenian to the Adriatic Sea. Hence, an anti-Catholic and anti-Church program proved very profitable to past generations of Italian politicians of all colors, as they could exploit the repressive and unenlightened politics of the Church. Today the highest percentage of Communists is to be found not in the industrial cities of the North, but in the territories joining Rome to the lower Po valley where the Popes governed until the unification of Italy. To a notable extent Communism in these areas represents the historical defense of revolution against ecclesiastical control.

But it is scarcely necessary to add that, as the modern Italian lay State developed, the defenders of the old order, in which the voice of the Church was heard as that of the supreme moral arbiter in all matters affecting the political community, did not altogether disappear. Many had remained faithful to the Church and to her political ideals. On them the Church continued to exert an influence which retarded the growth of a normal political life in the newly formed state, since she supported isolated groups not sharing in the political processes of the majority. This isolation of the faithful was deliberately fostered by the Church beginning in 1867 when the Holy See declared it to be "inexpedient" (*non expedit*) for Catholics to vote in Parliamentary elections. In 1895 Leo XIII, imagining that the new Italian State would collapse were all Catholics to refuse to participate in political life, transformed the *non expedit* into a compulsory prohibition (*non expedit prohibitionem importat*). The Italian State was to be considered as a usurper, as it had seized the temporal domains of the Popes, and its ultimate disintegration was to be brought about in part by the non-cooperation of the believers.

The practical importance of the Vatican prohibition should not be overestimated. The natural skepticism of the Italian people, their tendency to disregard directives of any kind, the sense of remoteness and detachment and often of defiance with which, especially in Southern Italy, the priest is looked upon, contributed to mitigate the consequences of the orders of the Church. As the

4

twentieth century began, Catholics resumed their political activities in increasing numbers and the Church introduced numerous practical exceptions to her ruling. But as long as the ecclesiastical prohibition survived on paper, it created a serious moral conflict in the more sensitive and more politically conscious Catholics torn between their duty to the Church and their duty to the political community. Progressive and democratic Catholics increasingly felt the need of participating fully in political life and of contributing to the revision of the Church's position concerning social and economic problems. But in their efforts they were baffled and hampered by an ecclesiastical stand which was rapidly becoming more anachronistic with every passing year. Nor was this all. Inevitably these Catholic votes, supposedly ready to be thrown into the political battle upon a signal from the Vatican, became in the eyes of the more astute Italian politicians a maneuverable mass which conceivably could be bought if the appropriate advances were made in the right quarters. The "Gentiloni Pact" for which Giolitti was responsible shortly before the outbreak of World War I was a good example of the consequences of the Church veto against Catholic participation in elections. Political events were forcing Catholics to take a hand in politics, but this was done by resorting behind the scenes to underhand deals in which all identity was lost as well as the chance to have the Catholic program accepted to any substantial extent.

II. Socialism and War

The growth of socialism and the outbreak of World War I broke the shell within which Christian Democracy was kept.

Ever since the publication of *Rerum novarum* in 1891 it had been clear that the Popes were aware of a new danger on the left. Conceivably Leo XIII may even have felt that the old bogey, the liberal bourgeois State, had lost some of its terror, as it was not making any impression at all on the vast masses of the working industrial class and as that class was getting ready to accept the materialistic creed of Marxism. With two enemies to conquer, individualism on the right and socialism on the left, the Church must have felt that a Christian Democratic movement, politically

5

active, could achieve much for the defense of its ultimate interests and could take over the fulfillment of those social obligations which the Church was no longer in a position to carry out but which had nevertheless to be carried out if the fabric of society, as the Church conceived it, was not to wither away. One of the first important statements of doctrine by the fledgling Christian Democrats, made in 1894 by Giuseppe Toniolo who was one of the leading Christian Democratic thinkers in Italy before World War I, bore the title of "Program of the Catholics Confronted by Socialism." [2]

But in its antiSocialist position, early Christian Democratic thought, as represented by Toniolo, never went beyond a concept of democracy ill suited to an industrial and rapidly changing era and never provided for the necessary division of jurisdiction between the political and the religious spheres. It is particularly interesting to see these points underlined and criticized by the present leader of Italian Christian Democracy, Alcide de Gasperi, in his 1949 preface to one of the volumes of Toniolo's complete works:

> [Toniolo's position] on the one hand failed to make clear the distinction between the spheres of action of the State and of the Church and to measure adequately the transformation of the modern State to which ever new economic and social functions are given. On the other hand it expanded the jurisdiction of the Church, as if it could undertake direct responsibilities in the political and social field. I am far from saying that Toniolo as a thinker is unclear or in error, but as organizer and in trying to maintain a united Catholic front with regard to social reform he was brought to define democracy in a vague manner neglecting that political character which by now democracy had assumed. Indeed, in trying to oppose to the future socialist state a Christian ideal, he overestimated, as part of the future democracy, the basic elements of the communal and corporative democracy of the Middle Ages. These were splendid and vital elements, but they represented the bright side of an epoch; the shadows of which had not been brought into sufficient relief. . . . It must also be added that in general his political and social thinking does not appear in his writings sufficiently related to the economic conditions of the society to

---

[2] "Programma dei cattolici di fronte al socialismo," reprinted in Giuseppe Toniolo, *Democrazia Cristiana, Concetti e indirizzi* (Città del Vaticano, 1949), Vol. I, pp. 3-14.

which it is to apply. . . . [But] at the end of the nineteenth century Marxism still asserted itself in Italy as an integral philosophical conception. Marx's dialectical materialism, built upon Hegel's dialectical idealism but substantially deriving from the total materialism of Feuerbach and therefore from a violent attack against Christianity, required an equally complete and total reply: such was the Catholic integralism of Giuseppe Toniolo.[3]

Toniolo's positions were not sufficiently flexible and modern to inspire an effective democratic movement.[4] The attempts made by Murri after the turn of the century to go beyond Toniolo did not achieve any significant advance. By then the new Pope, Pius X, had taken a position clearly opposed to any large-scale democratic movement of Christian inspiration in the political field. The crisis of the first World War was needed to bring to a head the liberation of political forces that until then had either expressed themselves unsatisfactorily or had been repressed.

Italy's successful participation in World War I and her increased strength in international affairs convinced the Vatican that the end of Italy as a nation was only a remote possibility. Within a month of Italy's entry into the war, the Vatican Secretary of State, Car-

---

[3] Toniolo, *op. cit.*, Vol. I, pp. ix-xi. It should be noted that this edition of Toniolo's complete works is being published in Vatican City. This adds to the interest of de Gasperi's polemics against the shadows of the Middle Ages, against the lack of a boundary line between State and Church and against a Catholic "integralism" which fails to take into account modern political conditions.

[4] One of the few to call Toniolo's thought democratic is Louis Terrenoire. He writes, "The ideas of the great Italian Toniolo are more democratic, more 'Christian democratic,' than those of La Tour du Pin. Profoundly attached to the cause of the working classes, he proposes at the same time as the reform of labour contract and the development of social legislation, the constitution of professional unions which shall resume the tradition of the ancient corporations. He counts on these unions to prevent and mitigate offences against liberty, right, and public order. He admits the principle of the compulsory syndicate and proposes as the basis of society, 'social organisms disciplined in a corporative regime which holds a balance between all classes without confounding them'." "Corporatism and Democracy," in *For Democracy*, edited by the *People and Freedom* group (London, 1939), p. 189. Terrenoire, for many years one of the leaders of the M.R.P., is now, of course, one of the leaders of de Gaulle's R.P.F.

dinal Gasparri, said, "The Holy See, as befits its neutrality, has no intention whatsoever of embarrassing the government; it puts its trust in God and awaits a proper readjustment of its situation, not from foreign arms, but rather from the triumph of those sentiments of justice which, it hopes, are steadily gaining ground among the Italian people." Later the Pope himself spoke encouragingly of Italy's war effort.

Above all, the war brought about an acceleration of the tempo of political life. It was clear that great changes were about to take place, that the war had given an impetus to Socialism and to movements of reform. It was impossible to maintain for long the fiction that Catholics should be cut off from the political life of a nation going through a period of serious political crisis. Thus it happened that when Luigi Sturzo, the founder of the future Popular Party, the first Christian Democratic party in Italy, asked Cardinal Gasparri a few weeks after the end of the war whether the Vatican was ready to lift the ancient official prohibition against Catholic participation in political life, an affirmative answer was promptly given.

With this formal obstacle eliminated, Christian Democracy did enter the Italian political stage early in 1919. Catholics were free to organize themselves and to prepare for the forthcoming parliamentary elections. It was a dramatic entry, for, starting from nothing, the Popular Party achieved within a few months the position of the second strongest Italian political party.

III. *Luigi Sturzo and the Popular Party*

From a long range point of view, the development of Christian Democracy as a political force was justified as a reaction against the more extreme policies of anti-clericalism and of laicism of the Italian ruling classes. Since their position was one in favor of a utilitarian positivism which denied moral values, and one of reduction of politics to the pragmatic satisfaction of conflicting individual material interests, there was room for a movement claiming to operate on the different premises of the essential relationship between politics and morality and of the permanent values of Christian ethics and of group life. Thus Christian Democracy appeared as a useful challenge to the routine approach and routine solutions of the old governing class, which was quite confident that it could face the revolutionary conditions of the postwar world with the ancient battle cries of laicism and individualism.

On the other hand, and again from a long range historical point of view, Christian Democracy represented a challenge to the control over the industrial and peasant classes exercised by the Marxian Socialists in increasingly monopolistic fashion since the beginning of the century. Against the notions of class war and violent revolution, of materialism and of total collectivism, for which the Socialists stood, Christian Democracy stood for the integration of classes, the method of freedom, the introduction of spiritual values, and a compromise between the rights of the individual and his duties to the community.

If the advent of Christian Democracy in 1919 produced a welcome change in the political atmosphere of the country, it antagonized a number of vested interests and it created what proved to be the insoluble problem of how to fit the new force into the existing framework. The old liberal ruling classes claimed, in effect, a monopoly of political power for themselves. In order to defend their monopoly they were often ready to concede the monopolistic claims of others in other spheres — to the capitalists, their right to restrictive cartels and tariff protection, and to the Socialists, their monopolistic right over trade unions and the life of labor. Since all political plums had been distributed, to the State a monopoly in education, to the Socialist a monopoly of syndicalism, to the industrialists a monopoly of decision on everything affecting the economic welfare of the people, the Popular Party appeared as an intruder and as upsetting the apple cart of monopolies. In wanting freedom of education, freedom of syndicalist organization, and economic freedom in the name of the interests of the community, the Popular Party was threatening the positions of nearly everybody. The newcomer was, therefore, rather poorly received.

The complexity of the issues raised by the advent of the Popular Party can be made clear by an analysis first of its leadership and of the quality of its democratic doctrine, and secondly of its relationships to the Church, to Socialism, and to the liberal democratic groups.

9

The contrast between the Christian Democracy which had been envisioned by Toniolo and the Popular Party which don Sturzo threw into battle in 1919, can be measured by looking at the traits of the founder and spokesman of Christian Democracy from 1919 until 1924, Sturzo himself. Sturzo brought to his task an exceptionally modern outlook, a wealth of information, and an awareness of the country's specific economic and social needs. Far from wanting the Popular Party to restore the legendary beauties of past centuries, he wanted it to face the problems of the present and of the future, and to contend with a school of socialism trying to reduce all ideals to a material level, and with a school of liberalism denying its own reason for existence by defending an illiberal conception of state power. Sturzo was a pluralist and believed in trying new economic and political techniques. He felt convinced that the liberal classes responsible for Italy's emergence as a national State were no longer capable of assuring by themselves the management of the State in the interests of the entire community. The workers had been "alienated" and they had to be readmitted under an aegis that would not be that of totalitarian socialism alone.[5]

Sturzo saw these problems through the eyes of the skilled administrator that he was, for his clear vision of the future was married to an extraordinary flair for the concrete. To be effective the modern state must be efficient at the administrative level. No political party can succeed if it fails to preoccupy itself with the real problems of the common management of public affairs. If the political class does not develop administrative skills or fails to understand the administrative process there will then develop an irresponsible administrative class over which the political class will have no control.

---

[5] "The central and characteristic theme of Christian Democratic culture is that of Sturzo's thought. Sturzo is the Messiah of reform. The reform movement of his time had a parasitic and utilitarian keynote and Sturzo had to deal with the concrete degeneration of political customs and of morality. He is the Messiah of reform because he seeks to prevent the catastrophe of atomism which is the inevitable result of socialist policies. Accepting Cavour's formula, he works with naive faith to make the people believe in the necessity of moral requirements for political life." Piero Gobetti, *Dal Bolscevismo al Fascismo* (Turin, 1923), quoted in Nino Valeri's anthology, *La lotta politica in Italia* (Florence, 1945), p. 531.

Sturzo's Christian Democracy was then in substance a modern liberalism, that is, it represented a belief in the essential worth of the human person to which was added a deep sense of community and group values and of the need for mastering the techniques of management of that community. In the summer of 1949 when, after twenty-three years of exile, Sturzo had been back in Italy for three years, one of his closest friends, shocked by the "liberal" color of some of Sturzo's recent articles, told him: "You have come back from the United States with liberal ideas." And the editor of a Milan Catholic newspaper publicly asked Sturzo to reveal "how and when he had become a liberal." In an article which appeared in a number of Italian newspapers on September 14, 1949,[6] Sturzo provided his own answer to these queries.

This is what he said. His own brand of liberalism was fifty years old and this was its substance. Beginning in 1899 he had fought the battle of local self-government and freedom, both as a Sicilian and as a regionalist, in the name of the liberation of local energies from the all-pervasive rule of the central government. The political education of the people at the local level was to be undertaken in the name of ancient municipal rights. Beginning even earlier, in 1894, he had fought the battle of free schools. In asking for private schools rights equal to those enjoyed by government schools he had taken a position against classical liberalism which understood scholastic freedom both in the sense of government monopoly and in the sense of a fundamentally anti-religious education. Beginning in 1901 he fought the battle of trade union freedom and of the public recognition of trade unionism at a time when classical liberalism was opposed to any government recognition of workers' associations. He continued the battle for the equal recognition of all trade unions and against the myth of working class unity twenty years later when the Liberal government, in order to harass and diminish the Popular Party, had recognized a Socialist monopoly on trade unions.

As for his political liberalism, Sturzo said that since 1899 he had accepted a Christian Democratic program which made the

---

[6] See, for instance, *Sicilia del Popolo,* 14 September 1949, "Il 'mio' Liberalismo."

11

guarantee of all political freedoms a basic point. In 1905 he had spoken for a party of Catholics but against a Catholic party with a confessional substance. In 1910 he had come out in favor of Rome as the capital city of the Italian state. In 1913 he had condemned the "Gentiloni Pact" whereby conservative Catholics had sold their votes for purely personal political gains.

This then was Sturzo's liberalism. It looked like a continuous and coherent body of doctrine and showed a member in good standing of the Catholic priesthood as a fighter for freedom, individual and social, and as a defender of a progressive outlook on the more complex economic issues of modern times. It indicated, moreover, that the years of exile in the United States had merely strengthened an already well-formed and thought-out body of doctrine.

Luigi Sturzo was indeed a priest. This was not the last of the paradoxes and problems presented by the Popular Party, for it revealed a member of the ecclesiastical hierarchy leading a party that pretended to be not only modern in its political democracy and economic outlook but also insisted on full independence from the religious structure of which its leader was an integral part.

The problem of the relationship of Christian Democracy to the Church is a basic one. Politically, the question is not: Can, in principle, a Christian Democratic party be founded which at all times will be free of Church control? It rather is: Have there been times when a Christian Democratic party has been free of Church control?

The second question can be answered in the affirmative. From 1919 to 1924 the Italian Popular Party was an independent movement free of Church control. When in 1924 the Church moved against the Party, it expressed its hostility towards a Party that was in effect, already dead as a result of the establishment of the totalitarian dictatorship of Fascism.

The Popular Party was started as an independent Party because Sturzo and his supporters wanted it that way. In March 1919, Sturzo said, "The Popular Party is born as a non-Catholic Party, an aconfessional Party, as a strongly democratic Party inspired by Christian idealism but which does not take religion as an element of political differentiation." Elsewhere he had said, "Our Party is a Party of national integration. It cannot and it will not take religion as its flag." Sturzo refused to have the Roman question, for so long the traditional battle cry of Catholics, even mentioned in the Party program. In defending this policy of complete separation between the Party and the Church, Sturzo was bound to displease those who, on the other hand, dreamed of a new alliance between altar and throne. But as long as he was at the head of the party the policy of independence was steadfastly maintained.[7]

IV. *The Popular Party and the Crisis of the Italian political system*

The Italian historian Guglielmo Ferrero said in 1919 that the appearance of the Popular Party had produced the effect of a bolt of lightning upon the Italian bourgeoisie. This is an accurate statement and one which can easily be verified by a glance at the election returns since 1900.

---

[7] Professor Jemolo has some difficulty in accepting this viewpoint: "The Popular Party has claimed to be an aconfessional Party . . . aconfessional because it did not have ecclesiastical assistance in its local Party offices, it was not part of the diocesan organization, the bishops did not have a right to issue directives to the Party, and the Holy See had stated that the Party did not represent or bind it. . . . But, in effect, I believe that everywhere and certainly in Italy one must understand in a very special sense the aconfessionality of a Party which, by putting forth, above all, the defense of Christian values and by acting, above all, for their fulfillment, requires the acceptance of those values for those sincere Catholics who have put them among their highest goals; of a Party which at election time must rely on the support of the bishops. . . . Aconfessional Party: but a conflict between local party leaders and the local bishop is unthinkable. . . . A Party independent of ecclesiastical authority, insofar as this authority shows a lack of interest in many of its activities . . . ; but the Popular Party, or any Catholic party, then or later, could never fight the [Vatican] Department of State on any matter, should the latter impose the acceptance of a directive. . . . A Catholic organization to fight the Pope has been for at least one century a contradiction in terms which cannot be realized." *Chiesa e Stato in Italia negli ultimi cento anni* (Turin. 1948), pp. 577-578.

13

CHRISTIAN DEMOCRACY IN ITALY

ELECTION TO THE ITALIAN CHAMBER OF DEPUTIES
(Percentages of votes cast)

Groups or parties	1900	1904	1913	1919
Conservative, liberal and democratic groups	73.7	65.5	61.0	36.0
Radical and republican parties	13.3	13.0	15.2	9.0
Socialist Party	13.0	21.5	22.8	34.5
Popular Party	....	....	....	20.5

The startling development of the 1919 elections was that the old groups of the conservative-liberal right lost the majority to which they had been accustomed for so long. They and their traditional constitutional opponents, the radicals and the republicans, found themselves reduced to the extremity of having to join forces with either the Popular Party or the Socialist Party if a government was to be formed at all. For the first time in the history of modern Italy the leaders of the old groups could only obtain a parliamentary majority by dealing with one of two strongly organized parties with specific and separate programs of their own. Since the Socialists were for the moment determined to remain in the opposition, only the Popular Party was left. To complicate matters further, the Popular Party was not a peasant party coming from the "illiterate" and undeveloped South, one, therefore, to be manipulated at will. The Party's greatest strength was in the North, and especially in the industrial cities, and was the result of the long work of schools, of study clubs, of workers' associations, of the activities, in brief, of some of the more "politically conscious" sections of the electorate.

A policy agreement rather than an old fashioned deal among politicians, had become necessary, for the new Popular Party was quite in earnest about the need of educational, political, administrative reforms, which would everywhere affect the existing structure of Italian society.

Proportional representation has been given a share of responsibility for the crisis of 1919-1922, as though Christian Democracy might have been repressed with a different electoral system. This seems to be a fallacious and anti-historical view, for it is not legiti-

14

mate to assume that the political upheaval represented by the appearance of Christian Democracy could have been avoided by manipulating the electoral machinery. The Popular Party was not a splinter party or a movement which could assert itself only gradually and with great difficulty. Once the necessary conditions were present, the movement could count on the support of a large fraction of the Italian electorate, regardless of the type of electoral law in existence.

This development came as a painful surprise to the traditional circles, since their historical hold on Italian political life was thus brought to an end. That objectively it should be viewed as a satisfactory development in establishing a healthier basis and balance of forces in party life is equally certain. The tragedy of the times, from the point of view of the survival of parliamentary institutions, was the inability of the old and of the new to understand each other. The old viewed the new as an intruder tainted with clericalism; the new dealt with the old with the excessive brashness and self-confidence of a young and victorious movement.

But the position of the Popular Party has to be defined also in relation to the other strongly organized party on the left. In 1919 the Socialist Party, with nearly 35 percent of the votes, emerged as the strongest single party. Socialism had achieved a steady growth before the war, but one which had not been significantly influenced by the introduction of universal suffrage. The greatest boost to Socialism was given by the postwar crisis rather than by the universal ballot. In 1919 the choice before Socialism was either to attempt to carry out a program of gradual social reform by agreeing to work within the existing institutional framework, or to give a free rein to revolutionary policies inspired by the success of the Bolsheviks in Russia and in so doing to continue to refuse to play its role within the parliamentary system. Socialism refused to accept its constitutional responsibilities and failed to make a success of revolution. When it tried to man the barricades in 1920, it discovered that its leadership was more at home in the cafés and in the parliamentary halls than on the firing line. It also found out that the few competent revolutionists to whom Socialism had hitherto given shelter, were ready to leave the party and assault it from a Communist redoubt to be created at the direction of Moscow.

Socialism was driven to its untenable revolutionary position when in August and September 1920 it supported the forcible seizure of all large northern industrial factories. In the previous months it had rejected the possibility of an agreement suggested by other constitutional parties. Now, having failed in its revolutionary attempt, it was subjected to a cross fire coming from both the left and the right: from the Communists, who now were getting ready to organize an independent party and who were criticizing Socialism for its failure; from the right, as the Fascists immediately sought to exploit the Socialist defeat. The chance for the peaceful affirmation of a democratic socialism, which had existed for a few fleeting months at the end of 1919 and at the beginning of 1920, had gone. With it, the fall of both Italian Socialism and of Italian free institutions was made inevitable.

After the elections of 1919, the survival of parliamentary democracy depended upon the realization of either of two main possibilities. The first was an effective coalition between the old groups and the Popular Party (capable of producing a majority of 56 percent in the Chamber of Deputies). Although this coalition was actually in being from time to time between 1919 and 1922, it was never a stable one based on reciprocal good faith. The leaders of the old groups could not accept the idea of having to deal with a Party totally new to political life and claiming to speak in the name of a reconciliation of politics and morality which many of them did not understand or found suspect. Worse still, there was the matter of the irrepressible and ever present secretary general of the Party, Luigi Sturzo, who besides having a definite program, a considerable nuisance in itself, was also a priest. Giolitti, the Piedmontese, the able administrator and clever manipulator, the perennial Prime Minister, who disliked plans and commitments to principle and was willing only to consider problems in their immediate practical significance, could not envision an understanding with Luigi Sturzo, for Sturzo was a Sicilian and therefore by definition an enemy of the centralizing policies in which Giolitti strongly believed, a crusader, a restless man who would have liked to see a good many things changed. Furthermore, like any good follower of the lay traditions of the nineteenth century, Giolitti could not accept conditions imposed by a priest, even though Sturzo's rank

16

in the ecclesiastical hierarchy was the very lowest.[8] To these psychological obstacles were added concrete difficulties which the general confusion of the times made insoluble. The Popular Party stood for administrative decentralization, educational autonomy in the sense of a greater recognition of private Catholic schools, freedom for the Christian Democratic syndicalist movement, and land reform. It is true that these programs were often presented with a rigidity which, though admissible under certain circumstances, could ill be reconciled with the need of compromise and moderation required by the very novelty of the situation. But it is also true that the older parties were fossilized in their traditional way of thinking and never grasped the extremity of the situation towards which Italy was drifting.

The other possibility was an alliance between the Popular and the Socialist Parties (capable of producing a majority of 55 percent in the Chamber of Deputies), that very same alliance which after World War II Christian Democracy and Socialism achieved in both France and Italy, in Italy a generation too late. In 1919, to have persuaded the bearers of the red flag with hammer and sickle to sit around the same table with the bearers of the white flag with the crusaders' shield and the cross, would have required a considerable effort and a good many compromises. No agreement was possible in the years of crisis which preceded the Fascist seizure of power. Sturzo himself writes of his efforts to achieve an alliance with Socialism as follows: "The author attempted several times to obtain a common front among Social Democrats, Socialists and Populars, and the formation of a government in which the Socialists would participate. But after various discussions, the Socialist leaders pre-

---

[8] In dealing with the Giolitti-Sturzo conflict, Benedetto Croce accepts the devil theory of history. He writes, "The Christian Democrats, that is, the Catholics, even though they supported other parties, were not wholly free in what they were doing for they depended upon the Vatican and upon the Vatican's particular interests. The Vatican vetoed the continuation and the return to office of Giolitti, that is, the only one of the old government leaders who, because of his unshaken liberal faith, was in a position to face, conquer and destroy fascism. It is well known that what prompted the veto was the law requiring the registration of all securities, the law which Giolitti had pushed through for the sake of fiscal justice, but which was opposed by ecclesiastical economic interests whose securities were preponderantly of the bearer type." *Per la nuova vita dell' Italia* (Naples, 1944), p. 16.

ferred to stay out, and at the end they gave support to the general strike of July-August 1922. The Italian bourgeoisie was alarmed by it and decided for Fascism." [9]

V. Fascism and the Church

The alliance that failed in 1922, at a time when its achievement would have been decisive, was sought again in the summer of 1924, in the midst of the deep unrest brought about by the Fascist assassination of the Socialist deputy, Matteotti. At that moment some illusions were still nourished concerning the possibility of liquidating Fascism without too much effort. The dictatorship was not yet entrenched. The popular revulsion against Fascist crimes had been immense. It was known that the King, not yet shorn of all powers and prestige, was consulting with pre-fascist political leaders. If a constitutional way out could be found, then the problem of a Socialist-Popular parliamentary alliance would re-present itself. The leader of Italian Socialism, Filippo Turati, in an interview granted to the Popular Party daily, *Il Popolo*, on July 1, 1924, pointed out that Fascism had enabled millions of people to get rid of worn-out clichés and had made it possible to bring all sincere democrats together. Political differences that a few years ago seemed irreconcilable could conceivably be settled. Turati maintained that Socialism had shed its old fashioned anti-clericalism, that it was ready to grant the fullest freedom to religious activities and to schools, and that it was certainly not going to insist upon a divorce law. A broad practical agreement was possible between the two Parties.

The answer to Turati's overtures came from de Gasperi who had, at about that time, taken over the leadership of the party following Sturzo's retirement. Speaking at a party meeting on July 16, 1924, de Gasperi attacked the "clerical-Fascist press" which had developed the theme of the absolute incompatibility of Socialist-Christian Democratic collaboration. "There is no reason to believe that Italian Christian Democrats will be found incapable or unwilling to maintain the integrity of thought and the autonomy of action that was demonstrated by the Christian Democrats of Ger-

---

[9] Luigi Sturzo, *Nationalism and Internationalism* (New York, 1946), p. 116.

many, Poland, and Czechoslovakia when, for well-defined purposes of parliamentary and government policies they sought or accepted participation in governments in which Socialists were represented. . . . Italian Christian Democracy believes that the gradual process of clarification with regard to Socialism, which has taken place everywhere in Europe since the war, must also be favored in Italy, as an important element of political and social stability."

These farsighted policies which, let us note, de Gasperi himself was able to fulfill in part more than twenty years later, were defeated in 1924 not only by the brutal force of Fascism, but by two other developments that are of greater significance from the point of view of an understanding of the persistent elements of the crisis of the Italian State.

The first was the negative attitude taken by the old conservative and liberal leaders whose advice was then being sought by the monarchy. When asked by the King whether their preference went to a government headed by Mussolini or to one which conceivably might have been led by a Socialist-Christian Democratic coalition, the trusted and venerable advisors of the Crown answered that a Mussolini government was preferable. If Fascism continued in power some "normalization" of political life might still be achieved. The Italian bourgeoisie, using its well-known manipulative capacities, might succeed in absorbing Fascism and in resuming the ancient ways. Mussolini was a buffoon without any intrinsic strength and he represented no danger to the survival of the *status quo*. But a Socialist-Christian Democratic government would be a revolutionary government. Given power, it would upset in a few years the established order of things by introducing structural reforms and by dethroning for good the bourgeoisie. The King accepted the counsel of the trusted advisors of the Crown and, therefore, as is well known, saved both the monarchy and the bourgeoisie.

The second development was the open intervention of the Church against a Socialist-Christian Democratic alliance. The Jesuit magazine, *Civiltà Cattolica,* speaking through the authoritative voice of its editor, said that a coalition between Socialism and a Party claiming to be Catholic must "cause anxiety to every serious citizen and still more to the ecclesiastical authority." Indeed, such a coalition would be "neither decent, nor opportune, nor lawful."

19

As for de Gasperi's argument that such coalitions had been effected throughout Europe, the fact was that no parallel could be found since Catholic parties in those countries had merely accepted collaboration with Socialist parties that were already in office, while what was being proposed in Italy was to call the Socialists to participate in the Cabinet for the first time.

Any doubt that the Jesuits might have been speaking only for themselves was soon removed by the direct intervention of Pope Pius XI, on September 9, 1924, in a speech delivered to a group of Catholic university students. "It is to be regretted that ideas indicative of dangerous immaturity are circulated among us. It is said for instance that any alleged defense of the public welfare is enough to justify cooperation with evil. This is false. . . . The collaboration of Catholics with Socialists in other countries is also cited but here there is a confusion due to the failure to distinguish between different circumstances. Apart from the differences in environment and in historical, political and religious conditions, it is one thing to find oneself faced with a party which has already reached power, but it is quite another thing to open the way and provide the possibility for that party to arrive at power; this is an altogether different matter. It is truly painful to the heart of the Father to see good children and good Catholics divided and engaged in mutual combat. Why, in the name of Catholic interests, commit oneselves in favor of a program which is aconfessional and which could therefore of itself even prescind from the Catholic confession?" [10]

The Pope who was speaking in 1924 was, of course, no longer the Pope who in 1918 had given his blessing to Christian Democracy as a political party. Pius XI, of conservative Lombard middle class origin, was disturbed by the rebellious and reformist attitudes of a party that claimed to be of Christian inspiration but even denied the existence of a Roman question and refused to make an open admission of confessionalism. On the other hand, Fascism was getting ready to restore the Church to some of its old positions

---

[10] See for the relevant texts, Stefano Jacini's *Storia del Partito Popolare Italiano,* with a preface by Luigi Sturzo (Milan, 1951), pp. 234ff. Jacini, a Christian Democratic leader of the right, is uncompromising in his criticism of the Pope's position.

and a settlement of the Roman question was not impossible. Under the circumstances it was better to disavow the Popular Party and assume towards it the Fascist line which had been proclaimed in Mussolini's grandiloquent style two years earlier. The leader of Fascism had written in his newspaper, on August 19, 1922, at a time when Sturzo had been engaged in conversation with Socialist leaders that, "with its ridiculous attempts to organize a Cabinet of the extreme left, the Popular Party has killed all remaining illusions; we are confronted by a Party infected by Socialism, hence by an anti-Catholic and anti-Christian party. . . . In high Vatican circles the question is asked whether the birth of the Popular Party will not cause a fearful harm to the Church." Mussolini got an emphatic answer on September 9, 1924.

In effect, the Popular Party, together with all other non-Fascist parties, was already dead when these events took place. Fascist pressure had been relentless and there had been a general underestimation of the power which Fascism already had at its disposal, even in 1924. The founder of the Party, Luigi Sturzo, had resigned on July 11, 1923 as Party secretary. Within a month of the Pope's address he was invited to leave Italy by a high Vatican official who provided him with a Vatican passport.[11] Sturzo left Italy for London on October 25, 1924, the first of the great anti-Fascist leaders to leave the country.

A restless commentator on the Italian political scene, who resides in the foggy bottom lands of progressivism, Arturo Carlo Jemolo, speaks of the failure of Christian Democracy at that time.[12]

It is rather the failure and the crisis of the Italian political classes that should be mentioned. It is idle to stress the particular shortcomings, rigid positions, inexpert handling of given situations, which Christian Democracy undoubtedly revealed in the seven years in which it existed as an organized party and, more specifically, in the four years in which it could operate in a free democratic framework. What matters is to see the decadence of the political system, and Fascism as the most visible manifestation of a constitutional, political, administrative, and economic crisis which could not be overcome by those who had the majority in the

---

[11] cf. Jacini, *op. cit.,* p. 189.
[12] Jemolo, *Chiesa e Stato,* p. 583.

21

country and in Parliament. On balance, the contribution of Christian Democracy to political life from 1919 to 1922 was a positive one, for it stressed the need of renovation and of modernization in the life of the country which, as later events well proved, were long overdue.

The Fascist attack against the Popular Party had been as sustained as that against the Socialist and Communist Parties. At the same time, helped by the attitude of the Church, Fascism had succeeded in taking over the clerical conservative elements of the Party. By 1925, at the end of that brief interlude which separated the initially weak and amateurish efforts of the dictatorship from the totalitarianism which followed, an interlude during which non-Fascist political parties still survived, the Popular Party was reduced to that condition of apostolic purity which its founder must have desired. The membership was smaller, the going was difficult, but the halfhearted had left and the party appeared in a new light. Here was a fiercely democratic and independent party, inspired by a future vision of a community drastically reformed and in which the ideals of the common good, of devotion to social duties, would triumph.

There exists an eye-witness account of the Fifth Popular Party Congress held in Rome from June 28 to June 30, 1925, written by one of the keenest observers of the Italian political scene of the time, Piero Gobetti who, still a young man, was to be killed by the Fascists within a few months. Gobetti had founded in Turin in 1922 the most important political journal of the postwar period, *La Rivoluzione Liberale,* which, as the title implied, was to be devoted to the goal of bringing about a revolutionary change in Italian society, but one that would respect the liberal tradition of the rights of man. Gobetti had been strongly attracted by Gramsci's utopian communism which appeared to him in those years to combine the promise of social renovation and of freedom for the working class. He had also been strongly attracted to Sturzo whom he considered a great party leader and one of the founders of the modern concept of mass democratic action. Watching the Rome Congress of 1925 Gobetti felt that here was a Party with very few priests and a great many young people. There was no trace left of clericalism and the party élite was made up of young men between the ages of thirty and forty-five, a generation Gobetti found missing in all other political parties. "While the ruling classes of the old political parties are made up of septuagenarians or of immature people or of pure intellectuals, Sturzo's party has new men accustomed to deal realistically with matters of politics and administration." His praise for de Gasperi is very high and in such men as Donati, Ferrari, and Gronchi he saw the nucleus of a modern political class.[13]

The men of 1925 demonstrated that, in spite of everything, including the open enmity of the Church, a small democratic party of Christian inspiration could survive and that its role in a restored democratic system was assured. It is true that the leader of Italian Communism, Gramsci, had special views of his own on the purposes to be served by Christian Democracy. He had written in 1922 in Gobetti's journal that the founding of Christian Democracy was for Italy what the Protestant Reformation had been for Germany. He saw a parallel between the history of the Jews and the history of the Catholics. The Jews, prevented from owning any real property, had developed a decisive power in the fields of trade and finance, as a result of which they could carry out economic reprisals against the governments which were oppressing them politically and spiritually. The Catholics, eliminated from normal participation in political life by the positivism and anti-religious attitude of liberalism, were now taking a leading part in the destruction of the bourgeois state. But the real winner would be Communism, Gramsci writes: "Christian Democracy is a necessary phase in the process of adhesion of the entire Italian proletariat to Communism. Christian Democracy creates forms of associated life outside of the industrial factory, that is, in areas where Socialism cannot operate because of lack of the objective conditions of a capitalistic economy. They are furnishing an initial orientation to the still-confused working masses who know that they are a part of a great historical process but who don't understand it because they do not live within the walls of a modern industrial plant." Where the factory and Socialism are not present then, Christian Democracy will fill the

---

[13] Cf. "Uomini e idee dei popolari," originally published in *Rivoluzione Liberale,* July 5, 1925, and reprinted in *Antologia della Rivoluzione Liberale,* edited by Nino Valeri (Turin, 1948), pp. 486ff. Cf. on the Fifth Party Congress, Jacini, *op. cit.,* pp. 260ff.

need of modern man for protection, group life and solidarity. Having accomplished this task, Christian Democracy will then die, Gramsci predicts, for the Christian Democratic masses, having acquired through collective action a sense of their reality and power, will reject their own leadership which presumes to invoke transcendental values in political and economic life. Communism will take over, much in the same fashion predicted by Marx for the proletarian revolution, which exploits the collective conditions of production and of work created by a fully matured capitalism.

VI. *The Resistance*

While waiting for the fulfillment of Gramsci's prophecy, let us look briefly at Christian Democracy in the long period between its final formal suppression by Fascism in 1926 and its rebirth at the end of World War II.

The Resistance was a decisive element for good or for evil in the life of all modern European political parties, as it marked the dividing line between the old and the new. It provided the test, accepted by the great majority, of the democratic or undemocratic qualities, of the eagerness for change or of the attachment to the past, of all those who claimed the right to political leadership. The effects of the Resistance period on the fortunes of Communism, Radical Socialism, Liberalism, in both France and Italy are well known. Christian Democracy was certainly not unaffected. In France, thanks in part to the Italian experience, Christian Democracy was instantly able to recognize the contrast between Fascism and democracy, in the crucial vote of July 10, 1940 on the granting of full powers to Pétain. As Goguel well shows in the second part of this volume, not all who voted that day for Pétain are to be condemned, but all who voted against him are certainly entitled to recognition as defenders of the democratic ideal. And all the members of the Jeune République and nearly all the members of the Popular Democrats voted against Pétain. This vote was the passport which rightfully admitted French Christian Democracy to the circle of democratic parties.

In Italy the situation developed along different lines and Christian Democracy never had a chance, as it had in France, of being reborn as an active and leading Resistance movement battling against both the foreign and the domestic varieties of Fascism. The Fascist night was a long one and for many years no resistance to Fascism was possible amidst the general applause which, from Churchill to Otto Kahn, was showered on Fascism. The leaders of Christian Democracy were in exile, Sturzo in England and in the United States,[14] de Gasperi in Vatican City once he was released from the Fascist jail. The best of the younger men were killed or died. Such was the fate of Donati and Ferrari. Others found it difficult to resist a process of gradual adaptation which the long period of "peace" from 1926 to 1941 made necessary for many.

We meet, however, a peculiar form of Resistance, that of the Church to Fascism. Having first given help in the destruction of one of the few vital forces that could have opposed Fascism, after 1931 the Church gradually discovered that between her own moral and political and social doctrine and the doctrines of Fascism there was a substantial incompatibility. At every point, on the doctrine of man, on the role of the family, on the nature of education, on the limits of state power, on the nature of war, the Church found herself at loggerheads with the regime which, by virtue of the Lateran treaties of 1929, she had done so much to strengthen and make respectable in the eyes of the world.

The opposition of the Church to Fascism became quite firm, and Pope Pius XI should be included among the forerunners of the underground. In carrying out her opposition to the government in power, the Church used many of the former Popular Party members. After 1943 these developments were to place the Christion Democratic party in a relationship to the Church rather different from that which prevailed between 1919 and 1922. While Christian Democracy was first born in Italy in 1919 as an independent political movement, it was reborn in 1943 as a movement owing much to the protecting hand and counsel of the Church

---

[14] While in London, Sturzo founded in 1936 the first *People and Freedom* group, not as a political party but as a nucleus of political action. According to Sturzo, "*People* means not only the working class but the totality of citizens, because all are to enjoy liberty and participate in government. *People* also means democracy; but democracy without freedom would be tyranny, just as freedom without democracy would become liberty only for some privileged class, never for the whole people." Cf. Sturzo, *Nationalism and Internationalism,* pp. 124ff.

during the later years of Fascism. The strong autonomy which had been so visible under Sturzo, became less visible under de Gasperi. This was not so much because de Gasperi himself entertained basically different views on the requirements of survival for a political party in Italy. Among these, in the long run, a firm show of autonomy vis-à-vis the Church is essential. But he could not fail to take into account the concrete circumstances and the specific relationship of power which had led to the rebirth of the party.

One of the key elements in the underground history of Christian Democracy between 1931 and 1943 was Catholic Action. As one of the few organizations which Fascism could not destroy, Catholic Action became one of the centers of a muted opposition to the dictatorship. Even by doing nothing, and this is what it did for the most part, it was anti-Fascist by reason of the simple fact of not being Fascist. In preserving the Party's cadres, Catholic Action played an immense role. As a result, one of the leaders of Catholic Action, Luigi Gedda, today feels entitled to assert from time to time his rights of control over the Party. The mortgage of Catholic Action, a lay organization under the direct control of the Church, weighs very heavily upon present-day Christian Democracy.[15]

Thus the Resistance had different consequences in France and in Italy, as far as Christian Democracy was concerned. In France it placed beyond doubt the democratic autonomous character of the M.R.P. In Italy, because of the generic protective role of the Church and because of the specific instrument used to salvage the remnants of the party, Christian Democracy was placed under a shadow. Many became convinced that, as far as the Christian Democratic Party is concerned, one is not dealing with an authentic Italian political force but with the Vatican itself.

---

[15] See *infra,* pp. 84 ff. for a further discussion of this point.

Chapter Two

THE PROGRAM OF CHRISTIAN DEMOCRACY
AFTER WORLD WAR II

Traditionally the United States has been more prepared to accept parties that tend to reflect in a flexible manner a country's varied political and economic problems, than parties based on any simple and rigid ideology. The United States has, therefore, welcomed parties that provide a common meeting ground where different groups bring their different attitudes, that act as a clearing house from which compromises emerge. This tradition satisfies a desire to avoid straight ideological and class conflicts likely to endanger the maintenance of common foundations and the survival of methods of political action accepted by all.

European political parties have tended to move in a different direction. As the impact of Marxism has deepened, as old religious issues have come back, as country after country has had to suffer the consequences of Fascism, political divisions along sharp ideological lines have increased. Political parties have acquired "mass" characteristics and flags and slogans to rally the faithful. The more colorful the flag, the more inflexible the slogan, the greater becomes the sense of mission. Much can be said against the perversity and the immorality of personal political factionalism, as opposed to the clean-cut qualities of those fighting for a precise ideal and ready to die for it. But with the disappearance of personal political groups, there also goes an element of compromise that can at times be precious. The clash of organized masses within the state can be more dangerous than the maneuvering of individuals.

The Christian Democratic movement, which, under different names, has asserted itself so strongly in postwar Europe, is far from having the easy going informality of the political parties of old. As a matter of historical necessity, as we saw in the preceding chapter, Christian Democracy had to organize itself strongly, if it was to fight successfully against the bourgeois State it wished to replace. The Italian Popular Party was a good example of the new techniques of program and organization.

But in Italy after the war, to organizational rigidity has been added the complexity of a much greater and varied base of popular support. The Christian Democratic Party revealed itself, beyond certain fundamentals, as a political movement of complex ideology, one attempting to gain permanent roots by being the image of many cross currents and of conflicting interests. The appearance of divergent trends, and the halting decisions which critics say are proof of weakness and illegitimacy, are, perhaps, to be taken as proof of the serious effort made to surmount the narrow class approach of other mass parties.

When the liberation of Italy was completed in 1945, it became clear that the reborn Christian Democratic Party was to be the country's largest and that to it was to fall, to a considerable extent, the task of creating a new democratic structure after the crisis of Fascism and of war. With what appeals, promises and programs did the party initially present itself to the people?

I. *The Christian Foundation and the Method of Freedom*

Christian Democracy was kept together by one fundamental common belief and by the acceptance, in most cases at least, of one method. The belief was the sum total of Christian religious and moral principles; the method, that of freedom.

The Christian foundation was the common ground upon which all met; the purpose of the party was the application of Christian morality to political and social life. Upon entering the Party, the Party member did not cut off the links which tied him to the Church, for "from the Christian patrimony he continues to derive the vital inspiration which will guide him in his public activities." [1] Only the Gospel, by affirming moral principles, dominated the life of centuries, while all doctrines which linked their fate to economic phenomena inevitably showed their decay as soon as those phenomena changed. No less clear was the emphasis on the method of freedom. "We can retrace our history well into the past and affirm that this exigency of freedom does not arise out of a contingent interest, but is the very substance of our thought. This

---

[1] Demofilo (de Gasperi), *Tradizione e "Ideologia" della Democrazia Cristiana* (Rome, 1944), p. **18**.

is why we feel we can be the foundation of a true democratic life." [2] And the leader of the Party, on the day of the downfall of Fascism, proclaimed that "Freedom will distinguish the new democratic regime, just as all men who are truly free will be pledged to the acceptance of the method of freedom." [3]

The Christian basis of the party was strongly and unremittingly stressed. Christian Democracy was to collaborate with representatives of idealist or materialistic philosophies in the solution of concrete social problems. It could walk hand in hand with Socialism and Communism in the achievement of the most daring reforms. But it would not in any way confuse itself with ideologies and conceptions of life which either fight, or prescind from, Christian precepts. The Party was not to seek the creation of a Christian State presupposing a unity of thought which did not exist, but it was not to forget that the history of Italy was part and parcel of the history of the development of Christian ideals.[4]

Confronted by such statements, the Church found the new Christian Democratic Party easier to support than the old Popular Party. This created difficulties for a Party claiming to be solely a political movement and not an ecclesiastical *longa manus,* and de Gasperi had to tell the Communists that the Party had never requested the intervention of the "Church apparatus." But speaking before the Constituent Assembly on July 25, 1946, de Gasperi sought to justify the preoccupation of the Church and her right to take a stand. "We are called upon to write a constitution. In the

[2] Gronchi, Assemblea Costituente, *Debates,* July 24, 1946; pp. 315, 317.

[3] De Gasperi, *Idee Ricostruttive della Democrazia Cristiana.* This was the first manifesto of Italian Christian Democracy, issued on July 25, 1943.

[4] See speeches by de Gasperi at various meetings of the Christian Democratic Party. *Popolo,* Rome; March 4, 1945, April 25 and 28, 1946. This stand allowed the Church to make an easy distinction between the several Italian political parties with which it had to contend once the simplicity of the Fascist system had vanished. The basic criterion became that of distinguishing between the parties which were for and those which were against a lay conception of the state. The Church was to fight those which claimed that in the field of political action the principles of Christian morality did not have to be taken into account; that the Church was to be ignored or merely tolerated, that a course of action independent of Christian teachings would be followed with regard to the problems of the family, marriage, education and schools. See pre-election statement by Cardinal Salotti in the Catholic Action paper, *Quotidiano,* Rome, March 24, 1946.

29

constitution we will not touch upon an economic and social program only, but we will also define principles concerning not only the rights of the human person, but freedom, education, and the relationship between Church and State. We need not be surprised that, on the eve, the Church has felt it her duty to speak. Our duty is to write a good constitution guaranteeing freedom and the Concordat."

This was only the most solemn declaration of the Christian Democratic view that fundamental Christian principles were to be not only the guiding political factor, but were to be to some extent embodied in the constitution. From the beginning Christian Democracy had made it clear that the new constitution was to recognize God as the fountainhead of all authority, that the religion of the Italian people was the Catholic religion, that the fundamental institutions of the State had to conform to Christian ethics, and that the State had the right to exercise only an auxiliary function in the field of education.[5]

These Christian ideals were to be realized in an atmosphere of freedom. The emphasis on the method of freedom implied the renunciation of the use of force by so-called "activist" minorities trying to confront the nation with accomplished facts in crucial fields of economic policy.[6] A true democracy could be born only if political decisions were taken through the full and conscious and free participation of the people. Through the method of freedom, the changing substance of political and economic freedoms could be realized gradually in a much more satisfactory way. These freedoms could exist only within the State and under its protection, but the premise was that the individual human being was a free agent endowed with certain inherent moral qualities. The solution to the problem of rights for the members of a community had to be found in a compromise between theories of the superiority of the State and theories which saw those rights only as a defense against the interference of the State. Thus following a pattern which

---

[5] Gonella, *Il Programma della Democrazia Cristiana per la Nuova Costituzione* (Rome, 1946), pp. 28, 29, 33. Tupini, "La Nuova Costituzione Italiana," *Popolo*, August 2, 1946.

[6] Motion approved by the national council of the party on March 2, 1945. Text in *Indirizzi Politico-Sociali della Democrazia Cristiana* (Rome, 1945), pp. 19-20.

was firmly established throughout Europe, the Christian Democratic Party added social and economic rights to the individual political rights of 1789; to the right of free expression of a man's personality it added the freedom from fear and want and the other limiting factors of our modern economic society; to the right of citizens to organize politically, it added the right of the State to issue juridical norms affecting the conduct of parties where their activities touch upon the public interest.[7]

II. *Bourgeoisie, Communism and Solidarism*

The dual emphasis on a Christian basis of politics and on the method of freedom, forced Christian Democracy to attack both the bourgeoisie and Marxism. Compared to the Popular Party attitude in 1919, there was nothing new in this position. It was necessary to achieve a renovation of Italian society, because the bourgeoisie was confined to a narrow materialistic outlook and had driven moral values out of political life. Its typical expression was a feudalistic capitalism which had to be replaced. It had developed an attitude of indifference towards basic institutions such as the family. Only the bourgeoisie favored divorce; the working people did not. The bourgeoisie preached freedom, and some of those freedoms were to be retained even though identified with bourgeois morality, but in many cases they were far short of what was needed in a democratic State. What good was the bourgeois freedom of the press if only the few had the means to make use of that freedom?[8] "The industrial bourgeoisie which in all countries has admirably created an industrial civilization and has pushed mechanical progress to the development of the atomic bomb . . . has left intact in man the instinct for violence, and has not reached his spirit and has failed to assure, together with material progress, the progress of spiritual values. The bourgeoisie has given us mechanical progress and not civilization, because civilization has above all a spiritual connotation."[9]

---

[7] Gonella, *Programma*, pp. 13ff., 40. It may be said here that, as in the parallel French case, nothing came out of these early proposals to provide for legislation regulating party life.

[8] Gonella, *ibid.*, pp. 32, 38, 43, 45.

[9] Gronchi, Speech at the first Party convention. *Popolo*, April 28, 1946.

But the enemy on the left was no less destructive, even though the deepening cleavage with Communism brought forth among left-wing leaders of the Christian Democratic Party a certain anxiety. Christian Democracy, they said, could not follow a purely negative policy of opposition without running the danger of strengthening the extreme opposite of Communism, Fascism or currents of Fascist tendency. Christian Democracy could not fulfill its role of "a center party of Christian inspiration and oriented towards the left" if it became merely the champion of opposition towards Communism. Giovanni Gronchi, among others, appeared as one of the leaders stressing the Party's revolutionary social and economic role and the need of economic democracy. To the conservative elements within the party he pointed out the dangers of an "obtuse" attitude of opposition to a united syndicalist movement, or of a reluctance to admit that Christian Democracy was a mass party. He underlined the inevitability of a fundamental change in the composition of the ruling and managerial classes and said that the times could be compared to the medieval shift from feudalism to the communes. The conservative classes, having finally proved their impotence, were being gradually replaced by new classes drawn from the working people. He praised the Socialists, who, he then believed, had given proof of being a vital Party, no longer a prisoner of fixed Marxian and Communist formulae but capable of evolving and of asserting its own individuality.[10] But even Gronchi's position was a clearly anti-Communist one, not only because he felt that Italian Communism was limited in its freedom of decision, but because of Communism's unavoidable appeal to violence. Ultimately, Communism could have no patience with a gradual evolution from a capitalistic to a socialistic society.

The Christian Democratic Party had to face the problem of relations with Communism, an issue the Popular Party had been spared. The issue arose quite early, breaking into print officially for the first time with an exchange of letters, in September 1944, between the two party leaders, Togliatti and de Gasperi. Togliatti's brief communication, on the occasion of the first meeting of the national council of the Christian Democratic Party, contained a

---

[10] Speech at the first Party congress. *Popolo,* April 28, 1946.

declaration of the Communist Party's "absolute respect for the religious faith of the Italian people," and the expression of a desire of a concrete political agreement with the Christian Democratic Party to create a "bloc" of popular forces sufficient to guarantee a "progressive", democratic regime. De Gasperi's answer stated that the one premise needed was the establishment of a climate of freedom and self-discipline. This climate was not being fostered by the Communist Party. Furthermore, the "bloc" and "front" tendencies would lead to the single party system.[11]

The Christian Democrats would not be satisfied with the Communists' avowed toleration of the Catholic religion. A spirit of mere toleration could not cause the Italian people to entrust to them the solution of the fundamental problems of family and school. Tactical shifts could not hide fundamental differences. Writing during the German occupation, de Gasperi had attacked "the totalitarian agencies bent upon seizing the whole individual in order to discipline him in ethical and philosophical and political and economic matters. Their heads are social philosophers and prophets as well as economists and statesmen, and their party is a philosophical system, a faith, a body of doctrines, and a vehicle for social and economic reforms." [12]

The grounds for the opposition to Communism, therefore, ranged from opposition to the materialistic conception of life which had spread among the masses, to the rejection of the centralizing techniques which Communism brings to governmental problems. Christian Democracy was against the Communist policy of leaving all primary education in the hands of the State; it was against what it felt to be the ultimate Communist tendency to collectivize all property; it was against the total transfer of all the means of production to the State; it was against a class conception of the State, a conception which primarily considered economic interests and rights

---

[11] See text of letters in *Indirizzi*, pp. 13-15. In the first circular issued in his capacity as Political Secretary of the Party, de Gasperi said, "Collaboration will have to be refused to so-called 'women's fronts' or 'youth fronts', already active in various localities, all of them of dubious origin and with even more dubious goals." *Ibid.*, p. 65.

[12] Demofilo, *Tradizione*, pp. 17-18.

belonging to members of given economic groups to the neglect of the rights belonging to all as citizens of a political community.[13]

Against these tendencies, Christian Democracy, seeking to reconcile divergent interests of various groups, offered the idea of "solidarism." Industrialists and property owners were welcome within the ranks of the Party if they accepted the spirit of its program. In this way collaboration and discussion could develop, through the participation of all concerned. Simple expropriation through State bureaucracy or government commissars had failed to produce the desired economic results and had jeopardized the principles of equity and of justice and the very freedom of the people.[14]

The bourgeoisie might be one of the enemies, yet it contained invaluable elements which had to be utilized. In recognizing the need of reconciliation, Christian Democracy not merely adhered to the method of freedom; it took into account its own interests and the success or failure of its own program. Claiming to be truly representative of the aspirations of all the people and feeling that, from a long range point of view, successful political action could not be based on the deliberate antagonizing of the various groups to which it appealed, the Party could not follow any other path. A pluralistic and flexible political and economic system was to be the instrument of the party's policies.

III. *The Constitution and the Economic System*

In the constitutional field pluralistic solutions were to be pressed forward; in the economic field, questions of method were considered at least as important as the ultimate goals to be achieved. Only in the field of syndicalism the basic tendency, as yet not contradicted, seemed to be one of unity and compulsion.

If certain elementary formulae about constitutional principles were developed early without too much difficulty, serious progress by the Party in thinking through these generic ideas was hampered until the spring of 1946 by uncertainties with regard to the issue

---

[13] See Gonella, *Programma*, pp. 38, 51; de Gasperi, speech before the national Party council, *Popolo*, August 2, 1945, *Quotidiano*, August 7, 1946.

[14] Speech by de Gasperi at the first Party congress, *Popolo*, April 28, 1946.

of monarchy versus republic, and, in general, by a lack of significant contributions and of real interest by Party members in constitutional problems. When any interest could be aroused, the resultant lucubrations had a strange air of unreality about them. The constitutional experiences of Estonia, Lithuania and Latvia were quoted as having established precedents of far reaching importance. The statement was made that "Nearly all the constitutions of the several European countries have set up, upon the example of the United States, supreme courts with the task of protecting the constitution, supervising its enforcement, settling the conflicts among the various branches of government and preventing abuses of power by each of them," without any apparent awareness of the failure of these alleged European applications of the American system and of the obvious reasons for this failure. But gradually a few guideposts emerged.

The new constitution was to be a written document. But the rigidity of a written constitution was to be tempered by the requirement of a pluralistic constitution stressing the functions of free bodies and associations active between the State and the individual citizens.[15] Mainly this meant the division of powers between the central government and a number of autonomous regions. The new structure of the central government, after the clipping of its old Napoleonic wings, would be based on a two-chamber system, a lower popular assembly, in which representatives of organized political parties would predominate, and a higher functional assembly made up of representatives of non-political groups such as syndicates, regions, universities, welfare bodies and the like. In the executive the Christian Democratic Party was ready to vest a greater power of control over the legislature than the French M.R.P. had been willing to admit. It was suggested quite early that ample powers of dissolution be given to the executive, and that a supreme constitutional court be given express jurisdiction to nullify legislative acts violating the constitution.

In facing the economic problem, Christian Democracy aimed to reconcile its pledge for radical reforms with its promises to safe-

---

[15] Speeches by de Gasperi at the first inter-regional Party congress in the North, *Popolo*, July 3, 1945; and at the first Party congress, *Popolo*, April 25, 1946.

guard the method of freedom and the role of individuals. The general statement of principles was simple enough. Economic life must take a subordinate position with respect to spiritual life. However, political freedom must be integrated by social justice. The task of the new constitution was to translate the novel economic concepts of our time into constitutional norms. The clash between capital and labor must be reconciled and as far as possible the interests of the two must be made to coincide. Beyond this point difficulties began, for concrete solutions had to be given to concrete economic problems.

The Christian Democratic Party was reluctant to commit itself definitely on any issue. The Party was pledged to a radical program of economic reform,[16] but "gradualism" was the norm, and all "simple" plans of agrarian reform were scorned.

A typical attitude was that taken with regard to property rights. One of the Party leaders, Paolo Taviani, offered these definitions: "In order to guarantee the freedom and affirmation of the human person, private property is recognized and guaranteed. In order to guarantee the personal and social functions of private property and the possibility for all to gain it through work and savings, the law will determine the norms regulating its purchase and transfer, its limits and the conditions of its enjoyment. When required by the exigencies of the common good and in order to avoid private privileged or monopolistic positions and to obtain a more equitable and convenient rendering of services and distribution of production, the law can reserve to the collective ownership of the State, of the region, of the communes or of other bodies of public law, the enterprises and the goods of specified and defined sectors of economic activity. Always in conformity with the above aims the law can transfer to the collectivity the ownership of specified enterprises or goods. The expropriation will take place against the payment of a just indemnity." [17]

These definitions could be adapted to many different and even opposite purposes, depending upon the mood of the legislative assembly called upon to construe them. In general, they did not contain anything to reassure traditionalist defenders of the concept

---

[16] Gonella, *Programma,* p. 47.
[17] *Popolo,* September 26, 1946.

of private property; indeed the Party was anxious in those years to dispel the belief that, except with regard to small property holders, it would take a conservative stand in the matter. If de Gasperi called Christian Democracy "anti-revolutionary," it was not to deny the need of radical change, but to stress the need for careful procedures and free consultation all along.

The main ideas of the Christian Democratic Party with regard to State intervention in general and nationalization in particular, appeared to be as follows: (a) No single solution would be adopted in the industrial field. When State intervention was necessary, it would vary from nationalization to joint private and public exploitation, or to simple control; (b) Present extensive State ownership in the industrial and banking field was to be recognized as real and not fictitious nationalization; (c) Planning was needed, but not of the kind which suppresses private initiative; while providing for the unifying direction of the State, planning had to call forth an increased private effort and the fullest coordination between public and private spheres of economic activity; (d) Particular care had to be taken not to bureaucratize the organisms of economic life; centralization of power was simple, but centralization of knowledge difficult. It was better, therefore, to provide for as many autonomous channels as possible through which knowledge could express itself without impediment; (e) Therefore, about 75 percent of industry was to remain free from State controls.[18]

In conclusion, Christian Democracy appealed for the support of the electorate by admitting its readiness to move in the direction of State controls or of outright State ownership of the means of production in given economic sectors and with the proper procedures.

---

[18] Tupini, *La Nuova Costituzione,* pp. 36ff.; Resolution of the national Party council, March 2, 1945, *Indirizzi,* pp. 29ff.; Speeches of de Gasperi before the Party's national council and convention, *Popolo,* August 2, 1945 and April 25, 1946. At the time, the French M.R.P. was moving with the same deliberate caution in economic matters. In answering the program of the "Délégation des Gauches," the M.R.P. said: "It is necessary entirely to transform the present spirit and methods of planned economy in the sense of a considerable decrease in the burden of administrative services and of a greater freedom in their application. It is also necessary to achieve the participation of all affected and organized groups in the elaboration and in the application of the plan to each of the economic sectors." (*Le Monde,* November 10, 1945).

But it added that it would not use the weapon of economic policy to bring about the forcible eviction and liquidation of entire social classes. The issue could be seen in its simplest terms in the case of the government-owned IRI (Institute of Industrial Reconstruction). The Christian Democrats accepted the ownership of banks and heavy industries which the State has long since achieved through IRI as a decisive fact, for it established the principle of government ownership in crucial economic areas. Through IRI certain basic industries had been nationalized, that is their ownership had been transferred to the State. But the "managerial" leadership of the nationalized industries had remained substantially unchanged. The Christian Democrats declared themselves satisfied with using, under proper controls, the old managerial classes who were considered too valuable to be discarded altogether. The Marxists, on the other hand, considered the transfer of ownership a mere legal transaction, and the imposition of over-all government controls inadequate. According to them, no revolutionary changes were possible so long as the old managers were not replaced by new ones who could be trusted to act in the interests of the "people". The country saw the issue as essentially a revolutionary one, and looked to the polls for its solution.

On June 2, 1946, when the Constituent Assembly was elected, the Christian Democratic Party obtained eight million votes, or 35 percent of the total, and emerged as the first party of the Italian Republic.

CHAPTER THREE

THE WRITING OF THE CONSTITUTION

Nearly two years elapsed between the election of the Constituent Assembly and the assumption of power under the new Constitution by the victorious democratic parties after the elections of April 18, 1948. During these two years, the writing of the Constitution was the main political task before the country. Therefore, the most conclusive and fairest initial test of the seriousness with which the Christian Democratic Party looked upon its ideal program is to consider the document for which that Party bears a great responsibility.

The Christian Democratic Party comes out of this test rather well. It took a successful stand on a number of important issues. When it yielded, it did so on points that debate had shown to be inherently weak. On the whole, the Constitution of the Italian Republic may be said to contain a recognition in principle of a majority of the items in the Christian Democratic platform. An analysis of six major constitutional areas will support this contention, and also show that, at the same time, the principles of a liberal and democratic constitution have, in general, been safeguarded.

I. *The Church and Religious Freedom*

On the mater of relationships between Church and State, the Christian Democratic Party succeeded in winning the constitutional recognition of the 1929 Lateran Treaties. The Treaties had ended the so-called Roman question by recognizing the sovereignty of the Pope over the territory of the Vatican City State and by providing for a Concordat defining the relationships in Italy between the Italian State and the Catholic Church. Few denied the desirability of the 1929 agreements. The main point at issue was whether the Constitution itself should formally acknowledge their existence. With Communist support the Christian Democratic Party saw its point of view accepted. Article 7 of the Constitution reads: "The

State and the Catholic Church are, each in its own sphere, independent and sovereign. Their relationships are regulated by the Lateran Treaties. Modifications of the Treaties, accepted by both parties, do not require the procedure of constitutional amendment."

Article 7 does not create any new situation. It provides a solemn and fresh recognition by the Italian Republic of the validity of the 1929 Treaties. In those Treaties the advantages secured by the Church are counterbalanced by advantages secured by the State. For instance, the recognition of the Catholic religion as the religion of State does not, as a result of long customary interpretation, mean more than that, whenever the State feels moved to share officially in any religious act, it will do so through the agency of the Catholic Church. In exchange the State is able to assert far reaching powers in all matters relating to the appointment of bishops and the administration of ecclesiastical benefices.

The fact remains that, as a result of Article 7, Christian Democracy has asserted the constitutional primacy of the Catholic Church, because it is for the Catholic Church alone that the Constitution makes such provisions as are contained in Article 7. However, Article 8 restores to a large extent the balance between the Catholic Church and other Churches by saying that if any other Church so wishes, it can make with the Italian State formal agreements aiming to regulate its relationships with the State in a manner similar to the 1929 Concordat with the Catholic Church.

In essence, Articles 7 and 8 are based upon the principle that separation of Church and State is not feasible in Italy and that concordatory policies are preferable. While those policies exist so far only in the case of the Catholic Church, they can be formulated at any time for all other denominations. At the end of 1951, Protestant Churches in Italy seemed ready to ask for a beginning of negotiations which would give them a legal status comparable to that of the Catholic Church. It is difficult to see why the Protestant groups should be anxious to reduce their freedom in this way, but this is their constitutional privilege.[1]

---

[1] This statement assumes, of course, that, even without agreements of any kind, the Protestant Churches can be free and that, if persecuted, they can find redress through the ordinary jurisdiction of the courts. These assumptions appear, so far, to be well founded.

If from the formal sphere of ecclesiastical rights we move to the spiritual one of religious freedom, then Article 19 seems to provide adequately for its defense: "All have the right freely to profess their own religious faith in whatever form, individual or associated, to propagandize it and to carry out religious functions in private or in public, provided this does not involve rites contrary to public morality." Again, the long established traditions of tolerance and freedom appear to indicate that on the basis of Article 19 Italy will enjoy a freedom of religious expression as unfettered as any other Western State possesses today. Christian Democracy is then to be congratulated for having given up its earlier inclination to make of the Constitution a document into which would be written a series of declarations of allegiance to Catholic doctrine. This has not happened and if Italy becomes a clerical state, the politicians and not the Constitution will have to be blamed.

II. *The Bill of Rights*

The Italian Constitution does not avoid the difficult task of trying to define both political and economic rights. In so doing, it provides for a more adequate bill of rights than the French Constitution, in which political and civil rights are sanctioned through an appeal to the Declaration of the Rights of Man of 1789. In the Italian Constitution political rights come before the economic and social rights and duties. Article 2 typifies the confluence of the old and the new: "The republic recognizes and guarantees the inviolable rights of men, whether as an individual or in the social groups through which his personality develops, and requires the fulfillment of the unavoidable duties of political, economic and social solidarity."

The traditional rights of man are restated in the guarantees of personal liberty, due process of law, freedom of movement, of assembly, of association, of speech and press. Article 21 does raise some doubts as to press freedom, for police authorities are granted powers of seizure which, though regulated and limited, might be abused. Article 21 indicates the urgency of a press law, promised by the Constitution, to remedy the possibility of arbitrary action by police authorities.[2]

The Constitution recognizes the right of the citizen to be left alone and free as well as his right to social freedom as member of a group. It recognizes his right to be left to the activity in which his life is fulfilled both as an individual and as a member of the community. It does more than bar the State from entering these areas of freedom: in its economic section the bill of rights directs the State to lend the active support of its machinery to secure those rights to work, to security, to welfare, to education, which are today an essential part of any political society. In exchange for these positive contributions to the citizens' happiness and welfare, the Constitution states that the community can exact from every citizen, according to the capability and choice of each, such tasks as will contribute to the material and spiritual progress of society.

The bill of rights includes as well some general statements concerning future economic policies. Definition is less precise, as the purpose is that of providing for the guidance of legislative bodies. It is also clear that Christian Democracy had to agree to a number of compromises between the claims of collective public policy and the claims of the defenders of private enterprise. The Constitution asserts the principle that the State may coordinate and direct towards social ends private economic activity. It declares that those economic enterprises which relate to essential public services may be turned over to the State or other public agencies or to cooperatives of consumers and workers. This is in keeping with the Christian Democratic theory that control of private business activity does not necessarily mean the setting up of centralized State

---

[2] These uncertainties, added to economic difficulties and political manipulations, have contributed to the present lamentable state of the Italian press. As in France, the failure of Italy to produce a strong, objective, well-produced, independent press is one of the great disappointments of the postwar period. In effect, the present Italian press is not much better than the Fascist press. The lack of objectivity, the partisan and narrow approach, the refusal to make the effort to be really well informed about the rest of the world, sensationalism, excessive national prejudice, these are the main characteristics of the press, with exceptions that are so rare as not to be noticeable. For proposed press legislation, see *infra,* pp. 60, 75-76.

administration, but can mean the creation of autonomous and decentralized agencies controlled by those directly interested, on the pattern of guild socialist doctrines.

Concerning land reform, Article 44 of the Constitution avoids any excessively simple declaration, in a tacit acknowledgment of the complexities of the agrarian problem. The law will impose obligations and restrictions on the private use of land, for the purpose of securing a rational exploitation of the soil and of establishing equitable social relationships. It will also fix limits to the extent of private ownership according to regional requirements. It will both promote and require land reclamation, the transformation of *latifundia,* as well as the reconstitution of more productive economic units. It will foster small and medium-sized farm ownership. Article 44, in effect, allows the future legislation to move in any direction required by a normally progressive and modern body of agricultural legislation. It seems to contain a specific mandate to act at two points: one, the fixing of limits of the amount of land that can be privately owned, and two, the transformation of *latifundia.* But even here the specific content of the required action is not made clear and the freedom of the legislator is not substantially restricted.

In the field of labor policies the Constitution recognizes the right of the workers, subject to the requirements of production, to collaborate in the management of business enterprises. It equally recognizes the right to strike within the limits of the laws which will regulate that right. It recognizes the freedom of trade union organization, but it imposes on trade unions the obligation of registration with appropriate government offices. No registration will be accepted unless the trade union provides for an internal democratic structure. On the other hand, a registered trade union acquires a "legal personality" and can enter into collective agreements which, within the jurisdiction to which the agreement relates, will be compulsory even for non-union members. There is more than only casual evidence here of the compulsive corporative tradition which has been so long a part of Christian Democratic theory. In an organic view of society, trade unions are not merely private associations, since they fulfill important public functions. The State must recognize them and, on the one hand, bestow certain benefits while, on the other, it exacts certain conditions. Christian Democrats will deny that this system bears any resemblance to the Fascist corporative State, for the trade unions are first the result of an autonomous workers' movement and are later recognized by the State, while Fascism, in effect, established a total control from the beginning. But the result in the end is to create in both cases a strong tie between State and trade unions and to give to the latter a monopolistic control over the entire working class.

III. *Legislative Power*

Perhaps the strongest influence of the corporative tradition on the Christian Democratic Party was seen in its proposals concerning legislative power. But here it was defeated.

While there was never any serious question on the desirability of bicameralism, a prolonged controversy arose as to what the nature of the upper chamber should be: whom it should represent and what powers it should have. Unlike the Communists, who wanted to see the powers of the upper chamber seriously limited, the Christian Democrats were in favor of equality of legislative powers between the Chamber of Deputies and the Senate. Their isolation was due to their belief that the Senate should not be elected on the basis of universal suffrage as the Chamber of Deputies would be, but on the basis of a complex system of interest representation.

To a Constituent Assembly chosen to establish a new democratic structure on the ruins of dictatorship, the idea of interest representation appeared too much like an effort to resurrect Fascist corporatism. But the Christian Democrats refused to concede the point. They argued that the representation of economic groups, divided into the major categories of agriculture, industry, trade, academic bodies, professions, artisans, white collar workers, and civil service, was needed to integrate universal suffrage and to counterbalance the role and influence of political parties which would dominate the state in the Chamber of Deputies. The monopoly of political life by organized political parties could not be a legitimate development in any country, since much of economic life, of social thinking, and, in general, of the activities of the citizens flowed outside the narrow boundaries of party life.

In what must now be recognized as a prophetic statement, the Christian Democratic leader Costantino Mortati said in the course of the Constituent Assembly debate of September 18, 1947: "Italian parties lack a strong attachment to the ideas of freedom; they are followed by an exceedingly small minority of the population, while the great mass is foreign to them. For this reason, political parties are dogmatic and fail to reflect the true needs of the country. Parties have as yet been unable to give birth to a technical and political aristocracy capable of meeting the difficult and specialized tasks of government." [3] In 1947 this attack on political parties was resented, for the country was just emerging from the rule of one party and was anxious to restore a free and varied party life to a position of eminence. But, read five years later, Mortati's statement reflects one serious aspect of constitutional life on the European continent, that is, the failure of parties to recognize the proper limits of their spheres of influence and activity once the line of government decision and of administrative action is reached. Mortati's strictures on parties and his defense of an administrative and political class capable of performing the "difficult and specialized tasks of government," provide an accurate commentary on the events of later years and on the attitudes of the party to which Mortati himself belongs. In 1947 the slogan, "politics above all," was the dominant one. To try to add, "but common sense from time to time," was bound to be unpopular especially when the attempt was made through the cumbersome machine of the cor-

---

[3] cf. Mortati, *Debates of the Constituent Assembly*, September, 18, 1947, p. 305. The main Christian Democratic motion on the issue of interest representation was, in part, as follows: "The Constituent Assembly—considering that a second Chamber, in addition to one elected by universal suffrage, is required for the integration of political representation, so as to reflect social reality, in all its politically significant interest and to guarantee to legislative work, which is of an ever-increasing technical character, the assistance of experts—resolves that these aims are to be reached by securing the participation in the second Chamber of the groups in which social activities spontaneously divide themselves." (*Debates of the Constituent Assembly*, September 17, 1947, p. 265.) The decisive vote on this motion took place on September 23, 1947, when it was rejected by 213 to 166, with practically only the Christian Democrats voting in favor of it.

porative state. It is difficult to believe that Mortati's solution of an upper chamber of wise, technical men would have overcome the difficulties which derive from the presence of political parties trying to sum up within themselves the totality of the political decisions of the community.

Following the defeat of their corporative Senate scheme, the Christian Democrats went along with the plan to provide for two chambers, elected in almost identical manner and having identical powers. For the first few years at least this system may create duplication and make for delay. In the long run, since the two assemblies are elected for different terms (the Chamber for five years, the Senate for six), they will come to represent different phases of the political temper of the country and presumably be able to perform useful functions of reciprocal control. On the other hand, this may lead to serious legislative stalemates and to more frequent elections in order to resolve them.

IV. *Executive Power*

On the issue of relationship between executive and legislative branches, the power of the President of the Republic is a sweeping one. Article 88 reads: "The President of the Republic may, having heard their respective presidents, dissolve both Chambers or only one of them." The only limitation is that he may not exercise such power within the last six months of his seven-year term of office. So anxious were the Christian Democrats to emphasize the absolute and autonomous power of the president in this connection that they wanted it to be proclaimed in the Constitution as a presidential prerogative to be exercised independently of the advice of the Prime Minister.[4] Having failed in this, they succeeded in defeating all efforts to add to Article 88 provisions similar to those of the French Constitution, which severely restricts the freedom of the executive with regard to the dissolution of the National Assembly.

The Constitution also establishes the leadership of the Prime Minister by saying in Article 95 that he "directs the general policy of the government and is responsible for it. He maintains the unity of political and administrative action and promotes and co-

---

[4] See *infra,* pp. 61-63, for later developments.

ordinates the activity of the ministers." The Cabinet is not only led by the Prime Minister: it can also be formed without any initial interference by the legislative branch even though it must at once seek a vote of confidence. Its survival against sudden parliamentary attacks is well protected in Article 94. Three full days must elapse before a vote of non-confidence (which must be by roll call and not by secret ballot) can be taken, and the motion of non-confidence must be presented by at least one-tenth of the total membership of either house. The same article, also, makes clear that "a contrary vote of one or both chambers on a government proposal does not carry with it the obligation of resigning."

In setting up executive power, Christian Democracy was not afraid to accept those constitutional precedents (in this case mostly British) which seemed to offer the best chances of successful application to the Italian scene and of rejecting the tempting French example. Democracy and reaction to dictatorship were not identified with weak executives. On paper at least the Christian Democratic Party saw clearly and built constructively.

V. *Regionalism*

Much less clarity and coherence is present in the Christian Democratic constitutional contribution to the regional problem. The dilemma was this: on the one hand, there was a commitment in principle, on Christian Democracy's part, to set up a regional system through which the autonomy of local government could be reintroduced into Italian life. On the other hand, there was the political and economic reality of the postwar world which counseled against any breakup of central organs of administration and reconstruction for as weak and small a country as Italy. The Christian Democratic regionalists could point to the past iniquities of a centralizing government and to the virtues of municipal society in the Middle Ages. The defenders of the unitary state could prove that this was pure political romanticism which, if carried out, would greatly hamper the recovery of the country. The establishment of local self-government did not require the setting up of regions with powers in spheres which, as long ago as 1787, were recognized by the Philadelphia convention as properly belonging to the central government even in a federal system such as the United States was to be.

The conflict occasioned by the theoretical phantasies of the Christian Democratic Party, has produced the least satisfactory section of the Italian Constitution. Strong claims of principle are made on behalf of the regions, which are to be constituted as autonomous bodies with their own powers and functions and to which the State may delegate the exercise of its own administrative functions as well. Some of the regions are recognized particular forms of autonomy in accordance with special statutes. An elaborate machinery of government is organized to fulfill these tasks.

If the appearance of regionalism is thus established, its reality is substantially weakened by two sets of provisions which contradict the spirit of a true regional system.

In the first place the jurisdiction of regional governments is severely limited. Most of the powers listed in Article 117 concern insignificant matters, such as communal boundaries, museums, mineral waters, peatbogs, hunting and fishing. The only important jurisdiction lies in the fields of public welfare and agriculture. But in this respect, too, there is the overriding limitation of the superiority of national legislation, for the Constitution retains for the central government the right to establish fundamental legislative principles in both these fields.

In the second place, however, even this subordinate and narrow jurisdiction is undermined by the provisions of Articles 124-127 which, in effect, grant to the central government the power to prevent the enactment of measures approved by the regional legislatures, and to stop regional executive action, whenever there is a conflict with the rights of other regions or of the nation as a whole. What is even more fundamental from the point of view of weakening the very substance of regional self government is the authority of the central government to dissolve regional parliaments and to force the resignation of regional executives, on a great variety of grounds, including "reasons of national security."

The section on regionalism, then, is vitiated by the vicious contradiction of first granting in principle something which is later withheld in practice. It can indeed be questioned whether the Christian Democratic Party has rendered a service to the tenable principles of regional autonomy, by creating the illusion that the Constitution recognizes them, but at the same time sanctioning a mechanism which deprives them of all reality. Subsequent experience, as will be seen later, had demonstrated the unpleasant consequences of a solution which is bound to breed a cynical view on the whole matter. By asking too much in the beginning, the Christian Democratic Party was forced to retreat. But the retreat has been a disorderly one, which has left behind an unmanageable constitutional problem.

VI. *The Constitutional Court*

Christian Democracy was equally committed to translate into constitutional terms one of their cherished philosophical ideals, that of natural law. Politically, and in the twentieth century, natural law could not mean much more than a belief in the relative permanence of certain fundamental principles concerning the life of man in society. Once those principles had somehow found their way into a written constitution, natural law doctrine required that the law of the constitution be placed on a higher level than statutory law, to give it a validity that could not be controverted by simple legislative action. For Christian Democracy the Constitution was to be the legal embodiment of the current political conception of natural law and was to provide the machinery whereby the validity of mere legislative action could be tested in the light of more permanent constitutional principles.

In spite of Communist opposition, the majority of the Constituent Assembly went along with the view of the Christian Democratic Party that a Constitutional Court with specific functions of legislative review was a desirable part of a Constitution which was to recognize the doctrine of a higher law and to establish a regional system which might lead to jurisdictional conflicts. There was also a strong feeling that here was a chance to do something that had proven so important in the strongest and most lasting of all constitutional systems. Had not the Supreme Court of the United States, ever since Marshall's days, asserted its right to be the supreme interpreter and defender of the federal Constitution? The judicial review of Congressional acts had been a milestone in the development of American government. Thus, on a decisive historical occasion, a younger democracy would also show its readiness to curb the reckless majority will of legislative bodies trying to assert themselves against the permanent views of the community. It did not matter that, owing to the provincialism which is a painful consequence of twenty-five years of frozen isolation imposed by Fascism and which in so many ways has cut off Italy from the stream of change that went on throughout the free world, the Christian Democratic deputies who propounded a judicial body to review legislative acts obviously did not know that ever since 1937 the voiding of Congressional acts by the Supreme Court has not appeared either fashionable or necessary. In any case, the idea of a Constitutional Court is a good one even if it turns out to be something else than what its originators imagined. For in the broad area of defense of human rights and of freedom, the Italian Constitutional Court can find a steadily increasing body of useful precedents issuing from the Supreme Court of the United States.

In the details concerning the organization of the court, the Constitution provides for essentially satisfactory solutions. The tenure of the fifteen judges is fixed at twelve years, which is not much below the average term of office of a justice of the Supreme Court of the United States. The power of appointment of the judges is distributed among three sources, only one of which could be said to be political: five are to be appointed by the President of the Republic who, as head of the State and protector of the Constitution, should be above narrow partisan considerations; one third by Parliament in joint session, and one third by other higher courts of the land. Nor is the choice of the appointing agencies free. The appointments have to be made from among judges of the higher ordinary and administrative courts, from full professors of the university faculties of jurisprudence, and from members of the bar with at least twenty years of practice. All the necessary guarantees for a competent and independent court seem to be present. What so far appears to be missing is the will to set in motion the institution itself.[5]

---

[5] See *infra*, pp. 63-64, 76-77, for later developments.

CHAPTER FOUR

VICTORY AND POWER

I. *The Conditions of Victory*

By 1948 Christian Democracy had to its credit three preliminary achievements of great importance.

1. It had developed a program appealing to a large body of people. It was conservative enough to satisfy those who wanted, after the disruption of Fascism and war, a period of quiet reassertion of the older values of individualism. It was progressive enough in its criticism of capitalism to satisfy those who knew that no return to "normalcy" would meet the demands of the postwar emergency. It was sufficiently anti-Marxist and anti-Communist to please those who, most of all, wanted to fight the danger represented by Soviet power.

2. It had put through a good Constitution. The Christian Democratic Party could say with justification that the Italian Constitution was better than the French. In spite of some empty promises at the regional level, it provided the framework within which an effective and balanced parliamentary system of government could be developed.

3. It had withstood the temptation to use its initial grant of power to achieve the temporary advantages that inflationary policies always produce in the economic field. By turning over the management of economic affairs in the spring of 1947 to non-Christian Democratic hands, it showed that party politics and prestige were not placed above the welfare of the nation. The economic policies followed since May 1947 and for which the Christian Democratic government assumed responsibility did much to create the framework of stability within which a meaningful discussion of future policy could be carried out.

Therefore, when the first elections under the new Constitution were called for April 18, 1948, the Christian Democratic Party started from a position of notable objective strength. But the Communist issue, the Marshall Plan and the intervention of the Church, dramatizing the tension of the times, proved to be added factors of equal importance in bringing about the Christian Democratic victory.

There was no hesitancy in the Christian Democratic attack on Communism. The loss of political freedom under Communism was the main theme and it was pressed home with relentless vigor. The Balkan trials, the Czech crisis, and, even closer at hand, developments of Yugoslav-occupied Istria, provided abundant material for the Christian Democratic campaign. Christian Democracy did not have too much difficulty in establishing the fact that in Istria even small peasant holdings had been taken over by the State, that all non-Communist parties were suppressed in Communist-ruled countries, and that the freedom of movement of the workers themselves was being drastically curtailed by Communist regimes. The Italian industrial workers themselves were getting restless as a result of overbearing Communist tactics inside the factories, for their tactics made it impossible to distinguish between the rule of the Fascist and that of the Communist bosses.

Christian Democracy made it clear that its refusal to compromise with Communism was due to the latter's denials of the values of Christianity and of political freedoms. Christian Democracy remained strongly critical of the capitalistic system and in favor of industrial and agrarian reforms. As de Gasperi said in an electoral speech, "We are not fighting the Communist party because of its economic program, with regard to which an agreement might be possible, up to a certain point." When large numbers of industrial workers in northern Italy voted for Christian Democracy, they were not voting for clericalism and reaction but for a party which, having promised to safeguard them from the loss of freedom which Communism would entail, would at the same time guarantee those social reforms to which they felt entitled. In this mood, they cast their vote for Christian Democracy, even though fully aware that clerical and reactionary influences were present within the party and would have to be dealt with later.

The championship of political freedom, however notable in itself, would not have been enough to carry the day for Christian

Democracy had it not been accompanied by the more concrete hope offered by the Marshall Plan. Without the Plan there would have been no alternative to the setting up of a dictatorship to carry the country through a period of economic readjustment and of even lower standards of living. The only party in a position to do that would have been the Communist Party. The Marshall Plan, by holding out the hope of the reintegration of the country within the Western economic system and of a slow improvement of the standard of living of the people, instead of restricting Italy's freedom of choice, introduced that freedom for the first time, and made the Italian elections free in the substantial meaning that a ballot could be cast in more than one way.

But the intervention of the Church must be considered as another element of almost equal importance. We have seen how Christian Democracy was born in Italy in 1919 as a lay party of leftist tendencies based upon a foundation of Christian morality. The formula of complete independence from the Church but of acceptance of its teachings on the nature of man and of his role in society, was devised by the party's founder, Luigi Sturzo, as the only one capable of developing the new political party in competition with the others. The division which had, for centuries, split Italy between Guelphs and Ghibellines had not been forgotten and no political ammunition was going to be given to the anti-papalist forces by any suggestion that the new Party was the creature of the Church.

When in 1943 the Christian Democratic Party was reorganized, there was greater difficulty in stressing with equal decision the separation between Party and Church. For the reasons that were noted earlier, Catholic Action and the ecclesiastical organization became the almost natural vehicles through which the structure of the Party could be rebuilt. There was, also, the increased intensity of religious feelings, the result of war and despair and of increasing dissatisfaction with the cynicism and materialism of opposed political groups. The net result was that the Christian Democratic Party was less willing than the Popular Party to renounce the tutelary benevolence of the Church. Indeed, Christian Democratic leaders were often anxious to show that they were the children of the Church and were ready to make—within a political context—

public acknowledgment of the supreme spiritual authority of the Pontiff.

These changes became obvious during the political campaign, which was waged, as far as the Church issue was concerned, on terms quite different from those of 1919 and 1921. Party leaders maintained that the hopes of Italian freedom, unity, and independence were based on the acceptance of a Christian program and upon the moral protection afforded by the Holy See. Even de Gasperi, immediately after the elections, said that during the war, the Pope had appeared to all as Italy's protector and savior, and the clergy had cooperated valiantly in the task of liberation from the enemy. "We know that the State is completely independent in its relationships with the Church. We want, as the Church itself wants, to maintain this independence. But we know that we have first of all the moral duty and, since the Concordat, the juridical duty as well, to surround the Holy See with the most absolute respect. And we must above all remember that in the last hundred years of Italy's history the activity of the clergy has been directed to the moral reconstruction of Italy and to that of healthy and free democratic institutions."

As far as the Church itself was concerned, the outcome of the Italian elections was a matter too serious for neutrality. The Church, therefore, supported with all available means, the anti-Communist side. The clergy and Catholic Action issued a call to vote for those who promised adequately to protect the interests and the principles of Catholicism. There was disquiet in many quarters when excessive ecclesiastical zeal considered only Christian Democratic candidates to be in that category. Some party leaders sought to undo the damage by pointing out that the primary duty was that of voting against Communism and not for Christian Democracy. There was disquiet, too, at the thought that Church intervention had tended to widen the cleavage between the two political groups, evoking in one of them the strong and burning resentment which is always felt at the intrusion of the religious arm in temporal matters. Finally, there remained, after the elections, the unsolved question of what the continued existence of the political committees of Catholic Action (the "civic committees" led by Luigi Gedda) would do to the freedom of action of the party itself.

II. The Arithmetic of the 1948 Elections

The outcome of the 1948 elections can be summarized statistically as follows. In the vote for the Chamber of Deputies, a total of 26 million citizens went to the polls, or about 92 percent of the registered voters, as against 23 millions in 1946. Almost 13 millions cast their ballot for Christian Democracy in 1948 as against 8 millions in 1946; about 10 millions for Marxist parties, as against 9 millions in 1946. All remaining parties and groups obtained about 3.5 million votes as against nearly double that number in 1946. The tendency, already so clear in 1946, towards the disintegration of smaller parties, became even more apparent in 1948; in certain regions of northern Italy they disappeared completely, and the South alone offered some haven to the groups which ruled Italy for the sixty years before the advent of Fascism.

The popular vote obtained by the Christian Democrats was about 49 percent of the total in 1948, as against 35 percent in 1946. The strength of the Party increased throughout the country. In about a dozen electoral colleges it polled substantially more than 50 percent of the total, and well beyond 60 percent in certain provinces of northern Italy, which continued to be the stronghold of Christian Democratic strength. In the "reddest" provinces of the Po Valley, where, in succession, Socialism, Fascism, and Communism have found their most fertile breeding ground in the last fifty years, Christian Democratic strength—starting from a rather low level—increased by one half over 1946. In the South, where Christian Democracy had never been very strong, the Party made equally significant progress, although as a whole it remained weaker than in the North. Throughout the country it benefited from the increased vote, from wholesale defections from the smaller groups of the center and of the right, and, in a smaller measure, from Socialist votes.

Contrary to the Christian Democratic pattern, the strength of the Marxist parties remained uneven. It surpassed 50 percent of the total vote in the lower Po Valley and in Tuscany. It reached 48 percent in the industrial provinces of Turin, the birthplace of Italian Communism. It dropped very sharply to less than 30 percent in several Venetian provinces, and to 20 percent or even less in some Southern provinces. The ten millions of Marxist voters were divided, moreover, into two hostile factions: the Communist front which polled about 8 million and the Democratic Socialists, who polled nearly 2 million votes. The elections proved that the strength of the independent Socialists was greatest among the skilled industrial workers and the middle classes, while Communism proved to be strongest among the workers of the mass industries and the poorer agricultural laborers and peasants. In a few areas in northern Italy the strength of the independent Socialists was almost one half that of the Communist front.

Outside of the two Christian Democratic and Marxist blocs, the biggest losses were sustained by the two center parties. The Action Party, whose main function was once described as that of acting as the guardian of the purity of the Communist Party, was completely swallowed by the latter, which did not care to have anyone as the keeper of its conscience. The Republicans, having won their main goal, the establishment of the Republic, suffered the dispiriting consequences of having no further justification for their existence. The Liberals saw most of their followers disappear into the Christian Democratic fold. The Sicilian autonomists were defeated by economic realities which demanded union with the mainland. The extreme right maintained its strength to a greater degree, and succeeded in polling almost 2 million votes against 2.5 millions in 1946.

III. *Coalition Government*

It is important to realize both the unprecedented and the decisive nature of the 1948 elections. Unprecedented, because, for the first time in the history of the country, one Party had achieved, as a result of a free election, an absolute parliamentary majority. Christian Democracy elected 305 out of the 574 members of the Chamber of Deputies and 131 out of 237 elected Senators. The Christian Democratic Party by itself could form a government enjoying an adequate parliamentary majority. Gone were the necessity of negotiation and compromise with other parties, the uncertainties of coalition life, the weaknesses of minority governments. At long last and when mostly needed the machinery of government was placed in a position to work effectively, backed by a brand-new Constitution. Decisive, because, in a real and not at all rhetorical sense, a strong and democratic government could now begin to apply itself to the solution of the disastrous heritage of thirty years of crisis, war and dictatorship, with the full support, economic and moral, of the leading country of the West, the United States.

Christian Democracy, between 1945 and 1948, asked for the full responsibility of power. It obtained it under the most favorable possible circumstances after the elections of 1948. The impartial observer is, therefore, forced to apply the strictest tests in measuring the party's achievements since 1948 and to accept as extenuating circumstances only those clearly suggested by the objective difficulties of the problems to be solved.

The beginnings augured well for the future, for in spite of its overwhelming victory the Christian Democratic Party decided to continue to welcome other democratic allies and to share with them the burdens of government. ' Liberals, Democratic Socialists, Republicans, had all contributed, in ideas and men, to the Christian Democratic victory. It was a demonstration both of humility and of generosity for Christian Democracy to seek the participiation of the smaller parties. Although not needed from the point of view of a majority in Parliament, coalition government was needed in order to create the widest possible solidarity among the defenders of the democratic system. It was also needed to fill obvious gaps in the staffing of foreign and economic agencies. Small in numbers, the minor democratic parties were relatively rich in brains. It was, finally, a wise policy to follow from the point of view of the future, for it established the practice of the Christian Democratic-Socialist collaboration which might again become a necessity.

The coalition policies, which Prime Minister de Gasperi has always strongly supported, have met with varying degrees of success since 1948. At times, all three minor democratic parties have participated in the coalition. Later, only the Democratic Socialists and the Republicans were left when the Liberals withdrew in protest against the allegedly radical economic policy of the government, especially in the field of agrarian reform. At the end of

57

1951 only the Republicans were in the coalition. The Democratic Socialists, in the course of what was described as a march towards Socialist unity, had broken up into quarreling groups which could no longer agree on Cabinet participation. Mere Republican participation gives a shadowy appearance to the coalition, but the idea is still alive and may be reinforced again if the Democratic Socialists finally succeed in achieving unity, and if the obstacles to reconciliation between the revived forces of laicism and clericalism can be eliminated.

CHAPTER FIVE

THE USE OF POWER

I. *Constitutionalism*

The new Constitution of 1948 needed implementation both in spirit and by legislation. By exemplary living and concrete deeds the government of the Italian Republic had to show that it considered constitutionalism as the distinguishing mark of the system so painfully instituted. The first phase of Italy's national political life, from 1870 to 1922, had been notable for the pervasive influence of personal, even though essentially democratic, government; the second phase, the Fascist one, had been a period of totally repressive dictatorship; the third phase of Italy's political development had to be founded upon an effort to combine democratic practice with respect for the Constitution, and to provide that elusive system of constitutional democracy which is the best guarantee of both freedom and progress.

The Constitution needed more than spiritual allegiance to its norms: it needed to be implemented by legislative action wherever this was indicated by the document itself. Some of the more important instances were those of press and labor legislation, regionalism and the Constitutional Court. In all of them the Constitution had specifically left to subsequent legislation the task of further definition of the principles and of setting up the necessary institutions. Without such legislation the Constitution would remain in several important aspects a mere declaration of intention without concrete application.

Four years after the passage of the Constitution, it must be said that the efforts both of spiritual and of legislative implementation have either not been made or, when made, have had a negative result. Many reasons may be adduced to justify inaction and action: the exceptional difficulties of the times, the disruptive influence of Communism, a recognition of what might now be considered the mistaken emphasis of certain sections of the Constitution. But some of these justifications are not relevant to the issue, and the conclusion must be maintained that the constitutional experiment started in 1948 has not yet been taken seriously. Enough evidence is at hand to support this view.

a) *The Press.*

The weaknesses of Article 21 on press freedom have been increased rather than eliminated in the government proposals for a press law. The police power to seize newspapers even without a court order, a power which the Constitution recognizes only for crimes specifically defined by the press law, has been extended to include "incitement to crime." To give the police power to seize newspapers for alleged incitement to crime, would mean placing the broadest discretionary power, unchecked by any definable legal concept, in the hands of the government. In a country where the main purpose of newspapers is not the objective presentation of the news, but the violent and partisan polemic against opposed ideologies, parties and governments, few newspaper issues will be free from rhetorical appeals to open attack and rebellion against organized political power. Any government could, therefore, harass the opposition press out of existence.

The chief vice of the proposed legislation is that it predominantly concerns itself with setting up potentially dangerous restrictions, instead of trying to interpret and organize in the most liberal sense the basic principles of press freedom. The low state of the press is not sufficient reason to gear press legislation to the least satisfactory common denominator.

b) *Regionalism*

It is an ironical paradox that Christian Democracy, the most fervent propounder of regionalism, should, once in power, shy away from its fulfillment. The Christian Democratic Party in its practical handling of the realities of government has, in effect, nullified its theoretical commitments concerning regional autonomy. The reasons for this change in position are strong ones. In Sicily, the government has been faced by the demands of the Sicilian autonomists who, basing themselves on the clauses of the Sicilian Statute, have been clamoring for the defenestration of the authority of the national government from the island while continuing to put forth all-inclusive demands for financial support from the center. Freedom without responsibility has been their slogan. The reaction of the government has been to deny these claims, to thwart the efforts of the more extreme supporters of autonomy and to take measures which have the appearance of going against the ideals of regionalism. In such regions of central Italy as Tuscany and Emilia, the government has been confronted by a different situation. There, the Communists are in a majority. If the regional governments were to be set up, the Communist Party would control them. The chance that such Communist regional governments might proclaim their accession to the Soviet Union of Socialist Republics is one that the government is not ready to take. It is true that by falling back upon the relevant protective clauses of the Constitution the government could dissolve these Communist regional bodies, but the task would not be an easy one and might entail civil war. Thus, the existence of a Communist threat is enough to cause the government not to set up regional institutions at all, just as in Sicily separatism has prompted the national government to restrict the power of the existing ones.

Many, including some of those who, even before 1948, had opposed regionalism, feel that respect for the Constitution as it stands demands that the regional structure be created. The national government does not lack strong powers with which to deal with possible rebellious and anti-constitutional activities of regional governments. But it cannot pretend to fight effectively against unconstitutionalism if, in the meantime, by its inaction, it is guilty of nullifying an important section of the Constitution. The pragmatic justification of the policy of the government reinforces the belief that the Constitution is a scrap of paper to which no one need pay much attention.

c) *The Presidency*

Article 74 of the Constitution grants to the President of the Republic the power of suspensive veto. Any bill sent to the President for his signature may be returned to Parliament without it, if accompanied by a presidential message in which the reasons for the President's dissent are set forth. Upon receipt of the message, both houses of Parliament must proceed to a new vote. If the bill is' again approved the President must sign it. It was the intention of the Constituent Assembly to create an autonomous source of legislative control in the hands of the President, to enable him to call the attention of the legislative assemblies upon any serious question, constitutional or otherwise, raised by the proposed legislation. The Constitution does not set limits to the presidential power. Messages can be sent either when the wisdom or expediency of the bill is questioned or when doubts arise as to its constitutionality.

The intended autonomy of the presidential power is due to the nature of the parliamentary system of government. In all major instances, as well as in most minor ones, bills that emerge from Parliament are either due to cabinet initiative or are supported by it. If a bill is approved and is sent to the President for his signature, the presumption is that the government is for it. It is specifically because of this joint parliament-cabinet responsibility for legislation, that the Constitution placed this suspensive message power in the hands of the President who stands outside of both Cabinet and Parliament.

With what appears as untenable logic, strong groups within the Christian Democratic Party have sought to deny this power of the President by appealing to the doctrine of the "countersignature" required for Presidential acts. According to this view, since the message requires the countersignature of a cabinet minister before it is sent to Parliament, the President can submit his message to Parliament only following a prior decision of the Cabinet in favor of it. This view assumes that the Cabinet, having proposed a legislative measure, having fought for it before Parliament, and having succeeded in obtaining Parliamentary approval, is likely to change its mind at the last moment when the bill is ready to be signed by the President, and begs him to suggest to Parliament that the bill be killed.

It is difficult to see how there can be a tenable defense of this position. And indeed the legislation, which would propose it, is proceeding with difficulty in its initial pre-parliamentary stages. Under it, Article 74 would be abrogated and with it one of the constitutional guarantees intended to provide for renewed deliberation in those cases which appear to the President to deserve it.

The real explanation for the move lies in the unconstitutional view of political life held by certain elements within the Christian Democratic Party. These groups reject as intolerable the idea of the development within the structure of the state of an autonomous source of power, which does not owe a direct allegiance to the party in office. Anything that tends to create obstacles to the unchallenged will of the majority party, is to be eliminated. That this does violence to a basic principle of constitutionalism is of no concern.

d) *The Constitutional Court*

A parallel case, which again shows the failure to grasp the complex arrangements and the balance envisaged by the Constitution, is that of the Constitutional Court. First of all, the actual establishment of the Court was delayed. It is true that the Party stood for the defense of natural law, in principle. But, in practice, to have a Court which might conceivably prevent the party from achieving some of its specific goals while it was in office, was bad. Therefore, for three years, nothing was done to organize the Court. When it was clear that the arguments of Communism and separatism, which have a certain surface validity in the case of regionalism, could not be logically applied to the Constitutional Court (no Communist was likely to be appointed as a judge and the Court was unlikely to threaten the unity of the Italian State), a second line of defense was sought, that of giving to the party in power the right to appoint two-thirds, instead of only one-third, of the judges. With two-thirds of the judges on its side, Christian Democracy had nothing to fear. Again the Constitution interfered, for Article 135 grants to the party in power, that is to the parliamentary majority, the right of appointing only five out of the fifteen judges, with five to be appointed by the Judiciary and five by the President. The Christian Democratic Party thought a solution was at hand if it could take over the appointment of the judges reserved to the President. Legislation was introduced in the Chamber of Deputies to provide that the five judges to be appointed by the President were first to be proposed to him by the government, that is, by the parliamentary majority. Again the spirit and the letter of the Constitution was being violated but this did not prevent the Christian Democratic majority of the Chamber of Deputies from voting for the violation, leaving to the Communist Party the role of defender of constitutionalism. At this point the Cabinet became aware of the probable and most serious consequences of the vote of the Chamber of Deputies and, having accepted the validity of the representations that were made, it forced the modification of the bill by the time it reached the Senate. But if this political assault against the independence of the Constitutional Court was defeated, the Court itself has not yet come to life. It is as if Christian Democracy, stymied in its attempt to gain control of the Court, had decided to have no Court at all. Again, regardless of the final outcome, it is certain that these vagaries have weakened the role that the Constitution was supposed to play.

II. *Economic Policy*

In the field of economic policy Christian Democracy has had to contend with objective difficulties not of its own making. But, in addition, it has been the victim of its own Party machine, of the Fascist inheritance and of Communist pressures, a terrifying combination indeed.

In general, monetary and budgetary policies have been well conceived. Without giving up flexibility and the expansion of credit facilities when needed for productive purposes, the government has succeeded in maintaining a framework of stability, much needed after the inflationary forces that multiplied prices fifty times between 1938 and 1948.

Equally sound, even if excessively slow, has been the approach to land reform. Christian Democracy has refused to narrow the issue to one of a mere formal and precipitate redistribution of land. The redistribution of mostly arid and unproductive land is not a step forward. (There is no really good land that can be redistributed. When an "agrarian problem" exists in such fertile areas as the lower Po valley, the task must chiefly be that of the establishment of cooperative techniques.) What the landless and impoverished Italian farmer wants is not to acquire a property title to an acre of desert land but to establish a fruitful relationship (which often could well be other than a property relationship) to an acre of watered and green land on which some decent shelter has been built. The Christian Democratic government has recognized this fundamental principle, even though its fulfillment must perforce entail long delays and expensive efforts, such as are not required by the simple device of cutting up the large estates without regard for the consequences. In general the government has adopted the policy of setting up autonomous authorities managed by competent technicians. In the small beginnings of land reform so far achieved, many people rightly see the real promise of large scale future developments.

Less hopeful is the outlook for the *Cassa del Mezzogiorno*, a public corporation organized for the purpose of coordinating the economic development of the Italian South. The difficulty is due to the influence gained by the party machine in the management of what should have been an autonomous corporation run by competent planners and technicians. The initial planning of the corporation's work,[1] and the study of its relationship to the International Bank for Reconstruction and Development, which was to supply the necessary dollar funds, were carefully carried out. Both the experts and the Cabinet were in agreement on the need of TVA-like management. Their subsequent defeat, at the hands of rebellious Christian Democratic politicians, anxious to gain control over this exceedingly important instrument of economic policy, shows at its worst the crisis of constitutionalism and the difficulties of eliminating illegitimate party interests from the sphere of common welfare.

Fascist and Communist influences have not been successfully eliminated, either. Fascism left a tradition of severe control of the worker's freedom to strike. The tribulations inflicted by a Communist-dominated General Confederation of Labor perhaps explain why there are some resemblances between the labor legislation proposed by the Christian Democratic government in 1951 and the labor charter enacted by the Fascists in 1926. One of them is the monopoly enjoyed by publicly recognized trade unions. The

---

[1] See the excellent report prepared by Associazione per lo Sviluppo dell'Industria nel Mezzogiorno, *Economic Effects of an Investment Program in Southern Italy* (Rome, 1951, English ed.), pp. vi & 88, with 53 tables and charts.

other is the prohibition of strikes which do not fall within clearly defined categories.   In principle the right to strike is admitted (while the Fascists denied it) but the use of collective agreements in prohibiting strikes is encouraged to an excessive extent. Again, as in the case of press freedom, a cumbersome and potentially dangerous machinery is set up which can do away with the very freedom it is designed to protect.

Communist power has made itself felt on the issue of reconversion and reorganization of industries suffering from the aftermath of Fascism and war. The government holding company, IRI (Institute of Industrial Reconstruction), has not been given a sufficiently free hand to solve the problems of unemployment, technical obsolescence, misdirected plant use.   As a result, IRI, for the most part, has had to allow the survival of autarchic and bankrupt industries which should have been subjected to surgical reform.[2] Communism has thus been successful in forcing the government to accept its own policies of economic rigidity and stagnation.[3]

III. *Party Structure*

What the preceding analysis of constitutionalism and economic policy has revealed is that the structure of the Christian Democratic Party and the relationship of the Party itself to the government, have often been the cause of serious trouble.   Both points deserve, therefore, more detailed discussion.

It is by now a commonplace to say that Italian Christian Democracy is a complex movement made up of groups and individuals that differ substantially among themselves. Born amidst conditions of political chaos and at the end of a long period of Fascist dictatorship, Christian Democracy profited from both the fear of Communism and the rejection of the old pre-fascist parties and succeeded in attracting to its ranks a multitude of political followers. Thanks to its electoral successes in 1946 and in 1948, Christian Democracy has not yet undergone the purification which the 1951 elections have forced upon the French M.R.P. The present relative

---

[2] The notable exception of the modernization, with Marshall Plan aid, of the steel industry, must however be recalled.

[3] Cf. Einaudi, Domenach and Garosci, *Communism in Western Europe,* Ithaca, 1951, pp. 29 ff. and 42 ff.

simplicity of structure of the M.R.P. is still foreign to Italy's Christian Democracy. It is therefore important to analyze the party's composition in order to gain a correct understanding of what the party means in Italian political life.

The striking initial fact is that Christian Democracy has rejected the leadership of its founder, Luigi Sturzo. That Christian Democracy in Italy owes much to the thought, personality, and hard work of Luigi Sturzo is generally accepted as beyond discussion. That between 1919 and 1922 Sturzo led the Popular Party in a way generally designed to make of it a strong, independent and permanent feature of Italian political life, is also a statement which is not easily controverted. That thirty years ago, Sturzo struck a proper balance between reform and conservatism is also admitted. It is then remarkable to see Sturzo today so much at variance with the Christian Democratic Party and to witness the mutual irritation that exists between the Party and its founder.

This lack of compatibility is not due to the usual reasons which lie at the roots of the conflict of different generations—the old, supposedly reluctant to give up accepted modes of thought and of action, the young, eager to go forward and unwilling to accept the obsolescent advice of elder statesmen. For, in this instance, the reverse is true. As a result of the combination of vigorous intellectual faculties and of a keen interest in the problems and political experimentation of many countries, verified at first hand over a period of twenty-two years of exile in Great Britain and in the United States, Sturzo, at eighty, shows an extraordinary mental agility and an enviably realistic political awareness. He understands the requirements of a modern state, realizes the compromises and adjustments that must be made, and is reluctant to sacrifice viable solutions of government problems to vague theoretical obsessions. In comparison with his youthful approach, the "young" generation of Christian Democrats seems very antiquated indeed. Their economic thinking has been made cumbersome by the ancient and fallacious tenets of corporativism, whether Catholic or Fascist. Their political views are almost totally innocent of any comprehension of the exacting needs of the twentieth century state. In spite of this break, Sturzo's influence remains strong, to the extent at least that it makes the Party constantly ashamed of what it is doing. It is too early to say that in the end this will not be productive of some good.

With the elimination of Sturzo, the leadership of the party has been held by Alcide de Gasperi, an impressive figure, scholar, anti-Fascist, democrat and Christian. Unlike Sturzo, who is always interested in administration and in the specification of the details of political and economic action, de Gasperi shows a greater flair for the generic needs of political life. He is interested less in the purely programmatic aspects of government than in the restatement of the higher ideals of a democratic and free society. Apart from a question of personal temperament, this is probably due, on the one hand, to the pressure of Communism, and on the other, to the complexity of a Party made up of conflicting groups even greater in number than in Sturzo's times. The task of the leader has unfortunately become to an excessive extent that of providing the steadying influence that will keep the boat from capsizing. De Gasperi has done this with great skill, and at the same time he has prevented any group within the party from exploiting power to its own exclusive advantage. In a condition of semi-paralysis of the activities of government, de Gasperi has proved to be an ideal replacement for Sturzo and nobody else in the Party could match his qualities as a stabilizer. It is also certain that no one but de Gasperi could have so successfully steered Italy's relationship with the Western powers after Italy's defeat, and done so much to restore confidence in Italy's democratic purpose among the Western nations.

If we now proceed to analyze the forces with which de Gasperi has to contend, this is what we find.

a) *The Right*

The strength of the right was bound to increase after the war as a majority of the conservative element saw in the Party a bulwark against Communism. We find here, especially in the South of Italy, representatives of the land-owning classes, of the middle and upper bourgeoisie, which had been firm supporters of Fascism, monarchists, and in general those who hope to use Christian Democracy to salvage something of the past. But we also find representatives of an enlightened liberal conservatism, disinterested defenders of a tradition of individualism threatened by leftist totalitarianism, men like Stefano Jacini who represent a valuable counterweight to the collectivist wing of the party.

Since 1948 a good many of the groups first mentioned have become displeased with Party policies. Some of them have joined the neo-Fascist movement. Others are in open revolt against the Party. This is a healthy process for, if continued, it should free Christian Democracy of elements substantially alien to its ideal structure. Apart from possible future developments, the right has so far represented a heavy burden for the party.

b) *The Center*

Here are found, together with the survivors of the Sturzo era and the most reliable supporters of de Gasperi, large numbers of small peasant owners, artisans, all those — and there are many of them — who would like to see a God-fearing, honest, forward-looking but tranquil government carry on and protect the community from the dangers outside. To the center belongs the core of the Party machine, the colorless hacks who occupy a majority of the political positions and of Party offices. Their function, it seems, is that of preventing both the right and the left from taking over. Even if some comfort can be found in numbers, the position of the center is not a happy one. Being largely negative, it has led to the immobilism of Christian Democracy ever since 1948. The center, too, has shown a tendency to yield to the temptation of power and to consider it as a prize to be used to gain advantages and remunerative posts for the Party, both inside and outside of government. Party interests are given a high priority and often no effort is made to fix with rigidity a line of division between the temporal and the ecclesiastical. This is a kind of negative clericalism, perhaps not as dangerous as the clericalism of the left which at times seems to involve the establishment of a theocracy and not merely the distribution of a few practical advantages to deserving ecclesiastics.

c) *The Left*

The left is usually the most interesting and the most petulant segment of any party's structure. It claims to represent the future, it prods the reluctant leadership to action, it is against vested interests, it is for "mass" action and economic democracy. The Christian Democratic left stands for all of this and some of the results are rather startling.

There is first of all the generic left led by Giovanni Gronchi, vaguely progressive and socialist in its aspirations but primarily aware of the advantages to be obtained from a redistribution of the practical benefits of political power. Its chief reason for existence seems to be its hope of replacing de Gasperi in the future. It stands generically for peace and it expresses only a mild interest in the Atlantic Pact because it hopes to capitalize on any latent dissatisfaction with the hardships imposed by de Gasperi's firm adherence to the obligations of the Western alliance. It is to the left of de Gasperi because this is the only way in which a practical alternative to the rule of the center can be created. Were the generic left ever to succed in its efforts to replace the center in its control of the Party, no one expects to see any radical changes introduced in Party policies. The realism of the generic left is so great and it is so unburdened by any heavy intellectual baggage that caution and compromise would appear to be the rule in spite of contrary appearances.

Not so with the academic or corporative left. Among its leaders are Giuseppe Dossetti, Amintore Fanfani, Giorgio La Pira. Its most important organ, from 1947 to 1951, was *Cronache Sociali*.[4] It believes in the regulated freedom of the individual which can come to him only through a group. The State, as the supreme manager of political and economic life, must function through a complex hierarchy to which publicly recognized trade unions belong. The academicians' critique of capitalism and individualism is so complete that in the end their State is not sharply distinguishable from the Fascist one, even though it is said that the freedom of the individual is to be safeguarded through the acceptance of the morality and values of Christian religion.

---

[4] *Cronache Sociali* was born under harrowing circumstances on May 30, 1947. On that day de Gasperi succeeded in forming his first cabinet without Communist participation, thus bringing to an end the experiment in "tri-partism" dear to the academic left. The journal died at the end of 1951 on the morrow of de Gasperi's return from the United States where he had sealed Italy's Western alliance.

The concern for the poor and for the shocking deficiencies of Italian life, needing reform in so many fields, is well justified. In many instances, the leaders of the academic left are young, intelligent, and have appealing personal traits. They have the fervor of the crusaders and the rigor of the puritans. Many of them have fought courageously in the Resistance and still carry with them the vision of the ideal republic of which they then dreamed. It was often a vision dreamed jointly with the Communists, and the longing towards some kind of all-embracing "popular" democracy perfected in collaboration with a Western variety of Communism still persists. They looked upon the break of "tripartism" in 1947 as a calamity to be avoided. Today, they find themselves amidst the crudities of the cold war, torn between a desire to continue the "dialogue" with Communism and the duties of filial piety and discipline which they have to accept as children of the Church. As a whole, they have remained within the fold of the faithful and accepted the consequence of the Church position with regard to Communism.

To some extent they have shared in the responsibilities of government, as de Gasperi has not forgotten his own definition of Christian Democracy as a Party of the center moving towards the left. Fanfani has been Minister of Labor and was made Minister of Agriculture in 1951 and, therefore, placed in direct charge of one of the most sensitive areas of government action. The influence of the group is felt in the proposed labor legislation. Dossetti was for a while Vice-Secretary of the Party until his resignation on October 8, 1951.[5]

The difficulty of the leaders of the academic left is that, in spite of all their assets, they have only a dim realization of what a free

---

[5] The resignation was not generally viewed, at the time it was offered, as a kind of sabbatical leave from politics, to write a tratise on Canon Law, something Dossetti must do to win a promotion to full professor. On October 20, a new organization was launched by the supporters of the academic left, to coordinate the opposition to the official policies of their own Party. And a new magazine, *Iniziativa Popolare,* was started to replace *Cronache Sociali.* Since then these activities have been either reduced or suspended in what appears like a retreat under pressure, so as to leave to Catholic Action a dominant opposition role.

and efficient government is. They suffer most from one of the two occupational diseases of the continental intellectual, suspicion of the motives of Western constitutional democracies. In trying to set up defenses against the imaginary threat from the West, they are either forced back upon the acceptance of Fascist collectivism or they are forced to underrate the danger to freedom represented by Communism. They imagine that a neutral position is possible for a Europe which has not yet recovered the strength which alone can guarantee its independence. They are suspicious of all government action that does not reflect directly and all the time the influence of theoretical party programs. They rightly look to reform, but refuse to learn from the experience of free communities and are not afraid to shackle administrative action with the ties of Party control.

IV. *Party and Government*

The dilemma which the academic left refuses to consider in its analysis of the relationship between political parties and the State can be stated in these terms. If political parties are permitted to extend a decisive influence, and to carry out a continuous control, upon the activities of governments and of administrations, one or the other of these two alternatives will have to be accepted:

(1) Political parties will continue to be purely private associations whose life, structure, methods of selection of their own internal ruling groups, are all beyond public control. In this case, a private, extra-constitutional organ, the party, will replace the public constitutional agencies of government of the community.

(2) Or, if the first alternative is to be avoided, parties are to be regulated and granted public recognition. Political life is to be channelled and controlled by legislation so that parties will belong to the formal structure of the machinery of government. Party statutes will be added to the constitutions, and minutely determine the activities and inner organization of parties, so that they will conform to the pattern set by whatever force happens to have the upper hand. In this way the door is certainly open to the establishment of dictatorship, for the party in power will be able to manipulate party life in such a way as to guarantee to itself a legal

monopoly of power. This was the Fascist solution. And this is also the Communist solution. (Article 126 of the 1936 Soviet Constitution: "The Communist Party . . . is the leading core of all organizations of the working people, both public and state.")

The only way to avoid choosing either horn of the dilemma is for parties to accept a self-denying attitude and to recognize the limits that must be established to their activities. It is exacly at this point that the thinking of the academic left is most inadequate.

Its views are sometimes set forth through a critique of the British system, described as a system of cabinet "dictatorship," suffering from these chief disabilities: a) The cabinet never informs the House of Commons beforehand of the legislative action it intends to take. Rather it presents the House with the *fait accompli* of a finished bill, perfected in all its details. b) The Cabinet goes its own way, free from any real parliamentary control. It is true that the Cabinet may be overthrown by a vote of non-confidence, but — *horribile dictu* — it does not have to suffer from the petty daily harassments which apparently are believed to be the essence of parliamentary control over the executive. The rendering of accounts at certain solemn and fairly well spaced intervals is not enough. c) It follows that the House of Commons has been reduced to a mere rubber stamp even though at times high level general debates take place in it.[6]

As against the division of responsibilities which is the chief characteristic of the British system, the academic left of Italian Christian Democracy would like to offer the following constitutional scheme. All legislative measures to be proposed by the Cabinet are first to be submitted for acceptance to the parliamentary groups of the parties on whose support the Cabinet rests. Apparently a mere statement of future intentions by the Cabinet to Parliament as a whole is not enough. What is required is the separate submission to each of the majority parliamentary groups of the specific measures which the government intends to propose.

At this point the academic left is anxious to stress that, just as

---

[6]Cf. for a statement of these views, Leopoldo Elia, "Democrazia e gruppi parlamentari," *Cronache Sociali,* January 1951.

the freedom of the Cabinet is limited by the requirement of prior consultation with the parliamentary groups, so the freedom of decision of each parliamentary group is limited by its prior engagements towards its own party, whose simple appendage the parliamentary group is. Therefore the autonomy of the group must be at all times limited and circumscribed by the views which have been sanctioned by the Party congress and by the Party national directorate.

The cycle is now complete. The party directorate emerges as the dominant decisive element in the life of the state. The responsibilities of administrators, the decisions of Cabinet ministers taken in the light of information which alone is available to them, the over-all policy which is thought to be desirable in the light of the interests of the entire nation, all of this must presumably disappear if it is in conflict with the views of the directorate of the party. Perhaps this perversion of democracy is put forth in the name of the defense of noble ideals and programs, of the achievement of good against the evil of administrative practice influenced by the "hidden" interests which forever dominate the actions of government. However it may be, the only certain consequence is that the system makes positive and sustained government action impossible, that it destroys the autonomy and dignity of parliaments and governments. This is not a fanciful conclusion, as can be seen from an inspection of the record of the British and American governments on the one hand, where these notions of the rights of parties are for the most part rejected, and of the record of the French and Italian governments on the other hand, where the practice of the assumption of illegitimate power by political parties has not been resisted.

THE USE OF POWER

NOTE TO CHAPTER FIVE

The criticism of the constitutional policies of the Christian Democratic Party made in the first section of Chapter Five is founded largely on its record of inaction and on an evaluation of the consequences of its announced intentions rather than on positive and final actions taken by government and Parliament. Furthermore, the legislative history of the past years is a difficult one, owing to the tortuous path followed by many of the more important bills, first announced, then withdrawn, brought again to the light of day in different garb, then pigeonholed, perhaps debated in one of the houses but set aside in the other; never, in brief, reaching the point of becoming law. Bearing these comments in mind, some details will be given here concerning the more important points made in the text.

Shortly after the Constitution went into effect, a press law was approved by the Constituent Assembly (February 8, 1948). This was a stop-gap measure which left undefined the seizure clause of Article 21 of the Constitution. Article 5 provided for the compulsory registration of all newspapers at the local tribunal's chancery. Among the many merely formal conditions of registration (such as the signatures of the publisher and of the editor, the articles of incorporation if it is a joint stock company), there is a demand for a document proving the membership of the registrants in the newspapermen's professional register, in the event that such membership will be required by future laws on professional organizations. This, of course, was the device used by Fascism to eliminate anti-Fascist newspapermen. The Fascist dictatorship, as part of its corporative structure, made registration of newspapermen compulsory. Without membership card, no newspaperman could exercise his profession. The mass parties of the democratic Italian Republic have taken over the Fascist system, in the name, of course, of the "purification" and "professionalization" of the notoriously bohemian and free-wheeling newspaper world. Thus, in the name of morality and professional competence and responsibility, the freedom of the press can be suppressed. The legislation which is currently being prepared aims to complete the 1948 legislation with further detailed regulation whose only result must be that of seriously endangering

75

press freedom. (1) No Constitutional Court has yet been set up, but the proposed press legislation with remarkable foresight requires the resignation of any newspaper editor who may be appointed to the Constitutional Court. (2) Before any newspaper can be sold in the streets, four copies must be delivered to the local judicial authorities. (3) Seizure of a newspaper may, whenever the timely intervention of judicial authorities is not possible, be effected by officers of the judicial police. Even though the seizure must, within 48 hours, be supported by the proper judicial authorities in order to be legal, such apparent protection of press freedom by the courts is obviously of no practical meaning in the case of the daily press. For it does not help a daily paper to have the seizure of any one issue cancelled 48 hours later. (4) Seizure can take place under a great variety of headings including violations of Article 414 of the penal code which punishes all public instigation to the commission of a crime and of Articles 261 and 262 of the penal code which prohibit the publication of state secrets and of news whose diffusion the government has forbidden.

Some of the more serious difficulties on the question of regionalism have arisen in connection with the Sicilian regional statute enacted in the immediate postwar period (May 14, 1946). Article 15 of the Statute implied the suppression of the prefects who are, as is known, the most effective and important agents of the central government. On February 24, 1951 the Sicilian Regional Assembly approved a law providing for the replacement of the prefects with new regional officers. The representative of the central government in Sicily appealed to the High Sicilian Court (still in existence because of the failure to organize the national Constitutional Court) and by a decision issued by the Court on March 20, 1951, obtained the invalidation of the regional law. While in Sicily the regional experiment had led to a tug of war which has made both sides angry, throughout most of the country regionalism has not yet come to life. It is most unlikely that regional elections will be held in 1952.

The initial bill on the Constitutional Court was presented to the Senate on July 14, 1948. Approved by the Senate on March 17, 1949, it was transmitted to the Chamber of Deputies where discussion did not get underway until early 1951. It was on March 15, 1951 by a vote of 230 against 199 that the Chamber of Deputies rewrote Article 4 of the bill to read: "The justices of the Supreme Court whose appointment belongs to the President of the Republic are appointed by decree issued upon recommendation of the Minister of Justice and countersigned by the President of the Council." The entire bill was approved by the Chamber of Deputies the next day by a 243 to 146 vote and transmitted to the Senate for a second vote on May 5, 1951. The second permanent committee of the Senate again modified the text of the bill, to meet the objections which had been raised against Article 4, which now reads: "The justices of the Constitutional Court whose appointment belongs to the President of the Republic are appointed by his decree. The decree is countersigned by the President of the Council." But by early 1952 the Senate had not started discussion on the new version of the bill, which, after it is approved, has to go back once more to the Chamber. No forecast can therefore be made of when the Constitutional Court will, in effect, begin to function.

CHAPTER SIX

THE FUTURE

I. *The Elections of 1951*

The local elections of the spring of 1951 offer a convenient starting point for a discussion of the future chances of Italian Christian Democracy and of the major problems it has to face both domestically and internationally.

Comparisons between national and local elections may be dangerous. It is true that the local elections held in Italy in 1951 were "national" from the point of view of the issues that were debated, of the political leaders that confronted each other, of the determined effort of the government and the opposition, that is of Christian Democracy and of Communism, to make of the vote a test of their respective strength. In spite of all this, voting attitudes are likely to be different when the voter knows that his vote may decide the fate of the entire nation or when he feels that he is only electing a mayor. It is likely that in 1951 Christian Democracy lost the support of some voters who, in the next national election will be unwilling to take the risk again of putting the Communists in power.

Bearing these general comments in mind, it is still possible to say that Christian Democracy suffered a serious setback in 1951, as it lost about 20 percent of the votes it had polled in 1948. The analysis of the returns in the fifty-seven provinces where provincial elections were held on May 27 and June 10, 1951, shows these figures.

THE FUTURE

POPULAR VOTE IN FIFTY-SEVEN PROVINCES
(in thousands)

Parties	Provincial elections of May-June 1951	%	National elections of April 18, 1948	%
Christian Democratic	5,848	40.0	7,657	49.0
Republican	427	2.9	386	2.5
Liberal	547	3.7	335	2.1
Democratic Socialist groups	1,436	9.8	1,276	8.2
Communist-Socialist front	5,377	36.7	5,601	35.9
Neo-Fascist	578	3.9	190	1.2
Monarchist	141	0.9	151	1.0
Independent groups	286	1.9	....	....
Total	14,641		15,597	

It should be noted that the fifty-seven provinces included in the table are mostly in northern and central Italy. Had the local elections taken place in the entire country, Christian Democratic losses would have been more severe and Communist and neo-Fascist gains greater than the figures above indicate. As they stand, they show that Christian Democracy has already lost the unique position it had obtained in 1948 and that a coalition government after the national elections of 1953 is almost certain to be a matter of necessity and not of choice. The votes lost to Christian Democracy went, insofar as they were cast, mostly to the liberals and to the neo-Fascists, a development which should be welcomed by Christian Democracy as it tends to make it a more homogeneous body freed from some of the more extreme pressures from the right. The strengthening of the Democratic Socialists, though significant, is not impressive. Far greater stability and community of purpose must be achieved by the various Democratic Socialist groups before they can hope to become an important third element between the Communists and the Christian Democrats. This greater strength and

79

coherence of the Democratic Socialists is much needed, since they appear to be one of the key elements of the coalition that should govern after 1953.

The popular front alliance, made up of the Communists and of the Nenni Socialists, shows a slight increase from 35.9 to 36.7 percent of the vote. Had all of Southern Italy been included, the percentage increase over the national average of 31 percent obtained in 1948 would have been greater, indicating the substantial gains that Communism has been able to make in recent years in the South. An interesting shift has occurred, however, within the popular front itself: away from the Communists and towards the Socialists. In the elections of 1951, out of every 100 popular front votes, the Communists received an average of only 57 votes as against a similar average of 63 in 1948. The Communist vote was less than one half or barely one half of the total popular front vote in Veneto and Liguria and was between 55 and 60 percent in Lombardy, Piedmont and Tuscany. It was also noted that where the Communists alone presented a list of candidates their vote was substantially smaller than in comparable neighboring areas where both Communist and Socialist Parties presented candidates. This indicates the existence among many voters of an important distinction between a vote for a Socialist Party allied to the Communist Party, and a vote for the Communist Party. The distinction betrays the hope that, ultimately, all of Socialism will free itself of the bondage to Communism.

Apart from the statistics, the elections were taken as proof that the country had lost a good deal of its confidence in the Christian Democratic Party, even though it was still the country's biggest. And they were held to show that the party must now re-examine its own positions, both for its own sake and in terms of what is needed to renew in the future a strong coalition with other democratic parties and to check the still growing strength of Communism and its allies.

We are thus led to a discussion of the "ideal" program of Christian Democracy: of the relationships between Christian Democracy and the Church and the organizations depending upon the Church; of the relationship between Christian Democracy and non-Communist parties. Going beyond the sphere of national problems we will finally take into account the attitudes of Christian Democracy towards peace.

II. *The "Ideal" Program of Christian Democracy*

It was the view of that restless moralist and critic of our times, Emmanuel Mounier, that no one calling himself a Christian Democrat could be a satisfactory person, for he is a horrid and unaesthetic mixture of political and religious man. As Etienne Borne, a leader of the M.R.P. and an interpreter of Mounier, writes: "If young, he is too nice, even if he is in his forties, and has all the sickly traits of a prolonged adolescence, well protected by private schooling and 'scoutism'. If old, he is sentimental and will open his heart with overwhelming and tender rhetoric. What is missing, according to Mounier, is a virile and aggressive maturity. To be quite frank, the determinism of his kind makes of him a soft type and Mounier tolerated only the hard types. . . . A sweet animal without a temper and addicted to mental confusions, such is the Christian Democrat according to the pitiless analysis of Emmanuel Mounier. But it is weak ideas that create soft hearts. Christian Democracy, according to the doctrine of *Esprit,* is not a strong idea. To found a confessional party of the left in order to fight the scandal of a confessional party of the right, means to continue an equivocal game . . . a left of Christian inspiration will have no backbone and will surrender before the harsh requirements of the necessary revolution." [1]

In this interpretation of Mounier's thought, there is more than a hint that the softness of Christian Democracy is due to its refusal to consider what Mounier believer to be the requirements of revolutionary action. It is only with the acceptance of those requirements that a political party becomes "hard" and, therefore, worthy of surviving. But what Mounier is doing here is to condemn as despicably soft the "ideal" type of Christian Democrat, which is something different from the criticism of the concrete realizations of Christian Democratic parties. On his own ground, Mounier's position is not very strong. On purely ideal grounds it can be said

---

[1] Etienne Borne, "Emmanuel Mounier, juge de la Démocratie chrétienne." *Terre Humaine,* February, 1951; pp. 66-67.

that the Christian Democratic program is a stern one, for it requires the adoption of solutions which defy both the easy and traditional approaches of the past, and the acceptance of a simple minded deterministic interpretation of the revolution of the future. Christian Democracy has tried to show that in order to do justice to the longings of freedom and to the exigencies of social solidarity, both the individualism of the liberals and the collectivism of the Marxian materialists has to be rejected.

The sternness or difficulty of the ideal Christian Democratic view of the world can be seen if we assume that Christian Democracy has three major goals.

One, to retain for man the freedom and autonomy which is due to a divinely created being.

Two, to create for economic man the security and for economic society as a whole those collective policies, which the complexity and the solidarity of modern economic life require.

Three, to reassert and bring back to life the link between moral principles and the direction of political life and to reintroduce once more into political life, which had been reduced in modern times to a low positivistic and materialistic level, the values of the group and of the common good that are part of the Christian tradition.

This is a complex (even obscure) as well as a rigorous program. In principle it is not a soft program and it is because of its hard moral qualities that it has attracted wide support in postwar Europe. No one can successfully explain in terms of "clerical" pressures the sweeping surge towards Christian Democracy that occurred in France and Italy in 1945 and in 1946, years that were still controlled by the idealism of the Resistance. One would be tempted to conclude that it is precisely because it is impossible of realization, that Christian Democracy has run into the divisions and the obstacles which now face it everywhere.

The emphasis on personal freedom, on the value of the individual, on the importance of the method of freedom, is a basic element in Christian Democratic doctrine. Opposed to totalitarianism, Christian Democracy emphasizes the values attached to the human person. This "personalism," opposed to the atomistic individualism of the eighteenth century, leads to a spirited defense of the autonomy of man even in his relationship to social groups. But if it is interpreted in a predominantly traditional sense, it can lead to a conservative position and to a defense of the *status quo* as best suited to protect individual rights. After the war, large numbers of conservative elements, determined to support a strong champion of anti-Communism, moved into the Christian Democratic camp to do just that. The clash between personalism and individualism has had serious repercussions on the integrity of Christian Democracy.

The emphasis on social solidarity and on the need of collective techniques to solve modern economic problems, represents the second facet of the Christian Democratic theory. It has attracted the many who have shown an increasing awareness of the social and economic readjustments required by the world crisis, and who have criticized the capitalistic bourgeoisie for their egoism and lack of social sensibility. Such criticism involves the acceptance of a marked degree of public intervention in economic life, of publicly controlled bargaining in industry, of nationalization of basic industries, of structural reforms in agriculture. At the same time, recognition of small property rights, of decentralization, and of the fairly autonomous development of social groups and economic forces within society, distinguishes Christian Democracy from Marxism.

But the social program of Christian Democracy has also been used, as we have seen, by groups transmitting habits and thoughts acquired during the Fascist era. The numbers of so-called "progressive" Christians with a close affinity to Communism has never been very large in Italy. Larger, however, has been the number of those who, while declaring themselves to be anti-Communists, have unconsciously proposed to imitate some of the practices of Communism. Here we find the total planners, the monopolists, seeking to press total controls of labor and the introduction of compulsory arbitration in labor disputes. The quite understandable social preoccupation of these currents, their dissatisfaction with the slow approach to the solution of the basic economic ills of the country are all part of the legitimate substance of the left wing of Christian Democracy. But they contain the seeds of tendencies which would be incompatible with the spirit of a democratic party.

Finally, the emphasis on moral and religious values, while coloring the whole intellectual outlook of the Christian Democrats is hard to translate into concrete attitudes. It offers furthermore the possibility of endangering the political and temporal foundation of the party. No one was more careful than Luigi Sturzo to assert the lay character of Christian Democracy in 1919, and to fight for its recognition on a footing of equality with the other Italian political parties. The M.R.P. in 1946 accepted a definition of the French Republic as a lay State. But the long reliance on the Church and her subsidiary organizations during the twenty years of Fascism, while useful for the survival of an organizational core, has created in Italy today some doubt about the survival of Christian Democracy as a movement independent of ecclesiastical influences. For there exists in the background the potential danger of a sudden and massive intervention of such powerful organs of the Church as Catholic Action.

The "ideal" is lost at this point in the unpleasant reality of a struggle for power.

III. *Christian Democracy, the Church and Catholic Action*

Two factors have contributed to alter the balance of power between the Church and the Christian Democratic Party. The Church not only played a considerable role in keeping Christian Democratic forces together in the long period of the underground, she also influenced the elections of 1948 in general and through the specific activities of political action committees organized by Catholic Action (the so-called civic committees). With Christian Democracy in office since 1948, the issue of the relationship of the party to the lay organizations of the Church and to the Church herself was bound to make itself felt, more particularly in times of crisis or of dissatisfaction with the concrete accomplishments of the government.

The leader of the party, de Gasperi, has been aware of the distinctions to be maintained between the political and the religious spheres. He is too keen a politician and too wise a statesman to underestimate the unfavorable repercussions of any marked confusion between the two. Speaking in Florence on May 3, 1951, de Gasperi echoed the words spoken in 1919 by don Sturzo: "We cannot make an exhibition of our religious faith and above all we cannot exploit it for political purposes, use it as an instrument of power and boast of our tolerance to those who think otherwise. . . .

Religious faith and religious practice cannot become the distinguishing criteria for participation in a political party: true religious practice, doctrine and faith belong to the Church and we acknowledge that the Church moves upon a different as well as higher plane than that of politics." This is a strong, even if cautiously worded, statement of the political independence of the party. Not Catholicism but a common body of political beliefs will justify admission to the party. Religion and politics are separate and there is no place for the use of religious doctrine as a political instrument.

But these views are not shared by important groups within Catholic Action, which is the strongest of the lay instruments of ecclesiastical policy. Catholic Action is organized and controlled by the Church hierarchy for the achievement of those religious, moral, and economic purposes which are considered to be part of the earthly mission of the Church. When Catholic Action proclaims as its aim the "Christian reconquest of Italy," [2] a direct political intervention is implied. This is made clear beyond doubt by the repeated statements of the new president of Catholic Action, the organizer and leader of the strongest and most active of all political agencies of Catholic Action, Luigi Gedda. It was Gedda who organized and still heads the "civic committees", a political agency of Catholic Action used in the course of all elections held in Italy since 1948 to bring out the vote for the Christian Democratic Party.[3]

In increasing measure, Gedda has publicly expressed dissatisfaction with his ward, the Christian Democratic Party. Writing in the civic committees' official journal, *Collegamento,* shortly after the conclusion of the local elections of 1951, Gedda stressed the right of his committees to express themselves on political matters and in particular to show their dissatisfaction concerning the opening of a Cabinet crisis shortly after the elections: "The civic committees are not a political party, as everyone knows, but they form

---

[2] See the official Catholic Action daily, *Quotidiano,* May 4, 1951.

[3] The official Vatican organ, *Osservatore Romano,* maintains however that the civic committees are independent and separate from Catholic Action. (See, for instance, the issue of April 11, 1951). The difficulties of this position, even from a merely formal, juridical point of view, are great when we remember that the head of the civic committees is at the same time the head of Catholic Action.

an association devoted to political activities with the right of expressing its views on events in the political field. This right, strengthened by the considerable achievements of the civic committees in the course of the recent elections, requires that the committees should state their point of view more often than in the past. This they will certainly do, for under present circumstances their right becomes increasingly a duty which they must fulfill."

In the course of clarifying his position in the columns of the Catholic Action daily (an imprudent move if the fiction of the separateness of Catholic Action and the civic committees is to be maintained), and of disclaiming any intention of taking over the Christian Democratic Party, Gedda developed an interesting doctrine of authoritative freedom, which makes of him a potential Italian ally of de Gaulle: "That freedom of speech, of association and of the press is a right, cannot be doubted; but it is also true that we must carefully watch a shift from liberty to calumny, from liberty to license, from liberty to disorganization." The democracy for which Gedda stands is "an harmonious, coherent and authoritative system." For this system the civic committees will never be afraid to take a stand.[4]

In spite of denials, Gedda's position contains this dilemma for the Christian Democratic Party: either the party accepts the program of "authoritative democracy" sponsored by the civic committees of Catholic Action, or it faces the organization of an outright "Catholic" party that will carry out that program. This is the view of as objective and well-informed a journal as *Relazioni Internazionali:* "In recent years Catholic Action has not only developed lay programs paralleling ecclesiastical ones. It has also aspired to transfer into the field of political action the strength of its efficient organization, well endowed with local branches, numerous publications, a Roman daily, *Il Quotidiano,* and supported by men who already occupy public positions in the government, in Parliament, and in the civil service. Therefore talks concerning the founding of a Catholic party have been going on for a long time, prompted by charges against the Christian Democratic Party of excessive inde-

---

[4] The entire Italian press from August 5 to August 8, 1951, reported these developments.

pendence vis-à-vis of religious authorities and of weakness towards Communism." [5]

This leaves the Church in a difficult position. The Vatican has not failed to realize that anti-clerical forces would be greatly strengthened by any accumulation of evidence showing that an ecclesiastical "Catholic" party was seriously being considered. Speaking on May 5, 1951, Pope Pius XII said: "We have no need of telling you that Catholic Action is not called to assert itself in the field of party politics." After the August 1951 statements by Gedda which increased the fears of ecclesiastical intervention, the *Osservatore Romano* attempted a further clarification, appealing to the union of all Catholics: "From the necessities of the times there flows a common duty for all Catholics: the duty to continue that unity which they have shown ever since their social activity developed; the duty to acknowledge in this hour, everywhere, in all fields where they are active, that such unity is cemented and rendered essential by the fundamental and urgent interests of civilization and of the Christian fatherland." [6] This "clarification" of the Vatican position, while indicating that the Vatican is not taking sides with Gedda against de Gasperi, strongly supports the view that what is wanted is a reconciliation in the name of unity between Gedda and de Gasperi. In the cold world of political reality, this can only mean a substantial surrender of the freedom and of the political autonomy of Christian Democracy to Catholic Action. Thus the clarification leaves the future of the relationship between the party and the Church shrouded in the gravest doubts. The question remains one of the utmost significance for the political life of Italy.

The final position of the Church towards Christian Democracy cannot be determined now. There is probably a greater awareness in Vatican circles today of the danger of supporting, or of helping to power, authoritarian movements which have a tendency to develop into totalitarian dictatorships. For the Church has experi-

---

[5] *Relazioni Internazionali,* Milan, May 12, 1951.

[6] *Osservatore Romano,* August 6, 1951. This article was reported in the *New York Times* of August 7, 1951 under the optimistic headline of "Vatican Assures Italy on Politics; Says it will continue Policy of Non-Interference, Chides Catholic Action leader."

enced the unhappy consequences of both Fascism and Nazism with regard to its freedom. Without saying that the Church may not in the future take an unfavorable position towards Christian Democratic parties, it may perhaps be said that the Church would not openly attack them if, as in 1925, the alternative were to be some new variety of Fascism. At the very least one may maintain that as long as democratic forces show themselves capable of running a constitutional system of parliamentary democracy, the Church will not prefer Fascism and support it in its conquest of power. That this is so may be inferred from an editorial published in the *Osservatore Romano* on May 25, 1951, on the eve of the French elections. The Vatican newspaper, addressing itself to the Catholic electorate in France, expressed a preference for the M.R.P. as against the R.P.F.: "It would certainly be painful to see a part of the Catholic electorate choose, as against the Popular Republicans who are, in spite of their shortcomings, firmly committed to a well-defined program deserving of support for the sincere effort it shows of leading France toward a better future, a vague transformism of the right which fatally might [sic] slide into intransigence." The specter of Mussolini was haunting the vision of the editorial writer of the *Osservatore*. The experience of the Church with the later Italian dictator was in the end a most unhappy one. The Church witnessed the transformation of what was believed to be a generally innocuous and old-fashioned conservative tyrant, into a totalitarian dictator, a racialist, an aggressive imperialist, and a destroyer of the autonomy and substance of the Church.

IV. *Christian Democracy, Communism and the Future*

Apart from the issue of the survival of the Christian Democratic Party itself, the influence, real or potential, of the Church on political affairs has an important bearing on the strength of Italian Communism. For that strength is in part due to the presence of historical traditions which have linked freedom and democracy to the battle against ecclesiastical interference in temporal life. If Christian Democracy should appear to weaken on the matter of its political independence, or if Gedda's threats were carried out, Communism would gain as the Party most clearly opposed to the metaphysical principles on which the Catholic religion rests. Even today the pro-Communist tendencies to be found in influential intellectual circles are to a large extent a reaction against the advance of clericalism. The well known literary critic, Luigi Russo, is a typical representative of this point of view. He feels that the Church conquest of Christian Democracy is already complete and that a radical move from Fascism to democracy can be achieved only as a result of a deep revolutionary process in which the Communists are to play a leading part.[7]

The "dialogue" between the Communists and the Christian progressives, which is still maintained in loud tones in France, is barely heard in Italy. The so-called Left Christian Democratic Party quickly went out of existence and the only case to create even a modest stir was that of Franco Rodano, a young Catholic intellectual, who, because of his writings in the Communist press, was subjected to a personal interdict from his ecclesiastical authorities. Rodano believed that a distinction existed between dialectical materialism and historical materialism. As a Catholic, he had to reject the former with its implications of immanent necessity depriving men of all freedom. But as a democrat, he could admit the latter, for no Catholic in accepting the material and economic reality of the world could feel wounded in his faith. Concretely, only a people's democracy was acceptable to a Catholic both from the point of view of the good of the people and the good of the Church. Writing in the official Communist journal of opinion, *Rinascita,* Rodano stated: "Reality is only one: only a State both popular and democratic can give freedom to the Church, for only such a State can, by virtue of its structure, liquidate democratically, with concrete persuasive means, the political influence exercised over the people by the ecclesiastical apparatus. And the Church can, as a matter of principle, receive its freedom only from a State which possesses an organic and not an individualistic concept of freedom, one not metaphysically absolute, but historically limited, as was wisely observed by Vishinsky at the last session of the Gen-

---

[7] Russo's acceptance of Communism was exemplified by his readiness to appear on the Popular Front ticket in the elections of 1948. On Russo's views, see his collected essays, *De Vera Religione* (Turin, 1949), and his articles in *Belfagor,* a literary and historical journal founded in 1946 and brilliantly edited by Russo.

eral Assembly of the United Nations, by the idea of the common good." [8] Apparently not appreciating this gift of freedom from Vishinsky's hands, the *Osservatore Romano* published an interdict decree against Rodano on January 17, 1949.

If Christian Democracy has so far enjoyed a relative immunity from the particular kind of disintegration represented by Rodano, it is not because it has developed any outstanding way of dealing with the Communist problem, the one dominant influence to shape its course and determine its strength. After four years in power Christian Democracy is still confronted by a Communist problem of the same overwhelming proportions as in 1948. In facing the elections of 1953 the Christian Democratic Party must consider the matter of the relevance and adequacy of its anti-Communist policies.

The Communist problem cannot be solved by resorting to a crusade for the conversion, where conversion is needed, of men from an irreligious or materialistic position, to a religious and moral one. In any case a crusade of this kind cannot be undertaken by a government, and appeals by a Cabinet member or any other public man to the beauties of metaphysical life are without effect, just as a statement that a corporative system based on Christian morality would be different from one based on Fascist tyranny is not enough to transform a centrally controlled machine into one that is free and democratic.

Nor is anti-Communism of any consequence if it is based upon a repetition of generic slogans of freedom and democracy, when the discrepancy between the slogans and the practice remains too wide and shows no visible signs of narrowing.

If millions of people have so far refused to join the democratic side it is not because the democratic position is, in itself, considered unattractive. The average citizen in Italy realizes that democracy implies a continuous struggle starting from a relatively low level of welfare and efficiency. But what is wanted on the anti-Communist side is a prior demonstration that some of the basic principles of democratic life and of modern change are grasped, and that the policies following from those principles are actually set in motion.

[8] Franco Rodano, "La Battaglia delle Idee," *Rinascita,* December, 1948, p. 472.

It is here that proof of economic intelligence, of a modern touch in administrative management, of a flexible and balanced and self-restrained political life, is demanded. The party in power must give proof of its readiness to learn through experimentation and from fellow democracies, and also of its concern to achieve equilibrium and an end to narrow party factionalism. But such proof, by the end of 1951, was not too much in evidence.

If modernization of economic life and of political and economic machinery is required (more efficient civil service, retrenchment of party positions, more determined guidance in certain aspects of economic life), the question may be asked, is there any particular contribution that Christian Democracy can make to the solution of these problems? Are there any grounds to believe that Christian Democracy can handle them more successfully than Socialism or Liberalism? Or that Christian Democracy offers a basis for the establishment of a viable coalition among democratic forces which, separately, would be incapable of effective action?

Looking at the matter from the broadest possible point of view (one which, it may be confessed, has perhaps little in common with the programmatic reality of Christian Democratic parties) the answer might be yes.

a) Christian Democracy and Socialism

In the first place, Christian Democracy alone in Western Europe is so far free from the heavy burden of historical failure which weighs on the other democratically inclined parties. By and large, Socialism is linked in the minds of the Europeans with political and economic failure and with doctrinaire paralysis. Too often Socialism has been the victim of principles no longer related to the democratic reality, especially when the democratic reality has to be developed in terms quite different from Communist totalitarianism. Either the Socialists showed a lack of regard for individual freedom and joined the Communists as the majority of Italian Socialist leaders did, or they tried a half-hearted revision of Socialist doctrine along humanist lines, as in France, and had to witness the slow deterioration of the party and its loss of popular support, as a result of the collision with the "harder" Communist core. Furthermore, Socialists in power have offered few outstanding examples of expert management of public affairs.

The parties of liberal tradition have also suffered from their collusion with Fascism, from their excessive individualism, and from their refusal to give up the support of certain industrial classes whose practices could no longer be tolerated in expanding societies.

After World War II this situation gave the Christian Democrats a unique and irretrievable chance. Theirs was the compromise view between individualism and collectivism and the belief that a variety of approaches could be sought in dealing with economic problems. Theirs too was the belief in the common good or the common welfare which has come to mean so much in the life of twentieth century American and British democracies.

Theirs was the chance for leadership, given their tremendous initial popular support, in bringing about a reconciliation, on a permanent basis, between Christian Democracy and Socialism. By virtue of it, both would have been strengthened.

There is much that, in effect, Christian Democracy and Socialism have in common, when each movement reacquires the necessary freedom from obsolete dogmas, corporativist or Marxian. On the basic issue of raising the welfare of the masses of the Italian people who still live below minimum standards, there should be a ready understanding and possibilities of joint work for a generation. De Gasperi and Saragat, the leader of the Democratic Socialists, seem to realize that this is the case and that minor issues should not be allowed to interfere. For the alternatives are either a degeneration of Christian Democracy into a clerical tyranny, or a Communist crisis.

In preparing for the future, Italian Christian Democracy should learn from the French experience. It should learn the techniques of collaboration with Democratic Socialism and the conditions which are required to make that collaboration possible. The same applies to Democratic Socialism. For until it can present a united and coherent front and reconcile its endlessly quarreling factions, there will be small inducement for Christian Democracy to make any effort to establish a firm alliance with it. On the other hand, Christian Democracy can accelerate the process of Socialist unification by a show of authentic political autonomy, of readiness to undertake on the required scale the measures of social and economic reform which the country needs. If the reality of an independent and progressive Christian Democracy begins to make a permanent impression on the country, the vitality of other democratic parties will be increased.

But even supposing that a Christian Democratic-Socialist alliance is possible, there still remains the fundamental need of the shifting of the boundary line between the party and the government. The repression of the fatal slogan of "politics above all" must become one of the main goals of the future. In trying to achieve it, the Christian Democratic Party need only go back to its origins, to Sturzo's teachings and to the brave hopes of its founders who saw in the skills of a new administrative class one of the conditions of the salvation of the country. For "politics above all" leads to the opposite slogan of "the experts above all," a slogan equally destructive of democratic freedoms. What must come about is the proper coordination and definition of the respective areas of action of the politician and the expert. Of course, the politician who accepts this delimitation and coordination is no longer a politician but a statesman. But then the survival of freedom and the. gradual development of the ideals of the common welfare cannot be achieved otherwise.

It would be an extreme paradox indeed, if the historians of the future were to find that more of the program of Christian Democracy was realized in countries which had no Christian Democratic parties, and in which no single dominant, or politically conscious Church, was present.

b) *Christian Democracy and Peace*

In the second place, Christian Democracy seems to be uniquely placed on the continent of Europe to deal with the obsolescence of the concept of national sovereignty. Liberalism, even though often unjustly, bears the historical burden of its link to the rise of modern national States. Socialism has often led to policies of economic self-sufficiency which negated the idea of supranational integration. And Communism has developed into the strongest defender of the rigidities and the absurdities of the national sovereign unit. Christian Democracy alone seems in possession of the ideal of an international community, linked perhaps to the *res publica christiana* of the Middle Ages and based upon the common dignity and worth of human beings. And it would be difficult to controvert the importance of the contribution of Christian Democracy to international peace and national progress were it to lead a sustained attack against sovereignty.

For the unity which in the West is so deeply threatened by the decisive efforts of Communism, can probably be restored only through the assertion of the higher unity of stronger supranational communities. The deep national division of Western Europe can be healed through the higher unity of the European community. In all the constitutional documents in the writing of which Christian Democracy has had a hand, the sacrifice of the principle of national sovereignty is recognized. Nowhere more strongly than in the Italian Constitution, whose Article 11 reads, "Italy repudiates war as an instrument of offensive action against the freedom of other peoples and as a means of resolution of international conflicts; it agrees, on conditions of parity with other States, to the limitations on its sovereign power which are necessary to a system guaranteeing peace and justice among nations; it promotes and supports international organizations directed to that end." [9]

Christian Democracy was born as a result of a battle against the national European States, against its centralizing tendencies as well as against its nationalistic policies. Christian Democracy represents in principle a revolt against the foreign, domestic and religious policies of the modern State as it has evolved on the continent of Europe especially since the eighteenth century. Christian Democracy must therefore seek to substitute for the independent sovereign State, the dependent State as member of a higher international community, just as internally it must seek to achieve the limitation and the diffusion of the powers both of the stronger private sources of economic influence and of the excessively centralized institutions of government.

The historical circumstances of European life at the middle of the twentieth century appear ripe for a beginning in the task of translating the ideal of the European community into reality. The

---

[9] Similar provisions are to be found in the preamble of the French Constitution and in Article 24 of the Bonn Constitution.

strong Christian Democratic preponderance or influence in six key countries of Western Europe, France, Italy, Belgium, Holland, Western Germany and Austria, should encourage Christian Democratic parties to that joint activity and initiative across national boundaries which they can easily undertake.

It is difficult as yet to assess clearly merits and demerits. In France the leadership in European affairs has often been taken by one of the chiefs of the M.R.P., Schuman, whose name is linked to the most far-reaching plan yet devised to build a sound economic structure out of Europe's narrow national components. In Italy Christian Democracy has been consistently in favor of a broadly European policy, a position which the weakened status of the country has rendered in effect mandatory. The de Gasperi governments have supported all plans aiming at the establishment of European institutions: the French-Italian Union, the United States of Europe, the Coal and Steel Community, the European army.

On the other hand, there are signs of Christian Democracy yielding to nationalistic pressures. It is one of the tragedies of Italian life that, while the country stands, in effect, ready to support a transition towards a new internationalism, it should still suffer from the remnants of the virulent poison of nationalism. Italy, the last of the great European States to achieve the pattern of a national State, still has to contend with the question of Trieste which has been transformed by certain groups into the symbol of all the alleged injustices that the world is said to be forever plotting against Italy. Already in World War I Trieste played a disruptive role. In 1919 the neighboring city of Fiume led to a crisis between President Wilson and the Italian government and to the first manifestation of Fascism, the march of d'Annunzio's legionnaires. A third of a century later, the Western powers have not found the necessary strength to bring about the only legitimate solution of the problem, which is to recognize Trieste as part of Italy. But it is absurd for men in responsible positions in Italy to refuse to realize that the question of Trieste is only a minor issue in a contemporary European scene in which immense unresolved problems continue to exist and will continue to exist for a long time. To single out Trieste as a problem deserving particular consideration is to show again the narrow provincialism which is the characteristic of all

95

nationalists. It is doubtful whether Christian Democracy can hope in this way to steal the nationalistic thunder. Rather it will merely increase the general restlessness of the country and weaken its capacity for rational thinking about international problems.

* * *

It is only by keeping faith with itself that Christian Democracy can leave its imprint on our times, and reassert the original and peculiar contribution it can make to European political life. This will require:

A firm spirit of independence, and the assertion of a moral strength which must not be allowed to become subservient to extra-political forces and to translate itself into clericalism.

A continued recognition of the fact that national and not machine interests must prevail, and that the party must use its power for the training of the political and administrative class whose absence has caused the endless series of crises of the last forty years.

A readiness to provide by public intervention and example, the necessary leadership in the modernization of economic life which Italy needs.

A belief in the values of constitutionalism and in the principles of freedom and of supremacy of the law, which Italy now, for the first time in her history as a national unit, has a chance to see realized.

A supreme effort to bridge the domestic gap caused by Communism and the international gap caused by national sovereignties through a renewed and sustained acceptance of the ideal of the European community.

SELECTED BIBLIOGRAPHY

by Eleanor Tananbaum

I. Books

A. *The Theorists of Italian Christian Democracy*

Giuseppe Toniolo. *Indirizzi e Concetti Sociali.* Parma, 1901.
———. *Democrazia Cristiana: Concetti e Indirizzi,* two volumes. *Istituti e Forme,* two volumes. Vatican City, 1949, 1951.
Romolo Murri. *Battaglie d'Oggi.* I. *Il Programma Politico della Democrazia Cristiana;* II. *La Coltura del Clero;* III. *La Vita Cristiana sulla Fine del Secolo XIX.* Rome, 1901.
———. *La Politica Clericale e la Democrazia.* Rome, 1908.
———. *Dalla Democrazia Cristiana al Partito Popolare.* Florence, 1920.
———. *Fede e Fascismo.* Milan, 1924.
———. *L'Idea Universale di Roma—dalle Origini al Fascismo.* Milan, 1937.
———. *Alla Ricerca di Se Stesso.* Milan, 1939.
———. *Democrazia Cristiana.* Milan, 1945.
Luigi Sturzo. *Popolarismo e Fascismo.* Turin, 1924.
———. *Pensiero Antifascista.* Turin, 1925.
———. *Italy and Fascismo.* London, 1926.
———. *The International Community and the Right of War.* London, 1929.
———. *Politics and Morality.* London, 1938.
———. *Church and State.* New York, 1939.
———. *The True Life—A Sociology of the Supernatural.* Washington, 1943.
———. *Le Autonomie Regionali e il Mezzagiorno.* Rome, 1944.
———. *Inner Laws of Society—A New Sociology.* New York, 1944. (Sturzo's fundamental theoretical work.)
———. *Italy and the Coming World.* New York, 1945.
———. *Nationalism and Internationalism.* New York, 1946.
———. *La Mia Battaglia da New York.* Milan, 1949.
———. *La Regione nella Nazione.* Rome, 1949.
———. *Del Metodo Sociologico: Risposta ai Critici.* Bergamo, 1950.

B. *Christian Democracy Prior to 1946*

Raffaele Della Casa. *Il Movimento Cattolico Italiano,* two volumes. Milan, 1905.
G. de Rossi. *Il Partito Popolare Italiano dalle Origini al Congresso di Napoli.* Rome, 1920. (A contemporary account by a member of the Popular Party.)
Agostino Gemelli and Francesco Olgiati. *Il Programma del Partito Popolare —Come non è, come dovrebbe essere.* Milan, 1919. (The point of view of the Popular Party's clerical right wing.)

CHRISTIAN DEMOCRACY IN ITALY

Stefano Jacini. *I Popolari.* Milan, 1923. (A contemporary view of a leader in both the Popular and the Christian Democratic Parties, embodying the Conservative-Liberal school of Italian Catholicism.)
————. *Il Regime Fascista.* Milan, 1947.
————. *Storia del Partito Popolare Italiano.* Milan, 1951.
F. S. Nitti. *Socialismo Cattolico.* Turin, 1891. (Reflects the fears of the old political groups.)
Beniamino Palumbo. *Il Movimento Democratico Cristiano in Italia.* Rome, 1950. (A good, though slender, history of Italian Christian Democracy before 1918; seeks to link today's left-wing Christian Democracy to the past.)
People and Freedom. *For Democracy.* London, 1939. (Doctrinal discussions of Christian Democracy published by the English group of Christian Democrats founded by Sturzo.)
Tiziano Veggian. *Il Movimento Sociale Cristiano nella Seconda Metà del XIX Secolo.* Vicenza, 1902.
Ernesto Vercesi. *Il Movimento Cattolico in Italia.* Florence, 1923.

C. *Current Christian Democratic Writings*

In the following list, the position of the writer within the party precedes any comment on the book:
Antonio Amorth. *Il Problema della Struttura dello Stato in Italia.* Milan, 1945. (Intellectual-corporativist left wing.)
Dante Benedetti. *De Gasperi—Politico e Statista,* Rome, 1949. (Official biography of de Gasperi published by the Christian Democratic Party.)
A. Canaletti-Gaudenti. *Sturzo: Il Pensiero e le Opere.* Rome, 1945. (Center; essentially a political-propaganda publication of the Party.)
Alcide de Gasperi. *Studi ed Appelli della Lunga Vigilia.* Rome, 1946. (Party leader; studies of Christian Democratic theory and of its forerunners written under Fascism and containing the first programmatic declarations of the present Party.)
Josef Dobretsberger. *La Politica Sociale Cattolica al Bivio,* with preface by Antonio Segni. Pisa, 1949. (Dobretsberger is an Austrian Christian Democrat, Segni a member of the Italian Party's center and a cabinet minister; a call for "modernization" of Christian Democratic social thinking.)
Amintore Fanfani. *Cattolicesimo e Protestantesimo nella Formazione Storica del Capitalismo.* Milan, 1934. (Outstanding member of the intellectual-corporativistic left wing.)
————. *Il Significato del Corporativismo.* Como, 1937.
————. *Colloqui sui Poveri.* Milan, 1943.
Igino Giordani. *Noi e la Chiesa,* second ed. Rome, 1943. (Mystical member of vaguely center-left wing of party.)
————. *L'Unità della Chiesa.* Rome, 1943.
Guido Gonella. *Presupposti di un Ordine Internazionale.* Vatican City, 1942. (Cabinet minister, and political secretary of party.)
————. *Presupposti di un Ordine Sociale.* Vatican City, 1942.

SELECTED BIBLIOGRAPHY

Giorgio La Pira. *Premesse della Politica.* Florence, 1945. (The "Saint" of the intellectual-corporativistic left wing.)
Piero Malvestiti. *Parte Guelfa in Europa.* Milan, 1945. (Slightly left of center; the program of the liberal Catholics of the "Guelph" partisan groups of Lombardy.)
———. *La Lotta Politica in Italia.* Milan, 1948. (A collection of articles written during the war and immediately after the liberation by the leader of the Lombard Christian Democrats.)
Ferdinando Storchi. *I Cattolici e la Politica.* Rome, 1944. (Head of ACLI.)
———. *I Documenti Sociali di Pio XII.* Rome, 1944.
Paolo Emilio Taviani. *La Proprietà.* Rome, 1946. (Center.)

D. *Church-State Relations*

M. Bendiscioli. *La Politica della Santa Sede.* Florence, 1939.
D. A. Binchy. *Church and State in Fascist Italy.* Oxford, 1941. (An essential and excellent study.)
Vincenzo del Giudice. *La Questione Romana e i Rapporti tra Stato e Chiesa fino alla Conciliazione.* Rome, 1947.
S. William Halperin. *The Separation of Church and State in Italy from Cavour to Mussolini.* Chicago, 1937.
Arturo Jemolo. *Chiesa e Stato negli Ultimi Cent'Anni in Italia.* Turin, 1949. (An important study; especially full and well-balanced for the period prior to the immediate present.)
Francesco Ruffini. *La Libertà Religiosa,* two volumes. Turin, 1901. (*Religious Liberty,* London, 1912.) (An historic-philosophical study of religious freedom in the modern state; exceedingly helpful for an understanding of the problem in Catholic Italy.)
Luigi Salvatorelli. *La Politica della Santa Sede dopo la Guerra,* Milan.

E. *Catholicism in Italy*

On the history of Italian Catholic Action by leaders in the movement:
Luigi Civarli. *Manuale dell'Azione Cattolica,* two volumes. Pavia, 1932.
Luigi Gedda. *Addio Gioventù.* Rome, 1947.
Francesco Olgiati. *La Storia dell'Azione Cattolica in Italia, 1865-1904,* second ed. Milan, 1922.

Doctrinal statements by organizations and leaders of Italian Catholicism:
Angelo Brucculeri, S.J. *Meditazioni Sociali.* Rome, 1944.
———. *Meditazioni Politiche.* Rome, 1946.
———. *Problemi d'Oggi.* Rome, 1949.
Agostino Gemelli (rector of the Catholic University of Milan). *Idee e Battaglie per la Coltura Cattolica.* Milan, 1933.
———. *Il Compito di una Università Cattolica ed Italiana nella Lotta del Comunismo contro Cattolicismo e Fascismo.* Milan, 1936. (As indicated by the title, ardently pro-Fascist.)
Istituto Cattolico di Azione Sociale. *Per la Comunità Cristiana.* Rome, 1945.
———. *Costituzione e Costituente.* Rome, 1946.
———. *Il Lavoro.* Rome, 1947.
———. *I Problemi della Vita Rurale.* Rome, 1948.

CHRISTIAN DEMOCRACY IN ITALY

Clemente Morando. *Aspetti Pratici del Programma Sociale Cristiano.* Turin, 1949.

Studium Christi. *La Morale di Cristo e le Professioni.* Rome, 1943.

Università Cattolica del Sacro Cuore. *Economia Corporativa.* Milan, 1935. (Studies of corporatism in general and of fascist corporatism specifically, in the light of Catholic doctrines.)

―――. *Problemi Fondamentali dello Stato Corporativo.* Milan, 1935.

―――. *Chiesa e Stato.* Milan, 1939.

F. Current Political History

Francesco Compagna. *La Lotta Politica Italiana nel Secondo Dopoguerra e il Mezzogiorno.* Bari, 1950. (A balanced study, written by a "neoliberal".)

Michele Dipiero. *Storia Critica dei Partiti Italiani.* Rome, 1946.

W. Hilton-Young. *The Italian Left: A Short History of Political Socialism in Italy.* London, 1949.

Gabriele Pepe. *La Protesta Laica.* Rome, 1949. (The anticlerical protest against the Christian Democrats.)

―――. *Un Anno di Dominio Clericale.* Rome, 1949.

Giovanni Spadolini. *Il Papato Socialista.* Milan, 1950. (Christian Democracy charged with aiming at the foundation in Italy of "socialist papal" dominion.)

Nino Valeri. *La Lotta Politica in Italia.* Florence, 1945.

Leo Valiani. *L'Avvento di de Gasperi.* Turin, 1949. (A generally favorable history by a Democratic Socialist of the process by which de Gasperi became prime minister.)

G. Specific Problems

On the *southern and agrarian questions:*

Istituto Nazionale di Economia Agraria. *La Distribuzione della Proprietà Fondiaria in Italia,* fourteen volumes. Rome, 1948. (Thirteen area studies and a general report by the editor of the series, the outstanding agrarian economist, Giuseppe Medici. The first comprehensive study of the conditions of land tenure and productivity in Italy.)

Giuseppe Medici. *L'Agricolture e la Riforma Agraria.* Milan, 1946.

―――. *Italy: Agricultural Aspects.* Stresa, 1949. (A summary of the above.)

Manlio Rossi-Doria. *Riforma Agraria e Azione Meridionalista.* Bologna, 1948. (By a leading Italian agrarian economist.)

On *school problems,* the Italian Ministry of Public Education has published the following:

La Pubblica Istruzione nel Periodo della Costituente. Rome, 1948.
La Riforma della Scuola: Conclusioni dell'Inchiesta Nazionale. Rome, 1950.

The documents on the history of the break in labor unity in Italy are presented by the Communist-dominated Confederazione Generale Italiana

SELECTED BIBLIOGRAPHY

del Lavoro in *La CGIL dal Patto di Roma al Congresso di Genova*, Vols. 1 and 3, Rome, 1950.

On the LCGIL, the noncommunist labor organization, see: *La LCGIL per la Legislazione Sindacale*, Rome, 1949, and *Primo Anno: Relazione della Segreteria Confederale al Primo Congresso Nazionale*. Rome, 1949.

II. Newspapers and Magazines

Civiltà Cattolica, Jesuit fortnightly.

Collegamento, official fortnightly of the Comitati Civici.

Conquiste del Lavoro, official weekly of the Libera Confederazione Generale del Lavoro (noncommunist labor organization).

Cronache Sociali, organ of the Christian Democratic left wing led by Giuseppe Dossetti, published between 1947 and 1951.

Democrazia, organ of the Milan organization of the Christian Democratic Party.

Humanitas, Catholic cultural monthly.

Idea, Catholic politico-social monthly.

Informazioni Sindacali, official monthly of ACLI.

La Libertà d'Italia, "independent" daily of Rome; organ of Christian Democratic left wing led by Giovanni Gronchi; stopped publication in 1951.

Notiziario della Scuola e della Coltura, monthly issued by the Ministry of Public Education.

Orientamenti Sociali, fortnightly of Istituto Cattolico di Azione Sociale.

Osservatore Romano.

People and Freedom, publication of a Christian Democratic group founded in Great Britain by Sturzo. Useful for comments upon activities of the several European Christian Democratic Parties. —

Politica d'Oggi, organ of left wing Christian Democrats in Rome. Published from 1945 to 1948.

Politica Sociale, "Catholic labor weekly", organ of Christian Democratic left wing led by Gronchi and of minority wing of LCGIL led by Giuseppe Rapelli.

Il Popolo, official daily of the Christian Democratic Party.

Popolo e Libertà, official fortnightly of the Christian Democratic Party; fuller reporting of important speeches, internal organization and party activity.

Quotidiano, official daily of Catholic Action.

Realtà Politica, weekly of the "visible" right wing of the Christian Democratic Party.

Realtà Sociale d'Oggi, monthly of Milan branch of ICAS.

Sicilia del Popolo, official Christian Democratic daily for Sicily, published in Palermo.

Studium, Catholic cultural politico-social monthly.

La Via, left-center Christian Democratic organ, edited by I. Giordani.

Vita Sociale, Catholic monthly.

III. Pamphlets

   A. *Christian Democratic Party*

   No complete listing of Christian Democratic pamphlets is possible here. The party's propaganda office, SPES, published in 1946 several series of propaganda booklets. Included in these "Collezioni della Segreteria Spes" are: a series of ten pamphlets, "Guide del Propagandista"; a series of six on political movements in other countries, "Panorami"; a series of three, a pamphlet each devoted to Bolshevism, Socialism and neo-Fascism, entitled "Contradittori"; and one on "riforme". SELI (Società Editrice Libraria Italiana), the publishing house of the Party, has printed a large number of pamphlets, many of the first written by Sturzo or de Gasperi (under the pseudonym Demofilo) under the general heading "Quaderni della Democrazia Cristiana." It was this series which attempted to popularize the historical and ideological roots of Christian Democracy and, in addition, to present Christian Democratic thought on such problems as the school, labor and agrarian reforms; they are the single most important group of early Christian Democratic propaganda publications. The same task of propaganda was attempted by SELI, with smaller booklets, in the series "Piccola Biblioteca di Cultura Politica". Finally, SELI also undertook a series on "I Problemi della Ricostruzione", the results of the work of the Party's study commission. Number six in this series was Umberto Tupini's *La Nuova Costituzione.*

   Of primary importance are the party pamphlets *Indirizzi Politico-Sociali della Democrazia Cristiana* (April 1945) and *Orientamenti Programmatici della D. C.* (1947). The former is a collection of Christian Democratic appeals, council and directorate resolutions and study commission conclusions in the first half of 1944. It contains as well the first party statute (adopted July 1944), the first circular letter sent out by the party's political secretary (August 1944), and de Gasperi's "Idee Ricostruttive della Democrazia Cristiana" first published on July 25, 1943.

   For the first national Party congress, see the SPES pamphlets: Guido Gonella, *Il Programma della Democrazia Cristiana per la Nuova Costituzione* (1946) and Attilio Piccioni, *Repubblica o Monarchia* (1946). For the second congress: Piccioni, *Dal Congresso di Roma al Congresso di Napoli, Organizzazione e Azione Politica* (1947); Paolo Emilio Taviani, *Problemi del Lavoro* (1947); and de Gasperi, *Non Diserteremo il Nostro Posto* (1947). For the organizational assembly of January 1949: Taviani, *Il Partito: Compiti, Struttura e Funzionalità.* For the third Party congress: Giuseppe Cappi, *Dal Congresso di Napoli al Congresso di Venezia: Verso l'Avvenire* (1949) and Mariano Rumor, *Necessità Vitali del Lavoro Italiano* (1949).

   From time to time SPES also publishes in pamphlet form important speeches in Parliament by party leaders and special studies on economic and social questions. It published de Gasperi's speeches at the conference which drew up the Italian peace treaty, and a *Dizionario Sociale* prepared under the direction of Giuseppe Dossetti in 1946.

   Speeches at meetings of the international association of Christian Democratic movements are published in both French and Italian by the Nouvelles Equipes Internationales of Paris. Important among these were the speeches of Piccioni and Taviani at the "study convention" held in Fiuggi and Rome

SELECTED BIBLIOGRAPHY

in July 1948, and the speech of de Gasperi at the organization's meeting in April 1950 at Sorrento.

Local SPES branches have also published important pamphlets, among them: Amintore Fanfani, *Il Progetto di Costituzione della Repubblica d'Italia* (Segreteria "Spes" of Arezzo); Fanfani, *Quesiti di Lavoratori; Risposte di Governanti* (Editrice SEPO, Milan); and *La Riorganizzazione dello Stato Italiano* (the Bologna section of the party). On specifically Sicilian questions, reprints by both party and provincial governmental organs are available.

Special attention should be drawn to Sturzo's series of articles on the development of the South in *Il Popolo* from October 10, 1948 through May 27, 1949; to Senator Giuseppe Medici's articles on agrarian reform in *La Stampa* during 1949 and 1950; and the editorials of *Il Popolo*, which afford the clearest insight into the policies of the party's center with respect both to internal affairs and relations with other parties.

B. *Civiltà Cattolica*

In addition to the books of Father Angelo Brucculeri listed above, his series "Le Dottrine Sociali del Cattolicismo" is to be noted. These are studies on such questions as communism, social justice, the social function of property, capitalism, just wage, labor, the state and the individual, democracy and the strike.

Of special note is Father G. Giampietro's *Sviluppi e Limiti della Nuova Legislazione Scolastica,* published in Civiltà Cattolica's series "Questioni di Attualità".

In a class by themselves are the two booklets by Father Riccardo Lombardi: *Crociata della Bontà,* Rome, 1949, and *Per una Mobilitazione dei Cattolici,* Rome, 1950.

C. *Communist sources*

Communist propaganda pamphlets aimed chiefly at the Christian Democratic Party and the government include: a pamphlet of the CGIL, Communist-dominated labor federation, *Da Melissa a Modena,* Rome, 1950, and official party reprints of various speeches of Togliatti, among them: *Per l'Unità di tutto il Popolo contro il Governo della Discordia* (1947); *Contro la Politica Interna del Governo Democristiano* (1948); *Unità di Popolo contro il Governo Poliziesco e Clericale* (1948); *Tre Minacce* (1948); and *Piano Marshall, Piano di Guerra* (1948).

Of special interest is Giorgio Candeloro's history of the Catholic social, political and religious movement in Italy, *L'Azione Cattolica in Italia* (1949).

PART II

CHRISTIAN DEMOCRACY IN FRANCE

by François Goguel

INTRODUCTION

During the Third Republic, French political life was to a great extent dominated by the almost invariable opposition of the parties of the left and of the right. The former invoked democracy, progress and secularism, conceived not only as the neutrality of the state in religious affairs, but as an attitude in favor of the emancipation of the human mind from the dogma and the authority of the Church. The latter were conservatives, Catholics (or at least sympathetic to the social influence of Catholicism) and basically hostile to democratic principles even when, for tactical reasons, they seemed resigned to accepting them. In spite of the growing pressure of economic and social forces, the religious question, that is, the antagonism between Catholics and anti-clericals, always played an important role in the political struggles of the period between the two world wars. As late as 1930, André Siegfried could write: "No militant of the left has . . . learned to believe that the Church can sincerely work for the Republic." [1]

Several attempts, which we will have to discuss, had been made shortly before or shortly after the first world war to sever the bonds that seemed to tie Catholicism to the conservative right. They failed. On the eve of the second world war, the idea that a Christian Democratic Party, as democratic as those of the left and as devoted to the principles and to the interests of the Church as those of the right, might play a major political role in France would have appeared improbable to every competent observer.

However, in the months that followed the liberation, the birth and the rapid progress of the *Mouvement Républicain Populaire* seemed to prove that Christian Democracy could be established in France. The three general elections of 1945 and 1946 placed the MRP in the first or second rank among the French political parties. Since September 1944, and with the exception of one month at the end of 1946 and at the beginning of 1947, its leaders have constantly participated in the government. Georges Bidault was Prime Minister in 1946 and in 1949-1950 and Robert Schuman was Prime Minister in 1947-1948. At no time, from the first election which

---

[1] André Siegfried, *Tableau des Partis en France,* Paris, 1930, p. 62.

followed the liberation till June 1951, could anyone conceive of a majority being formed in parliament without the support of the MRP. The party came out of the 1951 election with enough parliamentary strength to allow it to continue to play an important role.

At the same time, the traditional division of French public opinion into only two antagonistic blocs, necessarily almost equal, has apparently disappeared. Until May 1947 a coalition including Communists, Socialists and Popular Republicans, that is, three out of every four deputies, governed against the opposition of only the small Moderate and Radical-Socialist groups. Then a majority of the center was formed, opposed on its left by the Communists and on its right by the Moderates and those Radical-Socialists most strongly attached to economic liberalism, as well as by the neo-Gaullists of the RPF. Despite some faltering this majority was reformed after each ministerial crisis and won the election of 1951.

It is obvious that the existence of the MRP and the position that it occupies are largely responsible for this situation, which is so profoundly different from that before the war. Of all the French parties it is, moreover, the only one which is not the continuation of a previous political organization. These circumstances should suffice to justify a thorough study of the MRP, for they are essential to an understanding of the political evolution of France since the liberation.

Having traced its origin and its ancestry, we shall then examine what the MRP would like to be and what it actually is. We shall conclude by trying to estimate its future prospects.

CHAPTER ONE

THE ORIGINS OF THE MRP

The immediate origin of the MRP is directly linked to the events of 1940-1944 and to the resistance against the illegal Vichy government and against the Nazi invader.

Although It considers Itself a young and different party, the MRP also boasts that it has revived a very old tradition. "All those who are here," said Maurice Guérin (deputy from the Rhone until June 1951) to the MRP's constitutional convention in November 1944, "and even the youngest are the children of a venerable ideal. Each one of you, politically, is more than a century old. Your ancestors were united around the movement *l'Avenir* with Lamennais, Lacordaire and Montalembert. Later another name was to be added to these illustrious ones: Albert de Mun, who was to be followed by the first social Catholics. Then the *Sillon* was to be born, with Marc Sangnier and so many others . . . ." [1]

Before describing the circumstances surrounding the actual decision to create a great Christian Democratic movement in liberated France, it is appropriate to trace rapidly the MRP's historical antecedents.

I. *Historical Antecedents*

The antagonism between the principles of the Catholic Church and those of the individualistic democracy that the Revolution introduced into France first flared up in 1790, upon the passage of the Civil Constitution of the Clergy. The conflict between the new state and the Church provoked the bloody insurrection of the Catholic provinces of the west and gave birth to the first popular opposition to the Revolution. Less acutely it lasted for the entire nineteenth century. Even after the signing of the Concordat of 1801, the Church did not accept the social structure which the Revolution had created. When, in the Charter of 1814, King

---

[1] Cited in *l'Aube,* November 28, 1944.

Louis XVIII provided for freedom of conscience and freedom of the press, Pope Pius VII expressly censured this surrender to the revolutionary principles. As fragmentary as the concessions made by the Restoration to democracy were, a school of reactionary Catholic thought, symbolized by de Maistre and de Bonald, arose in opposition to them and preached the pure and simple return to the institutions and to the principles of the Old Regime.

Other Catholics, on the contrary, turned toward the future; having decided to acknowledge history, they realized that it was not possible to erase completely the consequences of the events that had occurred since 1789 and they believed that it was necessary for Catholicism to adapt itself to them. Everyone understood that to do this the Church would have to recognize the legitimacy of the new aspirations and needs of the masses, whose advent to social maturity had been marked by the Revolution. But the degree of confidence they placed in these masses as well as the basic orientation of their thinking varied a good deal.

Some, like Lamennais, Lacordaire and, much later, Marc Sangnier were, properly speaking, the founders of Christian Democracy. Not only did they accept the new position of the masses, but they wanted political power to be entrusted to the people. Others, on the contrary, like Montalembert or Albert de Mun, only envisaged a social Catholicism. They wanted the Church to inspire legislative and group activity designed to defend the interests of the masses and the workers, but they never agreed to abandon in the political sphere the principle of hierarchical organization, whether monarchical or simply aristocratic. Although resigned in differing degrees, varying with the men and the circumstances, to granting certain concessions to democracy, they were never convinced democrats. The distinction between these two currents, that of the Christian Democrats and that of the social Catholics, is not always easy to make but it is crucial. Occasionally these two currents have united at least on the surface, but almost always only to separate quickly again.

It is odd that the founder of Christian Democracy in France, Lamennais, was originally motivated by the desire to provide a new and firm basis for the absolute authority of the Holy See over the national churches, in brief, by ultramontanism. It was in order to frustrate Gallican influence, which was still powerful under the Restoration, that he proposed to create an alliance between liberty and the Church, to have Catholicism express its confidence in popular sovereignty, and especially, to express its confidence in the regime in a very general manner. His friends, Montalembert and Lacordaire, abandoned him when the Pope condemned the doctrine of *l'Avenir,* but his pride made him disregard this. He then broke with the Church. In spite of this condemnation and this breach, the Christian Democrats today do not hesitate to point out the connection between their position and that of Lamennais.

Montalembert and his liberal Catholic friends, frightened by the revolutionary days of 1848, were becoming reconciled with the conservatives. Montalembert even rallied for a moment to the Second Empire. Sincerely concerned with the fate of the working classes, reduced to a proletarian condition by the industrial revolution, these liberal (but not democratic) and social (but not socialist) Catholics sought improvement in measures inspired by Christian principles. They did not conceive that it might be a question of placing confidence in the people to the extent of consenting to a real democracy.

During the first phases of the Third Republic, Albert de Mun's concern for the fate of the masses was accentuated. He worked to create an economic structure which would permit both the formation of workers' unions and the discussion of working conditions by the unions. A monarchist when he first entered political life, de Mun "rallied" to the Republic when Pope Leo XIII invited French Catholics to do so, but he did not repudiate his aristocratic and hierarchical conception of political organization.

Setting aside individual activity carried on, especially in the Nord, by certain priests, many of whom were involved in Pius X's condemnation of modernism, the real restorer of Christian Democracy in France, in the tradition of Lamennais and Lacordaire, was Marc Sangnier. The movement *Sillon,* which he founded in 1897, originally proposed "to create in Catholic circles groups both conscious of the moral and social forces at their disposal and able to dislodge Catholicism from the prejudices which weakened its position," in order to "disseminate Christian influence among indifferent or hostile circles."

Experience quickly demonstrated to the promoters of *Sillon* that the connection between Catholicism and the forces of social conservatism and political reaction constituted the most powerful obstacle to its expansion in a country where the majority of the people had obviously completely adopted the principles of democracy. Marc Sangnier and his friends saw in Catholic doctrine nothing that was incompatible with an active and unreserved acceptance of these principles. On the contrary, the democratic regime, which tended "to develop to the maximum the consciousness and the sense of responsibility of the citizens," appeared to them to correspond exactly on the civic level to the essentials of Christianity. Their movement, which was purely secular and had no connection with the church hierarchy, did not constitute what we would call today a branch of Catholic Action. Their goal, according to a letter written by Marc Sangnier to the newspaper *La Croix* in 1906, was "the realization of the democratic republic in France." This did not prevent, Sangnier added, the *Sillon* from also being "a profoundly religious movement. For the members of the *Sillon* clearly recognize that they need Catholicism, not only to insure individually their personal salvation, but also in order to produce the moral force and the virtue which are essential to the temporal work that they have set out for themselves." [2]

Sangnier declared more and more clearly the deep solidarity which, in his opinion, united Christianity and democracy. "In ancient times there were nine slaves for every free man . . . a man appeared who made the democratic principle prevail over political barbarism . . . this man is Christ. . . . It would be dangerous . . . to suspect the elements . . . of true Christianity in the revolutionary temperament and in the Declaration of the Rights of Man. This respect for the individual, this acute sense of the infinite value of a single human soul, this declaration that man has rights which his very nature confers on him and which are prior to all written law, all that is pure Christianity." [3] It was impossible to indicate more

---

[2] Cited by Havard de la Montagne, *Histoire de la démocratie chrétienne de Lamennais à Georges Bidault,* Paris, 1948, p. 160. This book is a polemic, violently hostile to the subject it treats, but it cites several interesting documents.

[3] Cited by Havard de la Montagne, *ibid.,* pp. 164-165.

clearly not that one was a democrat although a Christian, but a democrat because a Christian.

The successor to Leo XIII, Pope Pius X, who brought to the Holy See an attitude indicating less awareness of the realities of his era than his predecessor's, believed it necessary to condemn the *Sillon* in 1910. Marc Sangnier and his friends, unlike Lamennais, submitted to this condemnation and the *Sillon* was dissolved.

In 1911, the leaders of the *Sillon* founded the *Jeune République*. This was a purely political league whose very object made it immune to condemnation, while there had always been some ambiguity as to the relationship between the religious and the political aspects of the *Sillon*. The *Jeune République* took up the *Sillon's* themes of political action, concerning itself with the defense of the workers' interests and with the organization of international procedures designed to prevent war. It also struggled against nationalism and militarism, then still predominant in Catholic circles, and advocated bold social legislation granting a large role to the collective activity of organized workers. In this respect, the Christian Democrats to some extent approached the position of the social Catholics of the school of Albert de Mun, united in the political organization called *Action Libérale Populaire,* which was founded in 1901 by Catholics who had rallied to the republic while remaining somewhat reserved with respect to democratic principles. But while the latter remained very cautious and tried to preserve the authority, the initiative and the prestige of what de Mun called "the eminent classes," [4] *La Jeune République* had repudiated the chimera of a medieval-type corporatism and did not flinch before the idea of the strike, that is, the direct action of the working-class against the employers in order to defend its legitimate interests.

This involved, however, only a handful of men. Before 1914, the *Jeune République* never had a representative in parliament. The majority of Catholics remained hostile to the doctrines of Christian Democracy. And because the leaders of the *Jeune Ré-*

---

[4] "You are too busy with politics, and you are separating yourselves too much from the eminent classes." Letter from Albert de Mun to the Christian Democrats of the Nord (1897). Cited by Havard de la Montagne, *ibid.,* p. 135.

publique made no secret of their Catholicism, the parties of the left still confused them with the reactionary right.

After the first world war, the *Jeune République* had a little more success. Marc Sangnier was elected deputy from Paris in 1919, but only as a result of a certain amount of confusion, and as a candidate on a right wing list. Later, on the contrary, two or three deputies from *Jeune République* were usually elected in Catholic districts each time against conservative candidates and thanks to the support of left wing minorities. In 1936 the *Jeune République* took part in the Popular Front. If it had not succeeded in modifying the traditional political orientation of Catholicism as a whole, it had at least succeeded in convincing the parties of the left that some Catholics could be genuine democrats.

In the meantime, the men who founded the *Parti Démocrate Populaire* in 1924 made a new effort to extend Christian Democracy into Catholic circles. Doctrinally, the *Parti Démocrate Populaire* adhered to democratic principles in as active and firm a way as had the *Jeune République*. Socially, while definitely displaying more caution and while theoretically favoring the collaboration of classes (without, however, condemning the use of the strike in certain cases), it continued to advocate and perfect the principles of social Catholicism even going so far as to make veiled criticisms of unrestricted capitalism. Internationally, it had advocated the policy of Briand and the attempts to organize peace through the League of Nations.

Actually, although the militants of their party were definitely more daring than they, the popular democratic deputies did not succeed in clearly distinguishing their attitude in parliament from that of their moderate and conservative colleagues: from 1924 to 1926 they fought the governments of the *Cartel des Gauches,* from 1929 to 1932 they supported Tardieu and Laval, from 1932 to 1934 they voted against the radical ministries, then from 1936 to 1938 against the Popular Front. In contrast to the parliamentary representatives of the *Jeune République,* the deputies of the Popular Democratic Party were all elected in Catholic districts by right wing coalitions and against candidates of the traditional left. There were two or three exceptions: in 1928, in Vendée and in Morbihan, three popular democratic deputies were elected against conservatives thanks to the support of left wing voters. Four years later, however, these conservatives no longer ran and the popular democrats were re-elected against radical and socialist candidates.

The Popular Democratic Party never succeeded in expanding over all of France. With the exception of its president, Champetier de Ribes, elected in Basses-Pyrénées where he was personally very popular, its deputies, of whom there were about fifteen, were all elected in the west or in Alsace and Lorraine. It also had some strength in the Nord, where the Christian Democratic tradition had been rooted since the end of the nineteenth century, but it never succeeded in electing a candidate there.

At the end of the Third Republic, Catholic circles as a whole were still hostile to the attempts to wrest them from their politically conservative, nationalistic tradition, replete with distrust of democracy. Conservative social Catholicism, with its working-class and corporative preoccupations, inherited from Albert de Mun, had just about disappeared as an independent political force. Only in the special preoccupation with problems concerning the family found in parties of the right, like the *Fédération Républicaine* led by Louis Marin, could there be found a reflection of the Popular Democratic Party. Within the Popular Democratic Party, however, the merger of the traditional tenets of social Catholicism with those of Christian Democracy had produced quite a new doctrinal synthesis, whose boldness doubtlessly contrasted with the very cautious attitude of the parliamentary representatives of this party, but which nevertheless constituted a powerful factor in the transformation of the way in which French Catholics had until then approached political and social problems.

The attitude of the *Jeune République,* further removed from the traditional prudence of Catholic circles, had contributed towards opening a gap in the wall of reciprocal suspicion which had for a long time stood between them and the parties of the left. The unanimous hostility of the popular democrats to the policy of capitulation to Nazi Germany and Fascist Italy widened this gap during the very last years of the Third Republic.

In the last analysis, however, the efforts which some Catholics had been making for a century to introduce Christian Democracy in France had met with little success when the Third Republic came to an end.

II. *The Founding of the MRP*

The psychological shock, which four years later was to end in the creation of the MRP, was produced by the armistice of June 1940, the striking victory of Nazi Germany and the formation in France of a government disposed to capitulate by at least partially adapting the political and social institutions of the nation to the Nazi victor's principles.

These events provoked among a certain number of men, many of whom were then still isolated, a common reaction of hostility. This was not only the consequence of a patriotic movement against accepting both the defeat and the refusal to continue the struggle alongside Great Britain (by using the resources of France's colonial empire and her fleet, which remained intact) ; it was equally due to a basically religious aversion to accepting, even partially, the totalitarian and anti-Christian doctrines of Nazism. M. J. Hours, a professor of history at Lyon, who was one of the founders of the MRP, even considers that religious motives played more of a role in creating the attitude of resistance of his friends than did specifically patriotic motives. "The resistance of the Christians," he wrote, "had prepared them poorly for political activity because their motives were especially religious: they were less opposed to the German state as the destroyer of the French state and the oppressor of our people than to National Socialism, a racial fanaticism and veritable religion, in its very essence the negation of Christianity." [5] There is, perhaps, some exaggeration in this opinion. But it is certain that religious and patriotic motives were inextricably mixed in the source of the common attitude adopted in 1940 by all who were later to create the MRP.

In parliament, most of the Popular Democratic deputies and all those of the *Jeune République* refused to delegate constituent power to Pétain on July 10, 1940. They demonstrated a far-sightedness and an attachment to democratic principles superior to those of many radicals and socialists, and that contributed in no little way

---

[5] "Les chrétiens et la politique," *La Vie Intellectuelle,* May 1948.

to the recognition by the parties of the traditional left that Catholics could be sincere and confirmed democrats.

It was not only among political men that this reaction of rebellion was produced in June-July 1940. At London, the newspaperman Maurice Schumann rallied at once to de Gaulle. At Beirut, André Colin, the former secretary general of *L'Association Catholique de la Jeunesse Française*, launched appeals over the radio for the continuation of the struggle by all the forces of the empire.

In France the law professors François de Menthon and Pierre-Henri Teitgen, militants of the Popular Democratic Party, organized in September 1940 a resistance movement called *Liberté*. Former militants of Catholic Action or of Christian labor unions, monks and priests, non-Catholic humanists like Max André, to whom the Nazi outrages against the dignity of man were spiritually as insupportable as they were to Christians, and Protestants as well threw themselves into the resistance. They did this singly or in organizations which were not specifically Christian Democratic, but they did it for similar reasons, which were both patriotic (like those of all the resistants) and religious or philosophical. It is precisely this similarity of motives that led them little by little to become conscious of what united them.

There was, therefore, no Christian Democratic resistance movement, but there were Christian Democrats (or religiously minded democrats very similar to Christian Democrats) in all the resistance movements. Practically every Christian Democrat was in the resistance, at a time when conservative Catholics were content to believe that the "Communist peril" was removed, even though this security arose from the German victory. They deluded themselves into thinking that the "national revolution" of Pétain was going to revive France according to the principles of reaction, which were nearer, despite the vocabulary it borrowed from social Catholicism, to de Maistre, de Bonald and Maurras than to Albert de Mun and Montalembert.

The resistance organizations, at first isolated and preoccupied mainly with immediate action, progressively made contact with one another, partly under the influence of the Committee of National Liberation headed at London by General de Gaulle. They felt the necessity to undertake the study of the political and social problems

117

which would be raised after the liberation. The *Comité Général d'Etude de la Résistance,* whose president was François de Menthon, was formed. A wide program of research and political thought was undertaken, and this unveiled the affinity of the sympathies of all those people who had entered the resistance for the same reasons. When Georges Bidault, former Popular Democratic militant and editorialist of *l'Aube* (the Christian Democratic daily founded between the wars by the Catholic publisher Francisque Gay) returned from captivity, he contributed greatly to this crystallization of common ideas. The role of the Christian Democrats in the resistance or, perhaps more exactly, that of Christian Democratic ideas within the framework of the doctrine of the non-Communist resistance, appeared important enough for Bidault to be chosen as president of the National Council of the Resistance in 1943, after its former president, Jean Moulin, had been arrested by the Germans.

Preparing for the formation of a great Christian Democratic political movement at the moment of the liberation, seems, however, to have been specifically the idea of a young Catholic student at Lyon, Gilbert Dru.[6] A militant of *Jeunesse Etudiante Catholique,* Dru had been subjected not to the doctrinal influence of Christian Democratic ideas as they had been expressed on the political scene before the second world war, but to the influence of the personalist philosophy of Emmanuel Mounier, founder of the review *Esprit.* Opposed to the rationalistic individualism of the Jacobin tradition and hostile to the "established disorder" of liberal capitalism, Mounier's personalism was equally opposed to the dialectical materialism of the Marxists, conceived as a total philosophy. He retained as valid, however, for the explanation of economic and social evolution certain aspects of the Marxist method. *Esprit* had appeared at Lyon for several months after the armistice; its anti-fascist attitude and its scarcely-disguised sarcasm with respect to the Vichy regime soon led to its suppression. The position that it defended was nevertheless widely echoed among the young intellectuals who were instinctively hostile to collaboration with National-Socialism.

---

[6] See the biography of Dru by Jean-Marie Domenach, *Gilbert Dru, celui qui croyait au ciel,* Paris, 1947.

Because of this influence and that of several Catholic professors in the Lyon area, whose sympathies were Christian Democratic or personalist, and especially because of his own personal drive, Gilbert Dru was soon in the center of the Lyon student resistance. From June 1941 to June 1943, he administered the secretariat of the *Cahiers de Notre Jeunesse,* a Catholic review which openly struggled against the grip of Vichy and Nazism on France and which inevitably ended up by being suppressed. Then, within *Jeunesse Etudiante Catholique,* he contributed all his energy to exposing the sophistry of those people who advised the youth to submit to the *Service du Travail Obligatoire* and to go to Germany to swell the manpower of the Nazi war industries.

Gilbert Dru could not, whatever his current activity, fail to think of the future, and to think of it in political terms. He became aware during the summer of 1943 that "resistance and politics could only be one and the same thing, that the resistance was the only form of current activity and the mother, the teacher of future political activity." [7] From this time on he envisaged future political activity in the light of the clandestine struggle for liberation. Once the fatherland was liberated, the next task would be the liberation of man himself from the enslavement by the inhuman mechanisms of modern society and capitalism (already denounced by *Esprit.*)

The participation of Christians in this work seemed to him to be absolutely necessary. He did not believe that there were areas naturally prohibited to the influence and activity of Christianity. The similarity between these ideas and those of Marc Sangnier is obvious. They quite naturally led Gilbert Dru to envisage, in his turn, the creation of a political movement of Christian inspiration designed to create at last the genuine democratic republic, whose political, economic and social institutions would all be devoted to making possible the complete development of the personality of every man.

In 1943, Gilbert Dru wrote a kind of memorandum, summarizing his political conclusions. It was this memorandum, transmitted to the most important members of the Christian Democratic resistance, like Bidault, Gay and Colin, which was to stimulate the personal

---

[7] Jean-Marie Domenach, *ibid.,* No. 65.

contacts and the discussions that led to the decision to create the MRP.

"If we oppose," wrote Dru, "a pure and simple return to the old parties which are responsible for unfortunate parliamentary habits and whose representatives have, by a great majority, ratified a dictatorship born out of the defeat and betrayal; if we oppose any movement of fascist inspiration or of foreign allegiance, in the service of alien ideologies or of plutocratic powers, we think that the area of sane and genuinely national political activity is large enough to include several movements representing the broad political currents of our country.

"For example, we can see alongside our movement, the possibility of a grouping of the traditional forces of the right, but of a 'purified' right, released from the pernicious clutches of *l'Action Française* and the trusts.

"We are also thinking of Communism which, because of the attitude of its militants in the present drama, has unquestionably acquired a place in the community. Amid the decomposition of the parties of the left, this movement alone has proved itself capable of carrying on the political and social tradition of the French agnostics and 'materialists' and it will therefore be called upon to play, whether one likes it or not, an important role in tomorrow's politics.

"Nevertheless, if it declares itself to be the *only* revolutionary movement in our country, this would be a regrettable slur on the integrity of the French spirit which is so diverse and so rich with potentiality. Its very presence, which is both real and justified, demands the formation of a powerful movement capable of counterbalancing it and of collaborating with it.

"The birth of such a movement is really the first prerequisite of a fruitful collaboration which will be rendered possible by reciprocal loyalty and by the elimination of all foreign machinations." [8]

This statement is of paramount importance because it expresses very clearly most of the ideas—some of which were to be belied by experience—which are at the origin of the creation of

---

[6] *Ibid.,* pp. 78-80.

the MRP. There is the aversion for the "old parties," rendered responsible for the events since 1940 and for the political customs of the Third Republic (which, incidentally, the militants of the Catholic youth organizations knew only superficially as they always professed a non-political attitude). There is the conviction that it would be necessary (and the illusion that it would be easy) rapidly to free the conservative right from the grasp of the "trusts," doubtless by a series of nationalizations which would destroy the major bastions of capitalism. There is the belief in a "decomposition" of the old parties of the left (radical and socialist), based on the fact that they played as organizations no role or almost no role in the resistance and on an ignorance of the deep roots that they nevertheless retained in the country. There is, finally, the desire to "collaborate" with the Communists, while counter-balancing them, and there is the hope that they would eliminate in the future any foreign allegiance and act loyally toward their partners.

Dru's memorandum was submitted in the course of the winter of 1943-1944 to those people who were going to be the founders of the MRP. Because its contents corresponded thoroughly with what they themselves felt, perhaps in a less clear way, it is certain that this memorandum contributed decisively to the foundation of the new party. At first called the *Mouvement Républicain de Libération,* it eventually became the *Mouvement Républicain Populaire.* But Gilbert Dru himself was not to participate in the inauguration of the movement in whose creation he had so largely shared. Arrested by the Germans on July 17, 1944, at the home of Maurice Guérin, and found bearing documents which left no doubt as to his participation in the preparation of an insurrection, he was executed at the Place Bellecour a few days later in reprisal for an attack on the Gestapo.

The future leaders of the MRP had already secretly distributed in occupied France a preliminary manifesto, *Program of Action for the Liberation.* In August, with the liberation of Paris, the MRP appeared publicly. Three of its leaders, François de Menthon, Pierre-Henri Teitgen and Georges Bidault, entered the Provisional Government formed at Paris in September 1944 by General de Gaulle. An MRP group was formed in the Consultative Assembly. *L'Aube,* which had suspended publication at the time of the armis-

121

tice, began to appear. In the public life of liberated France, Christian Democracy therefore occupied, from the beginning, a position infinitely more important than it had occupied in 1939.

In order to maintain this position, it was necessary for it to establish its doctrine and to adapt it to the needs of the country, to organize itself not only at Paris but in all of France and to decide on effective tactics. A first congress, held at Paris at the end of November 1944, ratified the activity outlined clandestinely during the resistance and put into effect since the liberation: the MRP became a political party.

CHAPTER TWO

WHAT THE MRP WOULD LIKE TO BE

I. *The Doctrine*

The MRP is anxious to emphasize the importance which it attributes to the doctrine that guides its political activity. "It is . . . . clear," wrote Etienne Gilson in 1948, "that our political activity presupposes certain fundamental convictions that we implicitly admit without always being able to explain them, and that being incapable of doing this is a weakness." [1] The assistant secretary general of the MRP, Albert Gortais, opened his report on doctrine, which in March 1947 was approved by the congress of his party, by declaring: "It is only too obvious that one cannot act usefully without knowing where one is going. A day by day policy leads to the most deceptive ineffectiveness. The initiative which the course of events requires can avoid contradiction only if decisive choices are made. . . . Just as it is necessary to avoid abstract theories having no connection with real life, it is necessary to be careful not to sink into improvisation and incoherence for the lack of having been aware of the movement of history and of having understood the fundamental facts of the problems of civilization that our era raises. . . . " [2]

What is this doctrine characteristic of the MRP? It consists essentially of an interpretation of history linked to a conception of man and society. A doctrine relating to civilization as a whole, it is not directly an economic doctrine. We shall have the opportunity to see that the economic ideas of the MRP owe a part of their uncertainty and their ambiguity to the fact that they rest

---

[1] Etienne Gilson, *Notre Démocratie*. This is a series of articles published in *l'Aube* from April 25 to May 5, 1948, and later collected in a pamphlet.

[2] 2 Published under the title *Démocratie et Libération*, Paris, 1947, this report and Gilson's pamphlet are essential sources of the doctrine of the MRP. These quasi-official statements can be usefully supplemented by the critical and (because it is not designed as propaganda) franker study of Joseph Hours in *La Vie Intellectuelle*.

123

less on a specialized study of the problems of production and exchange than on a general conception of man and social life.

It is an interpretation of history: in this respect the MRP stems simultaneously from social Catholicism and from pre-Marxist French socialism. Like the former, it strongly criticizes the individualistic conception of the political, economic and social liberalism which sprang from the French Revolution. But, like the latter, it believes that the revolutionary doctrines are incomplete rather than false. It declares that the revolutionary principles imply not only the political democracy to which they have effectively led, but an economic and social democracy which is still to be created. Albert Gortais simultaneously emphasizes the "importance" and the "inadequacy" of the Revolution of 1789. It was important because it affirmed the equality of all before the law and because it struggled against the arbitrary, absolute royal power by obliging the government to respect the inalienable rights of every human being. It was inadequate because "the essentially individualistic and liberal ideology which inspired the young democracy was, through its economic and social consequences, to thwart its development. . . . The worker was free, but alone and defenseless." Individualistic liberalism, "developing across enormous technological progress, provoked both the concentration of economic power in the hands of a new aristocracy and the misery of a more and more numerous proletariat. . . . A flagrant contradiction on the human scene: a citizen in the political sphere, the worker remained in his working life a simple subject, subject to a power in which he had no share."

Etienne Gilson, on his part, after having stated in a positive way the adherence of the MRP to the democratic principle formulated by the Revolution—"sincerely to entrust to the people as a whole the task of administering themselves, to have confidence in their ability to do it progressively better and better"—explains in these terms the inadequacy of the revolutionary conception of liberty: "First of all there is political liberty: this is developed economically in the guise of an unbridled individualism in which equality consists of the right of everyone freely to develop himself at the expense of others; in order to react against the individualism of some, who cause it to suffer, the working class organizes and undertakes mass action; let us not be surprised, therefore, that wherever it succeeds its first care is to suppress this very political liberty from which, it knows, all its ills are derived."

In the perspective of such an interpretation of the evolution of the western world for a century and a half, and particularly of France, individualistic liberalism and collectivism appear, to use the expression of Albert Gortais, as "the two facets of a single error." The latter owes its birth and its development to the inadequacies and the excesses of the former but the latter is too intimately linked with the former to be able to rectify it.

According to the MRP, both these conceptions rest on a false notion of man and of human society. On the right as on the left, Etienne Gilson writes, one sees man "only as an individual among individuals." The liberals of the moderate parties and of radicalism say, "The abnormal development of some individuals harms others? Too bad for the others." As to the Communists, "They speak only of *masses* and *mass action:* this way they are saying exactly what they think, for the only way that Marxism has discovered to prevent a minority of individuals from enslaving the majority of others, is to merge everyone in a single mass where everyone counts for one indiscriminately."

For a democrat of the MRP, however, Gilson says, "There is in the word *mass,* when it is applied to men, something insulting and repugnant . . . because each man is not only an individual but a person." The MRP is the "party which has unanimously recognized this truth." An individual like stones, trees, animals, "man alone is also a person, that is, an individual being endowed with reason. . . . Capable of knowing, therefore free to choose, he can justify his acts and assume responsibility for them. . . . It is not the number of heads that counts, but what there is in them. . . . From this springs the precise meaning of the word *people:* a group of persons united for the conquest of the common good, which they pursue in the light of reason."

What such a conception of man owes to Christianity is obvious, although its specifically religious aspect is not clearly expressed in the preceding lines, doubtless because the MRP denies that it is a sectarian party, and along with a majority of Catholics, actually includes Protestants, Jews and agnostics. It is quite clear, however, that the liberty and responsibility of man as Gilson describes them assume all their significance only against a religious background, for it is a question not only of man's reason but of his soul. The MRP rejects liberal and competitive individualism because it treats too cheaply the "infinite value" of each of the men who are crushed by the merciless economic struggle which it creates. And if this infinite value is affirmed by humanists as well as by Christians, it is to the extent to which the former are the heirs of Christianity. Albert Gortais recognizes it clearly: "Just as rigorously as Communist doctrine stems from integral materialism, the doctrine which inspires the policy of the MRP . . . is founded on a *spiritualistic* conception of man, on a completely humanistic conception of society."

A society of persons thoroughly distinguishable from one another and in which each one is considered as having, at least potentially, infinite value, cannot really be conceived as the same as a society of interchangeable individuals: its structure will necessarily be much more complex.

The person and the community, says Etienne Gilson, are inseparable. "The goal of society is the perfection of the human person . . . the perfection of the human person is possible only in and by society."

Of what does this society consist? To this Gilson answers: "From his birth to his death, each man is involved in a multiplicity of *natural social structures* outside of which he could neither live nor achieve his full development." It is no longer a question, as in the liberal conception or collectivistic conception, of a simple structure; there is no *one* society in which every individual directly and exclusively participates. "Each of these groups possesses a specific organic unity:" first of all there is the family, "the child's natural place of growth," then there is the town which, according to Royer-Collard "is, like the family, prior to the state: the law finds it and does not create it."

"But really," Gilson asks, "what does the law create? It has not created the school, the college, the university, the hospital, industries or businesses, labor unions, political parties, countries or churches. It can systematize, define, adapt, arbitrate, order and coordinate all these groups, but it creates none of them and everyone knows that any attempt on the part of the state to substitute its initiative for theirs, results only in replacing the natural with the artificial, organs with organizations, in brief, in substituting something mechanical for something alive."

Society as it is conceived by the MRP is not a political group directed in every way by the state and composed of indistinguishable individuals. It is a complex and hierarchical structure composed of natural groups, each one of which operates in its own sphere and all of which are necessary for the personal development of the men who participate in it. "Because the perfection of individuals is linked to that of groups, our democracy," Gilson writes, "is, in a way, social by definition. But that is also why it cannot be *socialist* in the exact sense of the word." For the personal rights which serve the goals of the state, namely the protection and the perfection of individual existence, must not be transferred to the state. "Personal rights belong to persons, and to take them away from persons under the pretext of making them more secure would be a policy contrary to the very nature of things." Gilson does not expressly say that some of these personal rights are really exercised by the secondary social groups to which people belong and that the real question is to protect these groups against the control of an omnipotent state, but it is clear that this is his inner conviction. "Our democracy," he writes, "is completely alien to any form of statism and it is to remove this danger that it supports people in the social groups which are their natural surroundings. . . . The independence of natural groups, coordinated for the general welfare, is the only efficient guarantee of personal liberty against the spontaneous totalitarianism of the state."

What is the political role of the state? It is simply "to be the protector and the regulator of these natural social groups, which alone permit the free development of the human person in the direction of his own interest as well as in that of the community."

The state must, of course, intervene in the life of groups "and, through them, in the life of the citizens." But it must not "substitute itself for these natural social structures. It must intervene only for the purpose of helping them to achieve their individual goals."

In brief, in the conception of the MRP, natural social groups possess, like people themselves, inalienable rights, which must be respected by the state. The latter is simply the administrator of one of a variety of functions, the function of coordination, supervision, support, which can be executed only by respecting the specific functions and the independence of each of the secondary groups. And because man, the ultimate value of society, cannot achieve his full development without the support of the various groups in which he participates and toward each of which he therefore has certain obligations, the state has no right to enlist for its benefit all the activity of the citizens, nor to deal directly with them without proceeding through the necessary but independent intermediary of each of these groups.

Because of its complete adherence to the democratic principle, this doctrine is extremely different not only from the reactionary Catholicism of de Maistre and of de Bonald, but even from the social Catholicism of Montalembert and of Albert de Mun. "It is inconceivable," says Gilson, "that every human being . . . does not have the capacity to contribute to his own government" and, further, "man achieves his full development, as a person, only by the use of his will according to the light of reason." In order to be free he must "ultimately rely on himself, first physically, which means economic liberty, and then spiritually, which means political liberty, both the expression and the guarantee of the inviolability of the human person. . . . These two liberties are inseparable, for one must be either a hero or a saint to possess a soul without possessing a body." The democratic convictions of the MRP, therefore, appear to be intimately linked with its spiritual or even religious convictions. It is certainly a question, literally, of Christian Democracy and not merely a matter of passive and reluctant acceptance of democracy by certain Christians.

It must be emphasized, however, that against this background specifically economic problems of a technical nature appear to be secondary. Pre-marxist French socialism itself attributed to them greater importance while subordinating them also to the demand for justice. Marxism, with its analysis of the contradictions of capitalism, has raised them to the first rank and given them almost independent meaning. The harmony between the demand for justice and what Marxism considers the necessary consequence of the very evolution of the economic structure can be regarded, at least theoretically, as accidental. It is a purely economic analysis, bearing on the facts of production and exchange, which serves as the essential basis of its program as a whole.

It is an entirely different matter for the Christian Democracy of the MRP. For it, the economic element is subordinated to the human element, and its conception of economic life really does not rest on an original analysis of the phenomena of production and exchange. For Albert Gortais, economic liberalism is condemned because "history has proven that political democracy is to a great extent based on fiction if it is not accompanied by a truly economic and social democracy," and because "tied to liberalism, yesterday's democracy almost perished because of it."

What is the economic democracy which must replace the democracy of yesterday? On August 26, 1945, the national council of the MRP defined it this way: "Economic democracy is characterized by the effective participation of everyone in the management of economic affairs, by a more equal distribution of income and by respect for the rights of everyone.

"It is opposed to capitalism, which reserves economic leadership only for the owners of capital, and which determines the distribution of income and regulates the relationships between men on the basis of the superiority of capital.

"It is equally opposed to a totalitarian statism in which economic relationships are regulated exactly like legal relationships, between governor and governed, between administration and administered, and in which confusion reigns between the political apparatus of the state and the economic organization of the nation."

It is remarkable that this text, which constitutes the charter of the MRP's economic doctrine, contains no reference either to the development of production or to the necessity of insuring stable markets in order to avoid the cyclical crises of overproduction, the responsibility for which the Marxists attribute to the capitalist regime. The major concern of the MRP is of a human and psychological nature. It advocates that everyone working in an industry participate, in some way still to be determined, in the management of industry, and that management not be the prerogative of the capitalist. In addition to this concern, there is a desire for justice which is reflected by the desire for a more equal distribution of income.

There is nothing specifically economic in all this. It is the mere translation, in terms of industry and working men, of the more general conceptions of man and social groups which we have just analyzed.

It is therefore apparent that these conceptions form the core of the doctrine of the MRP. Distinct from the conceptions of the other French political parties, they give to the MRP's doctrine its originality.

The MRP is aware of this originality. Gortais, as we have already seen, defines liberalism, a doctrine common to the moderate parties of the old right and to radicalism, and Marxist collectivism, a doctrine to a certain extent common to the Communists and the Socialists, as "the two facets of a single error." And Gilson says: "It would be futile to look for the methods of our democracy either to liberal individualism, which is undisturbed when some men use others for their own ends, or to Marxist communism in which, for a provisional period whose duration is unlimited, the state subordinates every human being to the product of his economic activity. There is no mid-point between these two conceptions. The MRP cannot define itself as more socialist than the radicals but less socialist than the Communists. . . . We are . . . beyond them and not between them. . . . We are entirely different from them and this is why you have to take our movement as it is or leave it."

Nothing could be truer. The social organism of the MRP, its conception of society as a great complex organism composed of a combination of individual bodies each one of which has its own sphere of activity and its independence, and in which the state exercises only one function among many, doubtless a coordinating function, but one which cannot be substituted for those of the other social groups, is completely opposed both to the political traditions of the French right and the French left.

It is opposed to the tradition of the right because, supported by Gallicanism, the jurists of the old monarchy had established doctrinally and had attempted to realize in fact the absolute primacy of the royal state over the intermediary bodies inherited from the middle ages: the provinces, universities, corporations and even the

Church. It is opposed to the traditions of the left because Jacobinism carried on for the benefit of the democratic state the tradition of the monarchical state and, supported by the individualistic and rationalistic philosophy of the eighteenth century, it dealt severe blows to the independence of the social groups as they existed even at the end of the Old Regime. Later, pre-marxist French socialism, with its associationist and anti-statist tendencies, so boldly expressed in the work of Proudhon, marked a certain breach with the statist tradition that the left had borrowed from the right while considerably reinforcing it. But Marxism's grip on the French socialist movement has for seventy years again led it in the direction of statism. Different tendencies have continually appeared, of course — from Pelloutier, founder of the *Fédération des Bourses de Travail* at the end of the nineteenth century, to Léon Blum who wondered in *A L'Echelle Humaine* if the French Socialists had "sufficiently fathomed the meaning of the effort with which Jaurès had transformed the Marxist deductions"— but they have always been a minority. The MRP is therefore doctrinally isolated in French politics. It is squeezed between the individualists on its right who reject the intermediacy of the secondary communities between the citizens and the state, and the collectivists on its left who think that every right conducive to the emancipation of the individual must be transferred to the state.

This doctrinal isolation is of great practical importance. The absence of a common political language between the MRP and the other parties and the lack of an implicit common reference to certain fundamental principles of political and social organization have, since 1944, constantly created equivocation and ambiguity in its relationship with the other members of the political coalitions in which it has participated. They therefore explain, to a great extent, its failures and the lack of understanding which it has encountered.

The MRP, of course, breaking with the tradition of the French Catholic parties, proclaims itself to be favorable to the Revolution of 1789 and conscious of its importance (and at the same time, it is true, of its inadequacy). But, Maurice Schumann declares: "The MRP is the continuation of an effort, which dates from 1789, not only to reconcile the revolutionary tradition and Christian thought with each other but to foster them reciprocally." This formula

131

implies that the activity of the MRP, if it succeeds, will result in a certain modification of the revolutionary tradition.

The conclusion is the same when Etienne Gilson repeats the three slogans of the Revolution, *Liberté, Egalité, Fraternité.* "By restoring to them," as he says, "the meaning that they had for a long time before it (the Revolution), the meaning which, it seems, the Revolution, unfortunately for it and for us, partly forgot," it could not be more plainly indicated that the MRP is departing from the revolutionary tradition as it has historically unfolded. It is in favor of a synthesis or a correction whose importance is not in doubt, but whose very existence is enough to erect a barrier between the MRP and the parties which unreservedly adhere to this tradition.

The doctrinal originality of the MRP therefore contributes to its isolation and this is tactically dangerous. Because it is aware of this, the MRP, with an insistence and a constancy which raise its affirmation to the level of a doctrine, has never since its creation ceased to proclaim that it refuses to accept the traditional division of French public opinion into two opposing blocs.

Historically, this division emerged from the opposition of the anti-democratic and conservative Catholics to the democratic and progressive anti-clericals. Now the MRP is Catholic, democratic and progressive. It believes that the breach between right and left has been introduced into the political traditions of France because the problems have been badly presented. The very goal of its activity is to correct this situation, to reconcile, to use the expression of Maurice Schumann, the democratic tradition with the spiritual tradition and to foster them reciprocally, and, consequently, to put an end to the opposition of these two blocs by promoting political coalitions which will appeal simultaneously to various elements of both of them.

This is a difficult task: we will see later to what extent it has been accomplished. But it is, in the eyes of the MRP, an essential task, and it results directly from the doctrine which defines the broad outlines of "what it would like to be."

II. *The Program*

In order to understand what the MRP would like to be, it is not enough merely to be acquainted with its doctrine. As original as it is, it is stated in such general terms that one still is uncertain of the way in which the Popular Republicans think it must be reflected in facts, that is, in concrete laws and institutions. It goes without saying that, wedged between parties whose individualistic or collectivistic doctrines differ quite greatly from its own, the MRP has had but slight success in making its views prevail concerning the reorganization of the state and of society. Later we shall have to measure this 'slight success' when we study what the MRP is; we shall try to discover what it has actually accomplished. But first we must still deal with what it wants to be by seeking in the legislative proposals of its members, in the resolutions of its national committees and in the debates of the committees entrusted with drafting the constitution of the Fourth Republic, the concrete suggestions which it has made.

CONSTITUTIONALISM AND POLITICS

The specific position of the MRP on the constitutional question is to be found less in the draft proposal submitted by Paul Coste-Floret in the name of the MRP group to the second constituent assembly [3] than in the debates of the constitutional committee of the first constituent assembly.[4] Actually, after the rejection of the first constitutional draft in the referendum of May 5, 1946, a draft which it opposed in conjunction with the moderates and the radicals, the MRP considered it necessary to arrive at a compromise with the Socialists and the Communists. The Coste-Floret draft represents a compromise proposal rather than the specific points of view of the MRP. On the other hand, in the committee of the first assembly and especially in the discussion of basic principles which took place in the committee in December 1945 and January 1946, the representatives of the MRP defended — usually unsuccessfully — positions completely consonant with the doctrine of their party.

---

[3] *Journal Officiel. Documents Parlementaires. Assemblée Nationale Constituante élue le 2 Juin 1946.* No. 68. Annexe au procès-verbal de la séance du 4 Juillet 1946.

[4] *Assemblée Nationale Constituante élue le 21 Octobre 1945. Séances de la Commission de la Constitution.* Comptes-rendus analytiques imprimés en exécution de la resolution votée par l'Assemblée le 25 Avril 1946. (Paris, Imprimerie de l'Assemblée Nationale Constituante, 1946).

With respect to the structure of parliament, the MRP advocated bi-cameralism, but it proposed two legislative chambers having unequal powers. The second chamber, the one with less extensive powers, would have had, according to its views, the function of guaranteeing a more careful drafting of legislation ("What has been examined twice instead of once is examined better," said Paul Coste-Floret on December 5, 1945). It would also give more balance to the constitution by permitting a time lag in the event of a conflict between the executive and the legislative power, and it would especially prevent parliamentary representation from assuming a purely individualistic character. "Are there not regional and local interests which must be defended? At the very moment when we are moving in the direction of tightening community bonds, it would be illogical to give a purely individualistic representative system to the country. The second assembly should represent these collective and community interests," said Henri Teitgen. Maurice Guérin, discussing the integration of labor unions into the political structure, added, "We must associate economic forces with political power and enable them to affect the destiny of the country." In brief, alongside the first chamber, which would have the last word and which would represent individuals, the MRP wanted to establish a second chamber, also political, but having more restricted powers and representing not only geographical communities, as the old senate did, but also professional communities, that is, the unions.

The first chamber would, according to the MRP's views, have been elected by proportional representation, with voting compulsory. Contested elections would have been settled not by the assembly but by a special agency, in order to prevent political passions from affecting the validation of disputed seats.

The MRP especially wanted to establish a statute of political parties defining both their rights and their duties. "We must have an organic republic," explained Daniel Boisdon on December 7, ". . . the parties of the Third Republic lost the confidence of the country because they were not sufficiently organized . . . the voters were not able to determine the attitude of their representatives. . . . What custom has accomplished in the Anglo-Saxon countries must be accomplished in France by law." Henri Teitgen said, "Universal suffrage is sovereign but it is now unsystematized . . . to establish a statute of parties would be to give it a framework. The parties would then become what they should be, intermediaries between the country and the executive and the legislative powers. How can they play this role if they are not organized?" This organization would have consisted in defining political parties, by distinguishing them from ordinary associations within the meaning of the law of 1901; in legally conferring upon them a political role; in prescribing the fundamental rules governing their structure and their activity; and in establishing controls over their financial resources. The political groups in the assemblies would have also been given a legal statute, designed, just like that of the parties, to prevent their multiplication and, in addition, to guarantee their correlation with the parties themselves.

As to the executive power, the MRP, which was hostile to the separation of powers but in favor of the separation of functions, wanted a President of the Republic, the "arbiter of the parties," to be chosen by an electoral college composed of the members of parliament and an equal number of delegates from the departmental councils, from the large cities and from the overseas territories. Representing the continuity of the state and placed above parties by the electoral system, the President of the Republic would have chosen the Prime Minister, the leader of the majority, without being obliged to submit his choice for ratification by the assembly.

Charged with presiding over the council of ministers in order constantly to be informed of the course of affairs, he would also have directed the work of some non-political bodies, like the judicial council and the council of national defense. The guardian of the constitution, in this capacity he would have presided over a high court empowered to examine the constitutionality of laws. Finally, he would personally have exercised the power to pardon and he would have promulgated laws.

With respect to the government itself, the MRP adopted the Socialists' suggestions, designed to ensure ministerial stability by establishing fixed procedures for a vote of confidence and vote of censure. A ministry could be overturned only by a special majority and only after a specified delay had preceded the vote of the assembly. Ministerial responsibility would be collective because each min-

135

ister would apply the decisions of the cabinet and would therefore have neither an individual policy nor individual responsibility.

Hostile to "government by assembly," which was recommended by Pierre Cot and by the Communists (usually supported by the Socialists), the MRP opposed the delegation of legislative power to committees, for so-called laws of "application," fearing it would deprive the government of its traditional administrative power and actually create "a government by committee."

As to the judicial power, Fonlupt-Esperaber declared on December 18, 1945, in the name of the MRP, the need for consecrating and reinforcing its traditional independence by creating a high judicial council to be presided over by the President of the Republic. This council would be empowered to guarantee the independence of the judges and especially to regulate their promotion. From the text of Coste-Floret's proposal to the second constituent assembly, one gathers that the MRP would have wanted most of the members of this council, or at least half of them, to be selected among judges and other people concerned with the administration of justice rather than from the members of the National Assembly.

Finally, the MRP advocated control over the constitutionality of laws, desiring that this control be exercised through use of the referendum. Laws declared unconstitutional by a judicial committee elected by the assembly, whose own members would be ineligible, were to be submitted to popular ratification before they could take effect. "There are certain inalienable individual rights," said François de Menthon, "and the assembly must not be able to infringe upon them."

The MRP had the opportunity to define with precision the practical consequences of its doctrine when the declaration of rights came up for discussion. This declaration was to appear at the head of the constitution and, according to the MRP, its principles were to serve as criteria for judging the constitutionality of laws. On January 10, 1947, Daniel Boisdon said that, in the opinion of the MRP, the individual rights listed in the declaration should be supplemented with "the rights of communities, such as the family, the town, and professional associations," as well as by a definition of the sovereignty of the state and of the limitations that would be placed upon it by the nation's integration in an international framework. The same day, Fonlupt-Esperaber insisted on an affirmation of "the right of the individual to a full economic life" and a definition of "the character of property, which must not be an end in itself but a means of serving the general welfare." In answer to the representatives of the conservative parties who were recommending a declaration which would be accepted unanimously by the French people, Henri Teitgen said that it was necessary "to decide on a certain social structure which would be imposed on the future legislators," and Maurice Guérin said that it was necessary "to state in the declaration that we have entered a new era which is revolutionary from the economic and social points of view." The representatives of the MRP insisted that the principle of labor participation in the management of industry be written into the declaration. "A man engaged in economic life remains a man:" said Fonlupt-Esperaber, "his work is not separate from his person, and he must be, according to details yet to be arranged, master of the use of his productive efforts."

As was natural for a party whose support was largely Catholic, the MRP fought desperately to include the principle of freedom of education, and not just a theoretical freedom, but a freedom made effective by material aid from the state to private schools or to families who would like to send their children elsewhere than to free, public schools. Henri Teitgen said that "the father has a natural right, prior to and superior to that of the state." Rejecting "totalitarianism in every form," he explained that "the true design of the democracies to come is pluralism." And Teitgen concluded by saying that "in France, there are diverse spiritual families: it is not by suppressing this diversity that you will create national unanimity; on the contrary, you can do this by giving them the means of their development."

Defeated on this issue, the MRP through its spokesman, Henri Teitgen, allowed "the separation of church and state and the secularism of the state and of public education" to be declared "the best guarantees of the freedom of opinion, of the freedom of conscience and of the freedom of worship."

The same day, the MRP vainly demanded that "the rights of the family founded on marriage" be recognized by the declaration. It received no more satisfaction with respect to the rights of towns, or unions and, in a general way, of "all the natural communities, created outside the state, and which can neither be subservient to it nor identified with it and whose inherent powers limit the powers of the state." Most of the representatives of the conservative right and the radicals, favorable to individualism, actually voted against this suggestion along with the Socialists and the Communists, the partisans of a statist collectivism.

With respect to economic matters, on January 16, the MRP agreed to the insertion in the Constitution of "planning for full employment," the "distinction between a public sector" by "nationalization of monopolies and key industries" and the existence of a high council for the national economy, an advisory body to be consulted in the drafting of economic plans.

Is there any necessity for emphasizing the conformity of the constitutional program supported by the MRP with the doctrine which we have described? If the MRP had been followed by the other parties, the breach with the traditions of the Third Republic would have been accomplished by the dominance of an assembly chosen by universal suffrage on the basis of proportional representation, by the role of intermediary between the citizens and the state which would have necessarily devolved upon the political parties and by the affirmation of economic and social rights. A corporate orientation of institutions would have resulted from the proclamation of the rights of social groups, made effective by a procedure for deciding upon the constitutionality of laws; from the composition of the second house of parliament, elected by geographical and professional groups and perhaps even by family organizations; and from the independence of the judicial structure. Such institutions would obviously have been in harmony with the conception of man and of society held by the MRP. It is precisely for this reason that they could not be accepted by the representatives of the other parties.

Economic Life

The MRP has had no real opportunity to describe in detail the economic policies that it would like to see put into effect in France. It is not so easy in the economic field as it is in constitutional and political matters to specify the concrete policies that the MRP derives from its general body of doctrine. We have already pointed out that its general doctrine is influenced more by a philosophical concern with the nature of man and human society than by a specific analysis of the phenomena of production and exchange. It is not surprising, therefore, that the economic program of the MRP betrays some uncertainty and hesitancy. We shall, however, try to outline its major features.

There is one point on which the Popular Republicans have taken a firm position: that is the necessity for a reform of the internal organization of industry in order to bring about a democratic atmosphere through the participation of the workers in management. A 1945 ordinance and a 1946 law, with this end in view, created *comités d'entreprises,* which are elected by the personnel of a plant and endowed with rather extensive functions: "To study all the suggestions of the management or of the workers for increasing production, to oversee the general operation of the industry, to receive from the employer an annual general report and financial statement, to make suggestions for the disposition of the profits, to delegate two members to the board of directors who would participate in the discussion but not vote, and to direct or control social activities." [5]   The MRP participated, through its representatives in the provisional government, in the preparation of the 1945 ordinance, and through the support of its deputies in the first constituent assembly, in the passage of the 1946 law. Later, it followed the application of this law with a vigilance that demonstrated the importance it attached to it. When it became apparent that certain employers were trying to evade its provision, for example, by subdividing their businesses or by reducing the number of their personnel to just below the number fixed by the law as the criterion for the creation of a *comité d'entreprise,* it proposed a bill designed to thwart these attempts.[6]

The Popular Republicans, however, consider the *comités d'entreprises* as only the first stage in the reform of the capitalistic structure of industry. A bill presented by Paul Bacon in the name of the entire MRP group indicates what they regard as the subsequent

---

[5] This summary of the functions of the *comités d'entreprises* is drawn from Georges Lasserre, *Socialiser dans la Liberté,* Paris, 1945, p. 272.

[6] *Journal Officiel. Documents Parlementaires. Assemblée Nationale.* No. 1214.   Annexe au procès-verbal de la séance du 2 May 1947.

steps.[7]   This bill would create "a new type of corporation, the *Société de Travail et d'Epargne.*" It does not make compulsory the replacement of the traditional corporations, which are characterized by the dominance of capital over labor, with the new type. The goal of the bill is simply to create a new legal framework, and it is only after an important number of businesses have actually adopted it that the possibility of making the transformation compulsory would be considered.

According to Bacon's bill, the *Sociétés de Travail et d'Epargne* would be administered by a board of directors, at least one third of whom would be representatives of "the assembly of worker-associates" (which must include at least two thirds of the employees in the business); the rest of the board would consist partly of representatives of the assembly of stockholder-associates and partly "of members designated as permanent consultants, chosen among persons who have displayed especially creative activity in the founding of the company or in its development." The director, designated by the corporation's charter or elected by the board of directors, would in any case be revocable by the board. Profits would be distributed to the stockholder-associates and to the worker-associates according to a ratio fixed by the charter, but at least fifty per cent of the profits would be earmarked for the workers. The further distribution among the workers and the stockholders would be decided by their respective assemblies. Finally, in case of increases in capitalization, preferential subscription rights would be given to the workers, whose acquisition of capital would thereby be facilitated.

In brief, this bill would establish the equality of capital and labor in the power of management, while giving to the permanent consultants on the board of directors an ultimate power of arbitration. This differs from the traditional capitalistic conception, in interfering with the principle of the sovereignty of the owners of the business, just as much as from the socialistic conception, since it does not completely abolish the participation of the owner in the management of the business. It is therefore not surprising that Paul Bacon's bill has not been brought before the National Assembly for discussion. The bill is nevertheless representative of the dis-

---

[7] *Ibid.,* No. 96. Annexe au procès-verbal de la séance du 12 Décembre 1946.

tinctive ideas of the MRP concerning the structure of industry, and it is beyond doubt that the MRP would like to promote the compulsory establishment of the type of industrial structure defined in this bill.

The MRP has had one opportunity to defend before the National Assembly its ideas on the structure of industrial organization.[8] The occasion concerned the special problem of the Berliet factories. The Berliet company is an important truck manufacturing concern at Lyon. At the time of the liberation, the Commissioner of the Republic for the area seized the factories because the directors of the company had agreed to work for Nazi Germany during the occupation and were even accused of having gone out of their way to seek orders from the enemy. A provisional board of directors, controlled by representatives of the personnel of the factory, succeeded in getting the factory into operation again and, in 1946, a cabinet decree sanctioned this type of administration in the interim before a new legal statute would be given to the company. But, in the meantime, the former directors, having served the sentences that they had received for economic collaboration and having paid the fines which had been imposed upon them (and which, moreover, had been greatly reduced through commutation measures), tried to reestablish the property and managerial rights of the old stockholders or, at least, with respect to management, the rights of those stockholders who were under no legal disability. As was natural under a legal system which in no way recognized the new conceptions of property rights defended by Socialists or Christian Democratic circles, the *Conseil d'Etat* had to annul the cabinet decree which had confirmed in 1946 the provisional system of management under worker control and which had no legal foundation.

From then on, the legal problem ceased to exist, and the Berliet corporation (whose form had in the meantime been modified through perfectly normal developments) should have reassumed possession of the factories, with all the powers of management to which it is entitled under the capitalistic system. But before the *Conseil d'Etat* had announced its decision, several private or governmental bills, designed to give a special statute to the Berliet fac-

---

[8] *Journal Officiel. Débats Parlementaires.* Sessions of November 15 and 28, and December 6 and 8, 1949.

tories, had been submitted to the National Assembly. Adversaries of a reform of the traditional structure of the company naturally believed that the problem should be considered settled and that there was no reason to legislate for a particular case which theoretically no longer presented any legal problem. The advocates of a reform of capitalistic industry, however, took a position favorable to discussing the problem. Here was a real opportunity to confirm by law the obsolete character of the traditional norms regulating the ownership of the means of production and their management.

The MRP took a very firm position in this debate. Hostile to the pure and simple nationalization proposed by the Communists and to the nationalization combined with worker-management supported by the Socialists, it rejected these solutions by casting its votes with those of the Radicals and the Moderates. The legislative committee dealing with the problem proposed, on the other hand, to endow the Berliet company with a special statute similar to that of those corporations whose stock is partially owned by the workers and which are governed by a 1917 law. Conservative jurists objected to this proposition on the ground that a law must always have a general character. The MRP recognized the validity of this argument and therefore made a counter-proposal which did not deal specifically with the Berliet company. According to this proposal, every corporation administered on a temporary basis because some of its directors have been penalized for collaboration, must, on the request of a majority of its personnel, be transformed legally into a corporation of the type governed by the 1917 law.

Actually, this proposal was very similar to the committee's and, taking into consideration all the circumstances of the case, really guaranteed that the structure of the Berliet company would be altered in the direction of an association of capital and labor organized on the basis of a producer's cooperative. Legal principles had been protected and the law did not provide merely for one particular case.

The MRP's counter-proposal was taken into consideration by the National Assembly on December 6, 1949, by 261 votes (Socialists, MRP and cabinet members) against 247 (Communists and the right), with 100 abstentions. But this counter-proposal had to be examined by the committee, and the discussion was therefore interrupted: it never did begin again, and, in fact, the Berliet company is now managed by the representatives of the stockholders. Nevertheless, the attitude of the MRP in this debate enables us to understand its position with respect to the problem of the reform of the capitalistic structure. This position is characterized by a dual hostility to the principle of the pure and simple *status quo* and to that of systematic nationalization, and by an attitude categorically in favor of a reform based on the principle of co-management by the workers and the stockholders.

With respect to the nationalization of certain branches of economic activity, the position of the MRP is no less clear. It is theoretically in favor of it, and in 1945 and 1946 its representatives voted for the nationalization of the coal mines, the big commercial banks, insurance, and electricity and gas. But on the one hand, it does not believe that the formula of nationalization must be generalized, and on the other hand, it demands that the present bureaucratic and statist management of the nationalized industries be greatly modified.

Albert Gortais, in his 1947 report on the doctrine of the MRP, stated the first point in the following terms: "If it is more profitable for the nation as a whole that an area of activity be withdrawn from the private sphere in order to be conducted in the national interest, 'nationalization' is legitimate and necessary. The MRP has already stated the essential criteria which, in the present economic situation, can justify nationalization, while it established limitations at the same time:

—"where the business is a public service

—"where private finance menaces the independence of the state

—"where, in an area that is essential to the life of the nation, private initiative is bankrupt."

And Gortais added: "In the very interest of the community . . . nationalization can only be the exceptional case. . . . It must be accompanied by compensation in conformity with justice."

The concrete application of these criteria can obviously vary. The declaration prepared by the National Council of the MRP on August 26-27, 1945, envisaged "the taking-over of key industries by the state." [9] The MRP's program for action, submitted in Novem-

---

[9] Published in the *Fiches de l'Action Populaire*, No. 57, September 1945.

143

ber 1945 to the Socialist and Communist parties, defined key industries as follows: "transportation; sources of energy: coal, gas, electricity and petroleum; essential raw materials: fertilizer, heavy iron and steel industries." [10]

This program has not been completely fulfilled. Road transportation, the petroleum industry, the fertilizer industry and the heavy iron and steel industries have not been nationalized and there is no doubt that the MRP would, at the present time, oppose their nationalization. This is because the management of the industries now nationalized is not satisfactory to the MRP; it seems to the MRP to be necessary to improve the operation of the nationalized sector before extending it. One should notice, however, that according to Albert Gortais, nationalization must be the exceptional case, and it is by no means certain that if concrete measures were proposed the MRP would adhere to a policy of nationalization in order to exhaust the program prepared in 1945; just the opposite is probable.

With respect to the management of the nationalized industries, the MRP's point of view was expressed in an important bill dealing with a statute governing public and national enterprises submitted by Pierre Schneiter and the members of the MRP group.[11] First of all, this bill distinguishes between public enterprises and national enterprises. Public enterprises "carry on, as monopolies or quasi-monopolies, legally or factually, operations whose suspension, even temporarily, would cause in a short time . . . the cessation of the very life of the country," and their purpose is not just to make a profit or, in any case, a maximum profit. Ordinary national enterprises "may belong to the state, but they are businesses which are similar to private businesses and which, operating in competition with capitalistic enterprises, must be judged by the profits they make."

The former belong in the public domain and they must be centralized and controlled. Their directors, who are given wide powers and who must be responsible, are to be named by the state. If necessary, these industries can be subsidized. The latter must be modeled on ordinary corporations: a quadripartite board of direc-

---

[10] Published in *l'Aube*, November 9, 1945.

[11] *Journal Officiel. Documents Parlementaires. Assemblée Nationale.* No. 1522. Annexe au procès-verbal de la séance du 30 May 1947.

tors (that is, consisting of representatives of the state, of the personnel, of the consumers and of capable people in industrial or commercial affairs, specialists in each appropriate field) will direct them, will participate in the selection of the chairman of the board and will control their activity. If necessary, these industries can go into bankruptcy. But such a board of directors is dominated by private interests and it should be submitted to a certain amount of supervision by the state.

Some system must therefore be established to permit the intervention of the state in the management of the national enterprises as well as of the public enterprises in such a way as to reduce partisan considerations to a minimum and to permit the execution of long-term programs irrespective of political events. This is where the master-stroke of the MRP comes into the picture: a High Council of Public and National Enterprises, an independent agency to which the state would delegate most of its powers with respect to nationalized industries. "Its members," says the introduction to the bill, "named on the proposal of various people or organizations, are the deputies of no one and represent no one. They constitute a high judicial body and are given numerous guarantees of independence, as are other magistrates in a democracy." They would be appointed by decree for a period of five years; they would not be able to hold any political, union, or professional office; they would receive a high salary (equal to that of a *Conseiller d'Etat*) ; and they would enjoy strong guarantees of tenure during their period of appointment.

Who would name the candidates for membership on the High Council? The public enterprise section would consist of 11 persons: a magistrate from the *Conseil d'Etat,* chosen from a list of three names submitted by its vice-president; one member of the *Cour des Comptes,* chosen from a list of three names submitted by its first president; four civil servants designated respectively by the Ministers of Economic Affairs, Industrial Production, Finance and Labor; one worker and one foreman, each selected from a list of three names submitted by the boards of directors of the enterprises; and three consumers, chosen from lists of three names submitted by the presidents of the *Chambres de Commerce,* the *Chambres des Métiers* (independent workmen) and the *Chambres d'Agriculture.*

145

The national enterprise section would consist of only one civil servant, designated by the government, and instead of three consumers there would be two individuals especially qualified in industrial or commercial matters, chosen from lists of three names submitted by the presidents of the *Chambres de Commerce* and by the *Conseil National du Crédit*.

One will notice that this device corresponds very well to the general tendencies of the MRP's doctrine. It actually would create an agency independent of the traditional political and administrative control of the state. This agency would consist of a sort of special corporation, endowed with powers that the state, because of its very nature, is hardly able to exercise. This corporation is designed to protect the public interest in the management of the nationalized industries while taking into account the purely economic considerations which must inevitably arise.

Such an agency clashes with special interests: those of the labor unions and the parties of the extreme left, who want the specifically political interests for which they speak to continue to play a role in the management of the nationalized industries; and those of the representatives of the traditional state, in its political form (parliament) and in its administrative form (primarily the Ministry of Finance), who are reluctant to be deprived of their present authority over the management of the nationalized industries, even though their outlook is often much too narrow to promote satisfactory management. Once more, in brief, the corporative doctrine of the MRP clashes with the collectivists and the champions of the traditional liberal state.

The general position of the MRP with respect to economic liberalism is theoretically negative: it leaves no doubt that its doctrine really implies the "resolute intervention of the state," as Etienne Gilson remarks. The hostility of public opinion towards the measures of economic control (*dirigisme*) born out of the post-war scarcities has of course led it more than once to recommend a relaxation of the "bureaucratic controls" burdening "industry as a whole and especially medium-sized industries and small businesses." [12] But such concessions to liberal prejudices have always

[12] Statement of the National Council of the MRP, 26-27 April 1945. *Fiches de l'Action Populaire,* No. 57, September 1945.

been accompanied by an unequivocal statement of the necessity for a professional organization which will "permit various categories of members of the profession to establish together the rules governing their common activities." [13]

More recently, at a time when the Radicals and Moderates, advocates of economic liberalism, were directing their attacks against the government investments prescribed by the Monnet Plan, the MRP declared itself to be unequivocably in favor of the leadership and constant participation of the government, or at least the cooperation of the government, in the execution of the program of economic modernization which was adopted after the war. The concessions which the MRP has made to the liberal preferences of the majority of the middle classes, who represent a very large proportion of its electoral support, have been meager enough to enable us to conclude that its position in favor of a planned economy directly corresponds to one of its basic tenets.

THE SOCIAL PROGRAM

In social matters, the MRP applies its doctrine, in the first place, by paying careful attention to the protection of the interests of families. One can find this at the origin of most of the measures to increase government allowances to families and to represent family associations in the various administrative or advisory agencies for economic and social affairs. On the other hand, it has always defended the principles of the autonomous administration of social security agencies and it has fought against their absorption by the state. Though not opposed to a certain amount of state control over their activity, the MRP has succeeded in having this control exercised, not by an ordinary administrative agency, but by the *Cour des Comptes,* a judicial body whose independence is guaranteed by law. At the same time, the MRP is opposed to the conservative and liberal proposals which would tend to restrict the advantages which social security gives to the workers.

EDUCATION

The position of the MRP on educational matters is distinguishable from both that of the parties of the left and that of the parties

---

[13] *Ibid.*

of the right during the Third Republic. The former, advocates of the lay, state school, have always been hostile to the private, Catholic school; the latter frequently criticized public education. The MRP, for its part, does not think that the desire for Catholic education, and even the desire that the state relieve its financial burdens, must imply a hostile attitude to the lay schools. When, for example, parliament was discussing the question of appropriations for the construction of school buildings, made necessary by the wartime destruction and especially by the increase in the number of births, the MRP emphasized the necessity for the state to make a special effort to maintain lay education at the level of its requirements. But, at the same time, it demanded (unsuccessfully) that appropriations should also be made for the construction of private schools. The MRP has regularly supported proposals to authorize local communities to subsidize private education either directly or indirectly through the grant of financial aid to the parents of children who attend private schools. It has not been successful, no more than it was when it opposed the secularization of the old private schools belonging to certain coal companies which had been nationalized in 1945.

THE FRENCH UNION

In colonial matters, the doctrine of the MRP breaks with the old colonial conceptions. But it does not condone the separatist tendencies which the exacerbation of indigenous nationalism can create and it condones even less the exploitation of these tendencies by the Communist Party. "The strongest tie of the French Union," writes Albert Gortais, "is and will be a community of civilization within whose framework, guided by the eternal France, the overseas populations will rise in material progress as in human progress to the full development of their ethnic, economic and political personality . . . the more they become conscious of their own value and of common values, the more freely they will adhere to the Union. . . . In this respect, France has taken a heavy responsibility before history. It would fail in this mission by weakening before the internal and selfish foreign pressures which are already contributing to the dissolution of the Union without bringing the slightest guarantee of human progress to its people."

The MRP does not want, at any price, to move from federalism to separatism. It postulates that the development of the personality of the people overseas will attach them more to the French Union and, consequently, it is opposed to any faltering before the tendencies toward dissolution, which it regards less as a spontaneous phenomenon than as the result of calculated pressure.

This explains why, on the one hand, Daniel Boisdon, member of the MRP and the first president of the Assembly of the French Union (half of whose members are representatives of the overseas population), symbolizes in a way the adherence of his party to the new formula of cooperation between France and the native populations, and why, on the other hand, other representatives of the MRP, like Paul Coste-Floret and Jean Letourneau, successively Ministers for Overseas France, or Pierre de Chevigné, for a long time High Commissioner at Madagascar, have assumed (especially the first in Indo-China) responsibility for a policy of armed resistance to secessionist attempts and of systematic repression of these tendencies. The apparent contradiction between these attitudes disappears if one agrees that separatism cannot be a spontaneous phenomenon in the territories of the French Union, and this is what the MRP believes. In addition, the MRP does not accept the idea of any restriction of the political reforms which were carried out in the overseas territories after the liberation, and this distinguishes it from the Moderate and Radical parties that have accepted these reforms only with great reluctance.

INTERNATIONAL PROBLEMS

The initial position of the MRP on international affairs was very favorable to the United Nations Organization and to the attempts which were being made to create an international community, and also decidedly hostile to the formation of antagonistic blocs of nations.

At the time of the drafting of the constitution, the representatives of the MRP proposed that the French state freely renounce some of its sovereignty in favor of the international organization. According to their point of view, the national community, to which a hierarchy of secondary autonomous communities is subordinated, must agree to be subordinated itself, under similar conditions, to the international community.

This subordination, however, must be to the international community as a whole. This is the meaning of the MRP's opposition in 1945 to the policy of international blocs. " . . . We will never give our consent to a policy of 'blocs', more or less hypocritically opposing one another. The recently raised quarrel over the question of the 'western bloc' seems to us to be the prototype of a sterile quarrel. If anyone wanted to involve France in the politics of an 'eastern' or 'western' bloc, the MRP would be resolutely opposed, because of the danger of war which this policy would conceal." [14]

The MRP, however, has had to acknowledge that the development of international events has made its earlier opinion untenable. It has appreciated this all the more since, with the exception of one month from December 1946 to January 1947, two of its leaders, Georges Bidault and Robert Schuman, have constantly had the responsibility of directing France's foreign policy since the liberation.

Beginning in March 1947, with the failure of the Moscow conference, it was no longer possible for French diplomacy to pretend to ignore the growing antagonism between the USSR and the countries of the Soviet sphere on the one hand and the United States on the other. Obliged to make a choice, the MRP could choose only those who, like it, were attached to the western conception of political democracy. It has therefore advocated accepting the Marshall Plan and, later, the adherence of France to the Atlantic Pact.

There was, however, some hesitation on the latter issue in one faction of the MRP, among those members of parliament who feared that the pact would bring about a further increase in the antagonism between the USSR and the USA. The MRP as a whole accepts the Atlantic Pact because of its strictly defensive nature. Any policy directed toward a preventive war against the USSR would certainly meet its firm opposition, just as it would meet the nearly unanimous opposition of French opinion. In the event that it would appear possible to the Western European powers to bring about a lessening of the tension between the USSR and the USA,

[14] *Le MRP, parti de la 4ème République* (a propaganda pamphlet published in 1945).

an hypothesis which is unfortunately entirely theoretical, the MRP would certainly be in favor of it. On the other hand, it would fear the negotiation of a rapprochement without the participation of the European countries. A sort of division of the world into zones of influence by the two greatest powers would clash with the MRP's democratic conception of the international community. At the same time, it would be afraid that the American negotiators, insufficiently aware of the complexity of European problems, might resolve them in unacceptable fashion.

The position taken by the MRP with regard to the events which have occurred since the aggression of June, 1950, against South Korea has conformed to these principles. It approved the support given by the French government to the intervention of the United Nations against the aggressor, but it expressed the general fears of French public opinion, that rash policies might transform the resistance against aggression into an armed crusade against international Communism by enlarging the scope of the war to include the China of Mao-Tse-Tung.

In any case, experience has demonstrated to the MRP that the idea of an international community on a world-wide scale, to which it theoretically remains attached, has no possibility of being realized under the present circumstances. A more reduced community, however, on a Western European scale, seems possible, and the attitude of the MRP toward the efforts which have been made to bring it about have definitely been positive. It has taken part in the European federalist congresses and its speakers, during the debates on the ratification of the pact which created the Council of Europe and at the European Consultative Assembly at Strasbourg, have all indicated their desire to see a European federation created and have regretted only that British caution did not permit a greater advance at the beginning.

The problem of Franco-German relations is closely linked to the question of European federation. Here, the MRP shares the unanimous hostility of French opinion towards German rearmament, but this does not constitute an obstacle to a Franco-German reconciliation, for which no one in France has worked more tenaciously and sanely than Robert Schuman, the Minister of Foreign Affairs. The feeling for international life, which the MRP owes in part to its

151

Catholic origin, and the traditional hostility of the Christian Democrats to nationalism and militarism undoubtedly are the basic reasons for this attitude of the MRP, which wants to put an end to the old Franco-German antagonism within the framework of a federated Europe.

CHAPTER THREE

WHAT THE MRP IS

I. Organization

The MRP deliberately calls itself a "movement" and not a party. "From one end to another, the political activity that it carries on," says one of its propaganda pamphlets, "breaks with partisan political methods. . . . Formerly, to play politics and to belong to a party meant almost always to restrict one's activity to electoral considerations and to the quest for positions of influence. For the MRP, political activity . . . signifies other requirements . . . ; on every echelon the MRP directs its efforts so that its party workers, in close contact with the people, can continually study the problems which come up, seek their solutions, promote new ideas and make their opinions known to all governmental agencies. From the neighborhood group to the central national organization . . . the MRP wants to be an efficient instrument at the service of the welfare and the liberty of the people . . . ; a great movement which is building an authentic and complete democracy, by everywhere making the people contribute to their own liberation from every form of dictatorship, whether it be the dictatorship of money or a dictatorship which would suppress freedom of conscience." [1]

We shall see that the structure of the MRP is indeed different in certain ways from that of other French parties. But the most important differences between the MRP and the other parties are less in the structure itself and in the rules governing its organization than in its actual operation.

STRUCTURE

The MRP consists mainly of a National Center, Departmental Federations and Local Sections. The individual members belong to the sections. This analysis of the MRP's structure will consist mainly in showing how the general orientation of the movement is determined and how its members participate in determining it.

---

[1] *Le MRP, parti de la 4ème république, 1945.*

The local sections must consist of at least ten members who are led by a Bureau of elected officers. The role of the sections is to discuss the problems presented by the orientation of the party and by political circumstances, whether it be a question of the electoral tactics to apply on the spot or of the great problems which face the movement as a whole. This discussion culminates in specific resolutions which have an influence on the positions taken by the higher organs. At the same time, it acts as a means of civic and political education for the militants who take part in it. In addition, the section is responsible for propaganda in the town where it meets.

The departmental federations are the main organs of the MRP. They must include at least five sections and one hundred members. Their internal organization must be "democratic" and must provide for: periodic meetings of a federal congress, which debates and arrives at the policy of the federation and at which every member must be either present or represented; a federal committee elected by the congress which names a bureau or an executive committee; "specialized federal teams," especially for women, young people, workers, rural people, managerial groups and liberal professions.[2] The federations must grant the right to vote in every meeting of a section or a federation to members eighteen years of age or older. Their rules must make provision for a roll call vote whenever at least ten per cent of the members present request it, as well as for a secret ballot for nominations and elections and whenever at least one fourth of those voting request it for any other kind of ballot.

It is the federations (through their congress or their executive committee) which name the MRP's candidates for various elections, subject to the ratification of the executive committee of the movement. It is the federations also which bear the main responsibility for the propaganda and the political activity of the MRP in the departments.

The central organs of the MRP are the National Congress, the National Committee, the Executive Committee, the General Secretariat, the National Specialized Teams and the Research Sections.

The National Congress of the MRP is the supreme organ of the movement, the one to which, according to the statutes, "the leader-

---

[2] We will deal further with the very important question of the specialized teams.

ship belongs." It meets each year and it "settles sovereignly all questions concerning the movement."

All the members of the MRP can attend the congress. But only the delegates, or their substitutes, appointed by the departmental federations, have the right to vote and therefore to participate in the making of the decisions. These delegates are elected by secret ballot, during the month which precedes the meeting of the national congress. In practice, this arrangement compels each federation to hold a federal congress at that time and the work of these congresses are directly governed by the previous deliberations of the sections and, therefore, by the attitude of the local party workers.

The number of delegates at the congress or, more accurately, the number of "mandates" (that is, voting rights) to which each federation is entitled is fixed according to special rules: the number of each federation's mandates is not exactly proportional to the number of its members. Each federation is entitled to one mandate for every fifty members up to 200, another mandate for every 100 members up to 5000 and an additional mandate for every 200 members, or fraction of 200 greater than 100, from 5000 on. This diminishing progression is intended to prevent the federations which are most important numerically from becoming the masters of the movement. The major Christian Democratic party of the Third Republic, the *Parti Démocrate Populaire,* was very unevenly developed throughout the country. Britanny and Alsace, where it was strong, were therefore more likely to be receptive to the MRP's propaganda than the other provinces. If the MRP had adopted the principle of proportional representation for its departmental federations, it would risk having its leadership monopolized by the Alsatians and the Bretons, thereby hindering its progress in the other parts of France. The provisions of the MRP's statutes which we have just analysed reveal the desire of the MRP to expand throughout the entire country and to cede as little as possible to the regional particularism which was an element of weakness for Christian Democracy during the Third Republic.

At the congress, the right to vote is held by the members of the national committee and the MRP's members of parliament in addition to the delegates of the federations. This rule must be emphasized for it reveals a state of mind which is quite different from the distrust which reigns, for example, in the Socialist Party, between the parliamentary and non-parliamentary leaders. In the MRP, on the contrary, it is recognized that those men whose activity permits them to be especially well informed on political problems and who bear a responsibility in their solution, must enjoy at the congress greater influence than the ordinary local party workers. In this way, it is hoped that the difficulties which are constantly being raised between the parliamentary and non-parliamentary Socialists can be avoided.

The annual congress of the MRP elects the movement's president (who can be re-elected only three consecutive times) and its secretary general.[3] It hears the reports of the activity of the parliamentary groups and of the general secretariat. It debates (first in committees and then in plenary session) and votes the motions or declarations which establish the orientation of the movement, its program for the coming year and its tactics, especially its attitude toward the government and the other parties. Finally, the congress elects a financial control and auditing committee, composed of three members, and it hears the report on the financial operations of the central agencies by the committee elected the preceding year.[4]

The congress, the supreme organ, fixes the broad lines of the MRP's activity. But it does not meet frequently enough for the movement to be able to do without other organs of leadership to act during the intervals between congresses.

The first of these organs is the national committee, which meets every two months. The composition of the national committee is quite different from that of the congress: it gives less representation to the militants and gives much more representation to the leaders and members of parliament. In addition to the president and the secretary general, who are elected by the congress, the national committee includes: a) those ministers who are members of the MRP or five former ministers; b) the delegates of the

---

[3] Maurice Schumann was President until the Congress of 1949; since then, Georges Bidault has been President. André Colin has been Secretary General since the beginning.

[4] The MRP's budget is not published, nor is the budget of any other French party. It would have been otherwise if the Constituent Assembly had adopted the suggestion of the MRP and voted a *Statute of Parties.*

MRP's parliamentary groups, who must constitute one third of the members of the committee; c) the delegates of the MRP group to the Assembly of the French Union; d) the representatives of each federation, who are elected by their members; each federation is entitled to one delegate for every 4000 members and fraction of 4000 greater than 2000; e) twelve representatives of the specialized teams, named by the previous national committee on the nomination of the teams, and two representatives of the MRP's municipal and departmental councillors, named in the same way; f) lastly, ten militants named by the former national committee "because of their functions, titles or services," that is, chosen because of their individual importance.

Altogether, the representatives of the local party workers constitute no more than one half of the national committee. This committee, which has the job of adapting the decisions of the congress to the day-to-day political situation, has, in practice, a more important role than the congress. The great influence which the ministers and members of parliament exercise in this body always permits them to have their point of view adopted in delicate situations, in comparison with what happens in the national council of the Socialist Party, which is composed exclusively of representatives of the federations and which is frequently, if not constantly, in disagreement with the parliamentary group.

The national committee of the MRP names the treasurer of the movement. It can name one or more honorary presidents [5] and it decides on the creation of central agencies which may be useful to the movement and whose activities it controls and approves.

Because the national committee meets only periodically, every two months, a less cumbersome directing organ, which can meet more frequently, is necessary: this is the executive committee, which includes only about fifty members.

The president, the secretary general and the treasurer, the MRP

---

[5] The Treasurer is an industrialist, M. André Pairault, who was a member of the Council of the Republic from 1946 to 1948. There has been only one Honorary President, Marc Sangnier, the patriarch of Christian Democracy and founder of the *Sillon* and later of the *Jeune République,* who died in 1950.

ministers and the presidents of the MRP groups in parliament and in the Assembly of the French Union, currently sixteen people, automatically are members of the executive committee. In addition, the committee includes twelve members of parliament, two councillors of the French Union, eighteen representatives of the departmental federations and five militants chosen because of their personal merit; all of these are elected by the national committee from among its own members. If there were no MRP ministers at any given time, the parliamentary groups of the National Assembly would elect five former ministers.

The executive committee includes, therefore, only eighteen representatives of the federations (not chosen directly by their members) as opposed to more than thirty representatives of the party leaders and office holders. This means that the possibility of a conflict between it and the MRP members of parliament is virtually excluded. The contrast with the Socialist Party, which is sharp enough at the level of the national committee, is even sharper at the level of the executive committee; the corresponding organ in the Socialist Party, the steering committee, is completely elected by the congress and, according to the rules of the Party, no more than one third of its members can be members of parliament.

The general secretariat is the organ which carries out the decisions of the congresses, of the national committee, and of the executive committee. One of its most important tasks is to distribute to the federations memoranda commenting on the political situation, explaining and justifying the decisions of the movement and criticizing those of the other parties. These memoranda serve for both the political education of the militants and for the coordination of the MRP's propaganda throughout the country. The secretariat also exercises a certain amount of control over the activity of the federations. It sees that they do not deviate from the general line of the movement and in case problems arise it submits them to the executive committee or to the national committee.

It is assisted in its task of studying the problems which face the government and of preparing the solutions recommended by the MRP in the light of its doctrine by the research sections and the national specialized teams.

The research sections, which are presided over by a member of parliament, include party militants chosen because of their ability. They are auxiliaries of the general secretariat enjoying a certain amount of independence and are composed of congenial associates.

The specialized teams are something else. As we have seen earlier, their existence is required on the federation level and they also exist on the national level. The other units of the MRP, the sections and the federations, are organized geographically. The teams, on the other hand, consist of militants who are classified according to the social category to which they belong: women, young people, rural people, workers, managerial groups (engineers and supervisors) and the liberal professions. Their role is to study political problems in the light of the way they strike each of these categories, and, consequently, to express the attitudes of various social groups and to communicate them to the research sections, with which the delegates of the specialized teams cooperate.

The MRP attributes great importance to these teams, whose role was defined very clearly before the second national congress of the movement by one of the very first associates of the general secretariat of the MRP. "Doctrinally, the MRP has formed a clear notion of the existence and the role of 'classes.' . . . The delegates of the congress, meeting first in specialized teams, will study in the vocabulary of each class and in the light of the requirements and aspirations of each class the methods of education, action and conquest suitable for each class. Then, in plenary session, with each taking into account the interests of all the others but driven by the same enthusiasm toward the same goal, they will establish a program of action valid for the entire movement." [6] The teams represent in the movement the various categories of natural communities, the combination of which, according to the doctrine of the MRP, constitutes the French people as a whole. They therefore form one of the most original elements of the MRP's structure, something like the factory cells which characterize the Communist Party. It is thanks to them that the MRP can realize to a certain extent its ideal, which is that political activity must not have an exclusively electoral or partisan character. "The specialized teams devote themselves to continuous inquiries about the state and the needs

---

[6] Marc Scherer in *l'Aube,* December 12, 1945.

and the aspirations of the different professional and social groups." [7] The party is therefore not only a machine functioning from top to bottom; but it also provides for the education of the leaders by the militants, and one can understand better why it seems to the MRP to be an indispensable element in the structure of public life, serving as an intermediary between the citizens and the state.

In practice, the existence of the specialized teams might lead to some useless repetition and perhaps to some differences of opinion if they operated completely independently. This is why, in May 1947, their integration with the other organs of the movement was clarified by the creation of the research sections, to which the various teams communicate the conclusions of their specialized studies to be considered as component parts of full scale solutions.

UNITY

The MRP has been in existence for over six years: its structure, the operation of the organs of which it consists, and the discipline and faith of its militants have withstood the test of time and the political crises which France has known since the liberation. The results have been encouraging. If the creation of the *Rassemblement du Peuple Français* (RPF) by General de Gaulle in 1947 caused many of the MRP's voters and a few of its office holders to abandon it, its organization has resisted and its militants have remained faithful. In sharp contrast with the customs of the Third Republic, by which its members cannot fail to have been more or less influenced, the basic unity of the MRP has never been threatened with the formation of rival tendencies similar to those which exist in the Socialist or Radical Parties. In fact, the very diversity of the heterogeneous elements it contains determines the way in which it approaches political problems.

This result is certainly due to a great extent to the care with which the MRP's internal rules were drafted and to the precautions which were taken to enable the party leaders and members of parliament to make their opinions prevail, at least in the national committee and the executive committee, over those of the local party workers in the event of disagreement between the two groups.

---

[7] Jacques Fauvet in *Le Monde*, December 13, 1945.

It can also be explained by the fact that the great majority of the MRP's militants turned to political activity only recently, at the time of the liberation. In addition, they came into political life with a state of mind shaped both by enthusiasm and the desire to serve and, hence, different from the attitude of the Socialist or Radical militants. The latter are groups of people which were gradually formed during the Third Republic for various reasons, among which personal ambition was often of great importance. The idealism of the MRP's militants and, at the same time, a certain lack of political experience among many of them, explain the harmony which seems to reign between them and their leaders. It is beyond doubt that the religious training of a great many of the MRP's members and leaders and the habits which they acquired in Catholic youth groups also contribute to this situation.

Whatever the reasons, at none of the annual congresses that the MRP has held since its creation have there been the divergences in opinion and the struggles between tendencies and persons that characterize the Socialist or Radical congresses. However, at the Congress of Nantes, in 1950, the candidacy of M. Dumas, deputy from the Seine, was proposed by certain militants in opposition to that of M. André Colin for the post of secretary general. They wanted to express their wish to see the MRP take a stronger stand in favor of worker's demands than it had taken up to that time. M. André Colin was nonetheless designated, and one cannot say that this opposition did in fact mark the appearance of a "left-wing" tendency in the midst of the MRP. The homogeneity of the MRP, although it has been created by different means, reminds one of the Communist Party.

This does not mean that there are not different viewpoints among the Popular Republicans. But these shades of opinion do not crystallize in the same way as they do in the old parties. The specialized teams provide them with a natural outlet and enable them to contribute to the final conclusions reached by the research sections. The leaders of the MRP would not be human beings if certain personal rivalries did not occasionally divide them. But even in this connection, one must consider the circumstances which threw them together and amidst which they decided to carry out political activity on a national scale. The memories of the clandestine struggles of the resistance have created bonds of friendship and solidarity which may not last forever, but which nevertheless still represent one of the original features distinguishing the MRP from the other French parties.

The MRP's structure, the satisfactory operation of the organs of which it is composed, the ardor and the enthusiasm of its militants, which give a special atmosphere to its congresses, represent a significant political force. It has created a degree of cohesion which has enabled the movement to resist the wave of electoral desertions in 1947-1948, to remain true to itself and to undertake the arduous task of recovering its lost ground, on which the future of its role in French politics depends. It is impossible to state with certainty how many members the MRP has: the figures of 400,000 in 1949, and 100,000 in 1951, have been suggested.[8] This decline, however, is not unique to the MRP; it has affected all the parties. Moreover, the number of militants is less important than their solidarity, their confidence in their leaders and their attachment to the doctrine of their movement. That these crucial elements exist seems to have been confirmed by the history of the MRP for the last four years and by the way in which its organization has continued to function since the launching of the neo-Gaullist movement.

PRESS AND LABOR UNIONS

The structure and the organization of a party cannot today be studied without also discussing the power of the press and its relations with the labor unions.

With respect to the press, the MRP was favored at the liberation when newspapers could appear only with the authorization of the government (both for political reasons and because of the shortage of newsprint), because General de Gaulle had confided the Ministry of Information to Pierre-Henri Teitgen, a member of the MRP. Since that time, the MRP has operated *l'Aube,* a Parisian daily, and several provincial dailies.

L'Aube had been founded before the war by Francisque Gay, a Catholic publisher of Christian Democratic tendencies. Its editorials

---

[8] Jacques Fauvet, *Les partis politiques dans la France actuelle,* Paris, 1949, and *Les forces politiques en France,* Paris, 1951.

were written by Georges Bidault, then a professor of history at the *Lycée Louis le Grand*. It was directly connected neither with the *Parti Démocrate Populaire* nor the *Jeune République* but it reflected elements of the ideology of both these parties. Although it did not systematically support the Popular Front in 1936, it did not combat it like the press of the conservative parties. In international affairs, it constantly advocated resistance to Nazi and Fascist activity.

In 1944 and 1945, *l'Aube* met with far greater success than it had before 1939. Then, gradually, as a more conservative press began to appear and as the moderate elements which had supported the MRP at the beginning became more intransigently anti-socialist and anti-communist, its circulation began to decrease. From 230,000 in June 1946, its circulation fell in 1951 to about 45,000 copies daily (compared with 415,000 for *Figaro*, a moderate, non-Gaullist daily; 180,000 for *Ce-matin-le-Pays*, a Gaullist daily; 220,000 for *L'Humanité*, a Communist daily; and 40,000 for *Le Populaire*, a Socialist daily). By the end of 1951 it had to stop publication.

Today, the Parisian press is not distributed throughout the departments as much as it was before the war, and the decline of *l'Aube's* circulation is less serious for the MRP than it would have been then. This decline in circulation reflects the fact that Parisian opinion has to a great extent moved away from the MRP. In the provinces, the press acquired by the MRP at the liberation has fared better, in spite of the return to freedom of publication for newspapers and the reappearance of some great regional pre-war dailies, like the radical *Dépêche de Toulouse*. The main MRP provincial papers are *Ouest-France*, which is published at Rennes and which is circulated throughout all the western provinces, *la Liberté du Centre* of Limoges, *la Dépêche de St-Etienne* and *Nord-Eclair*.

As to the labor unions, it is traditional in France for them to pretend to be completely independent of political parties, but the truth is that they all have more or less close connections with them. The *Confédération Française des Travailleurs Chrétiens* (CFTC), which was founded after the first world war, always had some connection with the Christian Democratic parties during the Third Republic. The new significance that it has acquired since 1944,

163

combined with the appearance and the very rapid growth of the MRP, have naturally not ended this connection. But one should not speak of subordination, of either one or the other. While the *Confédération Générale du Travail* (CGT) obviously follows on every occasion the orders of the Communist Party, the CFTC has frequently taken positions completely different from those of the MRP, for example, on questions of wage increases. It has also tried to aid (and at the same time spur on) governments supported by the MRP, especially, for example, in its campaign for lower prices. Some militants of the Christian unions entered political life in 1945; they all sit in the National Assembly on the MRP benches. However, they abandoned their prerogatives as union leaders when becoming members of parliament.

The MRP benefits from the friendly bias and often from the support of the Christian unions. But it is not dependent on them (as, for example, the English Labour Party is dependent on the trade unions), and these unions are not subjected to it (as the CGT unions are to the Communist Party). This undeniable connection does not, therefore, preclude differences. And is not the mutual independence of the party and the unions an advantage for both of them?

II. *The Leaders*

The very importance that the structure of the MRP confers on its leaders requires us to sketch briefly the personality and the career of the most important of them.

Georges Bidault, now President of the MRP and former Premier of France, is fifty-one years old. He is a former professor of history who entered public life before the second world war as an editorial writer for *l'Aube*. The clarity of his articles and the vigorous way in which he asserted his opinions quickly attracted attention. Although he was a Popular Democratic candidate in the 1936 election, he was not elected. Captured by the Germans in 1940, he was freed because he was a veteran of the first world war and he became a professor at a *lycée* at Lyon, in the unoccupied zone. He immediately took part in the resistance and, upon the death of Jean Moulin, he was named President of the National Council of the Resistance, the group which coordinated the activity of the various internal resistance movements and which maintained their connection with General de Gaulle.

At the liberation, de Gaulle named Bidault, who had a large share in the decision to create the MRP, Minister of Foreign Affairs. But the President of the Provisional Government did not allow his ministers much freedom of operation, and it seems that Bidault was dissatisfied with this, while, at the same time, he became uncertain about the ability of de Gaulle to carry out the functions of a chief of a parliamentary government. After the resignation of the General, Bidault, who had been elected deputy from the Loire, remained Minister of Foreign Affairs in the Gouin government (January to June 1946), then in the government over which he himself presided after the election of the second Constituent Assembly. At that time he agreed to collaborate with the Communists and he was one of the MRP's leaders who persuaded the MRP to seek an agreement over the drafting of the constitution with the Socialists and Communists on the extreme left rather than with the right and the radicals. But he was far from satisfied with the Communists' methods and he felt the necessity for preparing a rupture with them; he let the MRP conduct the electoral campaign of November 1946 on the basis of the slogan "Bidault without Thorez." When the Constituent Assembly met, the Communists refused to vote for him as Premier. After the all-Socialist ministry of the late Léon Blum (December 1946 to January 1947), Bidault returned to the *Quai d'Orsay* in the Ramadier cabinet.

Until then, his foreign policy had been to try to maintain an equal balance between the USSR and the English-speaking powers. At the same time, perhaps out of an instinctive fear of seeing his old chief, General de Gaulle, reproach him for any capitulation on this question, he continued to support the broad lines of the first provisional government's policy toward Germany, with respect to the problems of German federalism, the Ruhr and the Saar. Beginning in March 1947, after the failure of the Moscow Conference, Bidault drew closer to Great Britain and the United States. The changes in the German policy of the French government which the new international equilibrium made necessary, and which were reflected in the decisions of the London Conference in the spring of 1948, brought about severe criticism and, in July 1948, after the resignation of the Schuman cabinet, Bidault left the Ministry of Foreign Affairs.

Back in his seat as a deputy, he quickly became the main leader of the MRP. When, in 1948, General de Gaulle sought to reach an understanding with the Popular Republicans, it was with Bidault that he spoke, although nothing came out of the conversation. In the spring of 1949, Bidault became President of the MRP. At that time, without in any way repudiating the doctrine of the movement, Bidault obviously tried to behave in a way which would be reassuring to moderate opinion. Endowed with a keen political sense, he foresaw a certain decline of the RPF and he undoubtedly wanted to prevent the old MRP voters who had been attracted to Gaullism in 1947-1948 from going over to the moderates and the radicals, that is, the strictly conservative parties. This calculated moderation of Bidault's attitude, just like the tone of personal respect which he has always used in his public statements about General de Gaulle, even when he was rejecting the ultimatums and condemning the methods of neo-Gaullism, explains why, in October 1949, after the resignation of Henri Queuille and the failure of Jules Moch and René Mayer to form a ministry, he won the support of many Moderates and most of the Radicals for his designation as premier. But he alienated this friendly attitude by presenting a budget balanced by new taxes which in no way undermined the nationalizations of 1945 and 1946 and social security. Politically, he again rallied to a formula calling for an alliance between the Socialists, the Popular Republicans and that fraction of the Radical Party which is least favorable to the simple restoration of laissez-faire capitalism. After the fall, in June 1950, of the cabinet over which he presided, Georges Bidault returned to his bench as deputy until the spring of 1951. He then reassumed the post of Deputy Prime Minister in the cabinet of Henri Queuille. He was reelected deputy from the Loire on June 17 at the head of a list of "National Union" formed between the MRP, the Independents and the Democratic and Socialist Resistance Union (U.D.S.R.) and affiliated with the Peasant, Socialist and Radical parties.

Georges Bidault's personality is attractive. He has a keen and quick mind, a sure political instinct and he is a cultured man. It seems, however, that his judgment is occasionally obscured, at least temporarily, by the too high opinion he has of himself: this is undoubtedly his greatest weakness. One can also criticize him for his propensity for sibylline formulas. But he possesses the two major qualities of a statesman: courage and political intelligence. He is very popular with the militants of the MRP and his prestige with everyone who participated in the resistance remains great. Many politicians from the other parties, especially those who remain attached to the traditions of the Third Republic, do not like him but they generally respect him.

Pierre-Henri Teitgen is, after Bidault, undoubtedly the most striking personality of the MRP. Forty-three years old, he is a law professor and comes from a Lorraine family traditionally attached to Christian Democracy (his father, former "bâtonnier" of the order of advocates, in Nancy, had been a deputy from the Gironde from 1945 to 1951). Before the war, he served in the ranks of the *Parti Démocrate Populaire* and was associated with a legal journal, *Droit Social,* which clearly advocated the establishment of a new set of relationships between labor and management. He took an active part in the resistance, having participated in the fall of 1940 in the creation of one of the first clandestine movements. Arrested by the Germans in August 1944, he escaped and, a few days later, became Minister of Information in the provisional government of General de Gaulle. He was elected deputy from Ille-et-Vilaine in October 1945 and since then he has held various government posts: Minister of State, Vice-President of the Council of Ministers and Minister of National Defense.

Of the leaders of the MRP, Teitgen is undoubtedly the one whose temperament is most similar to that of the Christian Democratic local party workers. A jurist, he has a particularly clear knowledge of the bourgeois conception of society which he rejects: he has spoken of property rights before the parliamentary assemblies in terms which scandalized the conservatives and radicals. He has a fiery temperament and he is little inclined to modify his original position for the purpose of conciliation and compromise. A more inflammatory orator than Bidault, he occasionally seems to be less in control of himself, less skillful. But he is certainly an element of strength, because of his faith and the ardor of his convictions, which undoubtedly create enemies but which also inspire lasting friendships.

André Colin, the secretary general of the MRP, is a former leader of *l'Association Catholique de la Jeunesse Française*. Forty-one years old, he took part in the resistance and, in 1945, he was elected deputy from his home department of Finistère. André Colin has been Minister of the Merchant Marine and Secretary of State for the Interior; but his influence is most greatly felt not in the government or in parliament but at his post at MRP headquarters. He has worked hard at organizing the MRP, in the departmental federations as well as in the central office, and he represents the tendency that wants the movement to exercise stricter control over the activity of its members of parliament. This steadfast activity that Colin is trying to carry on within his party does not prevent him from having many sincere friends. He is one of those who have contributed to the internal climate of the MRP the sentimental tone described by Joseph Hours as part of the heritage of the social Catholic groups.[9]

Francisque Gay, the founder of *l'Aube*, is considerably older than the other men we have discussed: he is sixty-six. A publisher (he is an associate of the famous Catholic firm of Bloud and Gay), he entered politics between the two wars by first publishing a weekly, *la Vie Catholique*, which firmly contested the sway exercised by *l'Action Française* over the groups attached to the Church, and then the daily newspaper, *l'Aube*. He exerted great influence at the time of the foundation of the MRP and during the first years that followed the liberation; elected deputy from Paris in 1945, he was for some time Minister of State and Vice-President of the Council of Ministers. But his prestige within his party seems to be declining. Handicapped by his age, by his somewhat old-fashioned appearance (he is one of the few Popular Republicans to sport a beard) and by a tendency to use a politico-religious vocabulary which impedes the development of the MRP in non-Catholic circles, he was sent to Canada for a year as ambassador and since his return to France in 1949 he has played only a subordinate role. His delicate health obliged him in 1951 to give up his candidacy for the National

---

[9] Joseph Hours, "Les chrétiens et la politique," *Vie Intellectuelle,* May 1948.

Assembly. His authority over the older generations of MRP militants nevertheless remains significant.

Robert Schuman, on the other hand, has seen his influence within the MRP and in political life in general increase greatly since 1945. He is a veteran member of parliament, having been elected for the first time in the Moselle, at the age of thirty-three, more than thirty years ago. At first a member of the conservative group, *l'Union Républicaine Démocratique,* Robert Schuman joined the *Parti Démocrate Populaire* in 1932. It is perhaps because he is a practicing Catholic that he was not made a minister before 1940. In June (before the meeting of the National Assembly at Vichy) Pétain made him director of the office which was dealing with the refugees. Schuman is the only one of the MRP leaders who voted for the delegation of constituent power to Pétain at Vichy on July 10, 1940. But his patriotism has never been doubted by anyone and the role he played in the resistance, during which the Germans vainly tried to capture him, was the reason why his ineligibility was removed in 1944.[10] Robert Schuman very quickly acquired considerable authority in the two Constituent Assemblies of 1945-1946 because of both his parliamentary experience and his personal integrity. At first president of the finance committee, he became Minister of Finance in the Ramadier cabinet (January 1947), then Premier (November 1947) and, finally, Minister of Foreign Affairs after the resignation of his own government in July 1948. He is, without doubt, of all the leaders of the MRP, the one whom the moderates and the radicals regard with most favor, partly because his strong social sense is accompanied by a very cautious approach to rash changes in the existing social order and partly because, having been a deputy for thirty years, he has been less involved than some of his friends in disparaging the Third Republic. His experience has also preserved him from holding dogmatic opinions which can later stand in the way of compromise. Respected within the MRP, whose most moderate wing he unquestionably represents, Robert Schuman owes to the friendships he has acquired among other groups part of the authority he enjoys in his own, because,

---

[10] Theoretically, the members of Parliament who voted for Pétain at Vichy are ineligible for elective office, but this disability has been removed if they played a role in the resistance afterwards.

of all the leaders of the MRP, Schuman is most capable of obtaining the support of the elements on its right.

Thirty-nine year old Maurice Schumann is a former journalist whose fame dates from the time when, as the voice of Fighting France over the London Radio, he was listened to every night, despite the occupation forces, by millions of Frenchmen. He is an old militant of the *Jeune République* and a Catholic who has easily won the confidence of the Christian Democratic militants of the Nord, which he has represented at the *Palais Bourbon* since October 1945. But his gifts as an orator have been less well received in parliament than they were over the radio during the war. He was President of the MRP until the spring of 1949, when he was, according to the rules of the movement, ineligible for re-election. The authority of Maurice Schumann in his party is considerable, greater in reality than it appears on superficial observation. He has never occupied ministerial offices, but, repeatedly, has designated certain of his colleagues at the request of a prime minister wishing to make certain of the collaboration of Popular Republican ministers. His articles in *l'Aube* enable him to keep in contact with the Popular Republican militants and his political, social and spiritual convictions are too similar to those of the militants for him not to continue to wield great influence in the party.

François de Menthon is Teitgen's colleague as a professor of law and a contributor to *Droit Social,* and is fifty-one years old, somewhat older than Teitgen. He comes from an old aristocratic family of the Savoie. His father has been a deputy from another department, the Haute-Saône, where he also owns property. De Menthon collaborated with Teitgen during the resistance and the Haute-Savoie has sent him to the National Assembly since 1945. The Haute-Savoie is one of the departments where the MRP is especially well organized: it controls that region not only during legislative elections but during the local elections as well. De Menthon has been a minister several times (notably Minister of Justice in the provisional government of General de Gaulle in 1944); he is president of the MRP parliamentary group at the National Assembly and his colleagues respect what he has to say. Coming from an aristocratic family of a moderate, if not conservative background, he is the typical representative of those sensible Christian Democrats who, different enough from their colleagues of proletarian origin, and occasionally inclined to sentimental views, can serve as a connecting link with the representatives of the more moderate parties. This position, which may occasionally handicap de Menthon before a group of MRP militants, is, on the other hand, useful in parliament.

We have said that there are no organized tendencies in the MRP as there are in the Socialist Party, and no personal struggles like those in the Radical Party. The friendship which unites the Popular Republican leaders is a deeper and firmer sentiment than parliamentary or party camaraderie, undoubtedly because it is based on common spiritual convictions. This sketch of the personalities of the main leaders of the MRP would not be complete, however, if we did not mention the names of some former members of parliament who have been for some time considered to be the *enfants terribles* of the MRP, and who have finally deserted their group on questions which seemed to them to be symbolic of certain crucial political atttiudes. They are men who cannot forget that the Communists claim to express the political will of the majority of the French proletariat. Although thoroughly distinct from the Communists in their most basic convictions, these men are troubled by the belief that any break with the Communist Party risks a separation from the proletariat. These men have abstained or voted against their party on the questions of the stern measures proposed by the Schuman government at the time of the insurrectionary strikes of the fall of 1947, after the interpellations on the miners' strike in 1948, after the debates over the condemnation of the native deputies from Madagascar and on the ratification of the Atlantic Pact in 1949.

Finally, they abandoned the MRP in 1950 and formed the little group of the Independent Left, which proposes to become the nucleus of a new left, non-Communist, but opposed to the MRP and to the S.F.I.O. as much in the domain of foreign policy (where it urges French neutrality between Russia and the USA) as in the field of social and economic policy (where it desires an immediate rise in wages and the return to a policy of socialization). The three members of this group, the marquis Charles d'Aragon (from Hautes-Pyrénées), Paul Boulet (Mayor of Montpellier, in the Hé-

171

rault) and the abbé Pierre-Groués (from Meurthe and Moselle) were defeated in the election of June, 1951. Close to them in certain respects, André Denis from Dordogne, and the abbé Gau, from Aude, remained in the MRP and were reelected on June 17. These MRP extremists say aloud what others believe but feel unable to say, and they express at bottom an ideal irreconcilable with the movement to which they belong: it is that which makes their position somewhat significant, at least with regard to the secret preferences of a fraction of the Popular Republican militants.

Less sentimental, Léo Hamon, an MRP senator from the Seine whose concrete responsibilities (he has been the *rapporteur général* of the budget for the city of Paris and president of the committee of the interior at the Council of the Republic) have protected him from enticing temptations, can, nevertheless, be compared with the deputies mentioned above. It is undoubtedly because of his friendship with certain Communists in the resistance that he has for a long time retained the hope that it might again be possible to work with the Communists. In addition, his complete lack of conservative inclinations explains his radical attitude as to how the native nationalist movements, especially in North Africa, must be treated. On both these questions he is sufficiently distinguishable from many of his colleagues to warrant mentioning his name; but his influence on the MRP, outside of the Seine federation, seems rather slight.

III. *The Electorate*

The voting body of the MRP has undergone profound modifications between November 10, 1946, date of the election of the first National Assembly under the constitution and June 17, 1951, date of the election of the second assembly. Great changes in the respective strengths of the parties have taken place as a result of the founding of the RPF by General de Gaulle.

These changes were first demonstrated in the municipal elections which took place throughout France in the fall of 1947 and in the cantonal elections (for members of the departmental councils) which were held in half of the cantons in the spring of 1949.[11] But the results of these local elections, except in the large cities, are always

---

[11] The departmental councils consist of members who are elected, one from each canton, for six years. Every three years half of the seats are renewed.

difficult to interpret. Often every party does not present candidates; personal considerations play as large a role in the voter's choice as do party labels, and many candidates try to conceal their political opinions rather than to exploit them. It is, thus, impossible ,to compare directly the elections of 1947 and 1949 with those of 1946.

The municipal councils elected in 1947 selected, in November 1948, the great majority of the members of the electoral colleges which, in turn, elected the members of the Council of the Republic in that same month. One can indirectly deduce from the results of this election the results of the municipal elections in 1947. However, only an approximation can be made, because the system for electing the Council of the Republic operated unfavorably for the minority parties in the villages, towns and small cities with fewer than 9000 inhabitants, and favorably for the majority parties.[12]

For the lack of more reliable data, however, we will study the electoral evolution of the MRP by comparing the elections to the National Assembly of November 10, 1946 with the elections to the Council of the Republic of November 7, 1948 and with the cantonal elections of March 20, 1949, before studying the results of the elections of June 19, 1951.

On November 10, 1946, the MRP lists received throughout metropolitan France 4,989,000 votes, or 25.9 per cent of the votes cast. Geographically and numerically, these results were very similar to those of the elections of October 21, 1945 (when the MRP won 4,780,000 votes, 24.8 per cent of the votes cast) and June 2, 1946 (when the MRP won 5,589,000 votes, or 28.1 per cent of the votes cast).

---

[12] The electoral colleges which elect the members of the Council of the Republic consist, in each department, of the deputies, the departmental councillors and the delegates of the municipal councils. The number of these delegates is not proportional to the population, but fixed in such a way as to favor the small and middle-sized towns at the expense of the big cities (a village of 300 inhabitants gets one delegate; a town of 3,000 inhabitants gets seven; a city of 30,000 inhabitants gets twenty-seven; a big city of 300,000 inhabitants gets eighty-eight). On the other hand, in the towns of fewer than 3,500 inhabitants, the delegates are elected by the municipal council by majority vote and in the others they are elected by proportional representation. But the municipal councils are themselves elected by PR only in cities with more than 9,000 inhabitants, so minorities in towns with fewer than 9,000 inhabitants have almost no chance of being represented in the electoral colleges of the Council of the Republic.

Map I

National Assembly Elections of November 10, 1946
M.R.P. votes (percentage of registered voters)

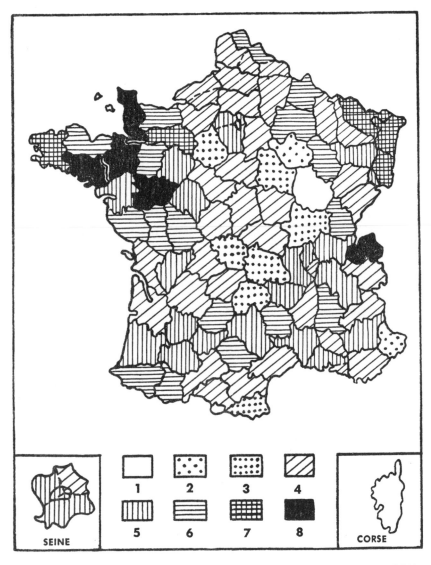

1 : None
2 : less than 5.9%
3 : from 6 to 11.9%

4 : from 12 to 17.9%
5 : from 18 to 23.9%
6 : from 24 to 29.9%

7 : from 30 to 35.9%
8 : more than 36%

Map I shows the geographical distribution of the main MRP bastions: the most important is the west, from Normandy to Poitou; then there is an eastern bastion, curiously divided, since it includes, on one side, Champagne and, on the other, Alsace and the part of Lorraine which had been annexed by Germany between 1871 and 1919, but it does not include the unannexed part of Lorraine (Meuse, Meurthe-et-Moselle and Vosges). In the other areas, the MRP seems to be stronger than it is generally throughout the country in a series of isolated departments which form a diagonal strip going from the western end of the Pyrénées to north of the Alps. Most of these departments are at least partially mountainous: Jura, Haute-Savoie, Drôme, Lozère, Lot, Tarn, Hautes and Basses-Pyrénées. Finally, the department of the Nord seems also to be a stronghold of the MRP.

A common characteristic of most of these regions is that they are mainly rural; the only exceptions are the Nord and, somewhat less so, Alsace and Lorraine. In addition, in most cases these are regions where the Catholic Church considers the extent of religious practice to be satisfactory.

Lastly, except for the Tarn and the Drôme, these are departments where, in 1946, moderate candidates received more than one-third of the votes.

It is, therefore, probably true that most of the MRP's voters in 1946 were moderate voters before the war or at least belonged to the same social groups as the moderate voters of old. This impression is confirmed by a comparison between Maps II and III. Map II shows the departments in which the moderates had won, in 1936, an absolute majority and more than one-third of the votes cast. Map III shows the departments in which, in November, 1946, the moderate parties and the MRP together won a majority and more than one-third of the votes.

The similarity between the two maps is obvious: it permits us to conclude that in 1945-1946 the MRP had penetrated social groups other than those which formerly voted to the right only in a few departments: Aisne, Ardennes, Saône-et-Loire, Isère, Drôme, Tarn and Charente-Maritime. It may be that this progress of a party of Catholic inspiration is due in these areas to women's suffrage.

175

Map II
Chamber of Deputies Elections of 1936
Moderate votes

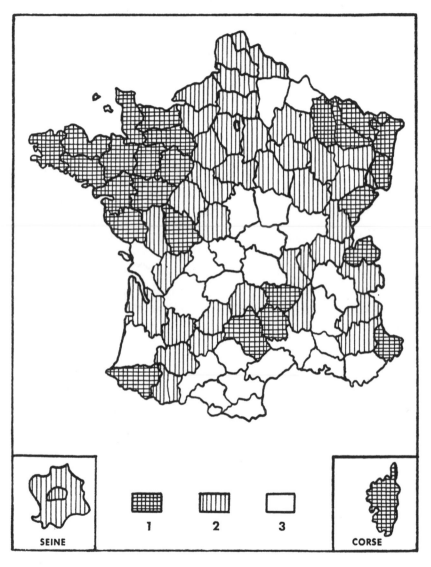

1 : absolute majority of ballots cast
2 : more than a third of ballots cast
3 : less than a third of ballots cast

Map III

National Assembly Elections of November 10, 1946
Moderate and M.R.P. votes

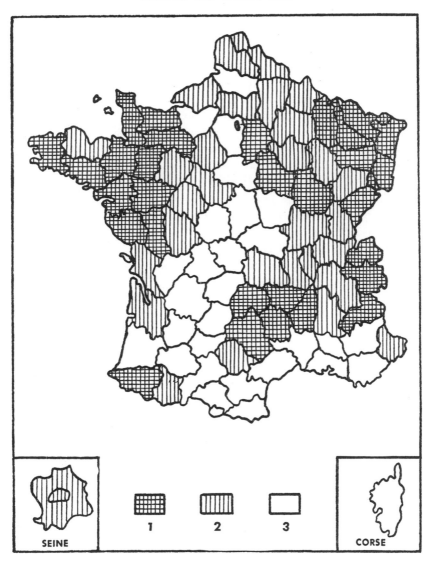

SEINE

1

2

3

CORSE

1 : absolute majority of ballots cast
2 : more than a third of ballots cast
3 : less than a third of ballots cast

177

In other departments, the total of MRP and moderate votes seems to have declined relative to the strength of the moderates of ten years ago. This is the case in the Somme, Eure, Seine-et-Oise, Loiret, Indre, Charente, Lot, Lot-et-Caronne, Tarn-et-Garonne and Gers. In all these departments, in 1946, the Radicals took a position very similar to that of the Moderates (who, at times, did not compete with them) and they received an important percentage of the votes from groups which formerly supported the right.

In 1946, in most cases, the great majority of the MRP electorate came from areas, and almost certainly from groups, which formerly supported the right. In some cases, the Radicals won at least the partial support of these people. In other and fewer cases, the MRP seems, on the other hand, to have received the support of old elements of what was called the left under the Third Republic. But the great majority of the departments where the moderates were weak in 1936, in central France and in the Midi, have remained impervious to MRP penetration.

This can be very easily explained. Religious factors played a considerable role in the political life of the Third Republic and in the departments where the right was weak in 1936 the Church had no political influence. It was obviously especially difficult for a Christian Democratic party to entrench itself in these areas after the second world war. On the other hand, it must be emphasized how easily, except in some Lorraine departments where the right had always been more nationalistic than clerical, the MRP in 1946 and even in 1945 penetrated the traditionally conservative regions. This may be explained by the fact that it was supported by groups traditionally rightist, largely under clerical influence, and by the discrediting of the old moderate groups or of well-known persons affiliated with the moderate groups because of their collaboration with the Vichy government during the occupation. The MRP, on the other hand, appeared as a party of resistants, of men who would be capable of exercising an influence on the state which had risen from the liberation. Giving every guarantee from the religious point of view, the MRP could implant itself without much difficulty.

It is, unfortunately, impossible, in the present state of the techniques of sociological research in France, to know the social categories to which the MRP's electorate of 1946 belongs. Certain monographs on electoral geography, which we have been able to consult,[13] completely confirm the impressions stated above: in 1946 the MRP appeared to be especially strong in the urban towns where the middle classes, businessmen and liberal professions are well represented. In the country, it was strong in the cantons which had traditionally voted to the right during the Third Republic. These studies, however, more detailed than those which consider the elections in the overly large area of the department, also show that in certain industrial zones of the Nord, of the Parisian area and of the east, the MRP is entrenched much more solidly than the old right was in towns or cantons with working-class populations. The phenomenon is less general and less universal than a simple replacement of the moderates of 1936; that is why it does not show on a map of all of France. But it exists and should be noted as the sign of the beginning of the success of the MRP in carrying out an important element of its political program: to persuade the popular classes, which have traditionally been tied to the extreme left, that Catholics (or, more generally, Christians) can sincerely and effectively defend their interests.

This fact is confirmed by a poll taken by the *Institut Français d'Opinion Publique* after the elections of June 2, 1946: [14] in France as a whole, out of 100 workers who were asked which party they had voted for, thirty-four said they had voted for the Communists, twenty-two for the Socialists and eighteen for the MRP, as opposed to only three for the Radicals and two for the right (the other twenty-one did not answer). The percentage of MRP voters rose to twenty for employees and civil servants, twenty-eight for farmers, twenty-eight also for persons with a small income from securities or pensions, thirty-seven for the liberal professions and thirty for businessmen and industrialists.

These figures, which would be much more interesting if regional polls had been taken instead of a single poll for France as a whole, indicate clearly that in 1946 the MRP was not essentially a worker's party, but they show that it was much more of a worker's party

---

[13] These unfortunately have not been published, with the exception of that by Pierre George on Bourg-la-Reine in *Etudes de Sociologie Electorale*, ler Cashier de la Fondation Nationale des Sciences Politiques, Paris, 1947.

[14] *Sondages*, July 16, 1946.

than the rightist and the Radical parties, and almost as much as the Socialists.

At the municipal elections of October 1947, the *Rassemblement du Peuple Français,* created the previous spring by General de Gaulle, presented at Paris and in all the big cities coalition lists which included, under its aegis, Moderates and Radicals. These lists achieved a brilliant success: the cities of Paris, Marseilles, Bordeaux, Lille, Strasbourg and a number of other important cities passed into the hands of RPF majorities. The Communists just about held their own with respect to November 1946; the Socialists generally declined. As to the MRP, at Paris it suffered a veritable collapse, losing about three-fourths of its 1946 votes. The appearance of a new right-wing group, free from the discredit which had struck the old moderate parties in 1945 and 1946, combined with the general discontent that the postwar difficulties had raised, clearly caused the MRP to lose the voters who were really conservative in their opinions and who had previously voted for it only for the lack of something better. In the part of Paris situated on the left bank of the Seine where, in the elections of 1924, Marc Sangnier had been a candidate for the Chamber of Deputies on a *Jeune République* ticket, the MRP received in October 1947 only a slightly greater percentage of votes than the Christian Democrats had received almost a quarter of a century earlier: 5.4 per cent of the registered voters instead of a bit more than 3.5 per cent.

In 344 cities with a population greater than 9,000, the number of MRP votes fell from 1,250,000 in November 1946 to 500,000 and, in the percentage of votes cast, from 23.8 per cent to 10.2 per cent. This means that its decline was greater in Paris than in the other cities.

As to the results in the countryside, it is difficult to evaluate them as many lists did not have a clear-cut political orientation. But polls taken in various departments where the MRP had received a respectable number of votes in November 1946 led to the conclusion that in the small towns the MRP had great difficulty in finding candidates willing to run under its name. The same thing happened to the moderate parties during the Third Republic. Leading citizens feared an electoral setback which might injure their social prestige. Their consequent reluctance to devote a part of their time to the management of the town's affairs, while neglecting their own affairs, had for a long time turned them away from seeking local elective offices, especially in the southern half of France. It was, therefore, not very likely that the MRP would control an appreciable number of towns after the elections of October 1947.

This is exactly what the senatorial elections of November 7, 1948 confirmed: the MRP actually won only sixteen seats out of the 246 for metropolitan France.[15] Map IV shows the geographical distribution of its votes.[16] To a certain extent, one finds here the same pattern as for the legislative elections of 1946, but the intensity of the colors is lessened. This difference indicates a decline which is undoubtedly due, in part, to the characteristics of the senatorial election which are mentioned above. The voters who had remained faithful to the MRP in 1947 in the towns with fewer than 9,000 inhabitants, where the municipal councils were elected by a majority system, could be represented in the electoral colleges for the Council of the Republic in 1948 only if they had been a majority, which was certainly unusual. One, therefore, cannot say that the actual decline of the MRP's influence in the country has been as marked as a quick, comparative glance at Maps I and IV would indicate. But there can be no doubt about the reality and the importance of this decline. Many MRP voters of 1946 passed, in 1947, to the RPF or to the independents or to the Radicals or, especially in central France, because of the lack of an MRP list, to the Socialists.

The MRP's decline was greater in the northern half of France,

---

[15] As the members of the Council of the Republic hold the title of senator, it is convenient to refer to "senatorial" elections.

[16] In order to make this map exactly comparable to Map I, a slightly different scale has been used. Both are based on the percentage of MRP votes relative to the number of registered voters. But in the elections of November 10, 1946, by universal suffrage, there were about 22 per cent abstentions. On November 7, 1948, there were almost no abstentions, as voting was compulsory for the delegates of the municipal councils. For this election we have used wider percentage ranges than for the map of the 1946 elections in order to show in the same way the departments where the MRP's percentage of those voting was the same in 1946 and 1948.

Map IV
Council of the Republic Elections of November 7, 1948
M.R.P. votes (percentage of registered voters)

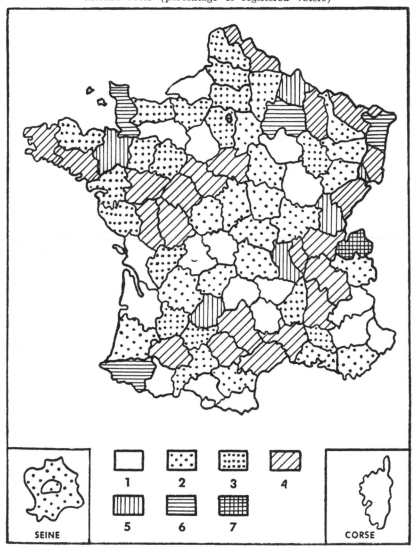

1 : no MRP candidates
2 : from 0.1% to 7.9%
3 : from 8 to 14.9%
4 : from 15 to 22.9%
5 : from 23 to 29.9%
6 : from 30 to 37.9%
7 : 39.2%

especially in the west, than in the Midi. This is in accord with the fact that the RPF had been much more successful in the north than in the Midi, where the MRP was able more easily to retain its voters.

The results of the cantonal elections of March 1949, on the other hand, seem to prove that the MRP's decline was checked and perhaps even that the MRP was recovering from the low-point it had reached in 1947. The MRP presented candidates in 479 of the 1508 cantons where elections were held, in those cantons, of course, where it thought it was strongest, and on March 20, 1949, received 676,000 votes or 9.1 per cent of all the votes. If one considers only those cantons where the MRP ran candidates, it won 20.9 per cent of the votes.[17] The number of its officeholders remained about the same after the election in the spring of 1949 as it had been after the elections of September 1945; but at that time it had proportionally fewer members in local offices than it had in the National Assembly after the legislative elections of October 21, 1945.

Map V shows the number of seats held by members of the MRP in the departmental assemblies; it includes councillors who were elected in 1945 and those who were elected in 1949. The number of seats varies from one department to another. One should not, therefore, draw too many conclusions from an examination of this map. None the less the essential features of the MRP's electoral geography which we have already mentioned stand out clearly; the west, the north, the east, the mountainous areas in the Alps, the *Massif Central* and the Pyrénées are where it is strongest. These characteristics are too similar to those of the geography of the moderate and conservative parties during the.

---

[17] The figures for the 479 cantons where the MRP presented candidates have been taken from *l'Aube* of March 23, 1949; the figures for all the registered voters come from statistics published by the Ministry of the Interior. It should be noted that the number of cantons where the MRP presented candidates represents 31.7 per cent of the cantons where elections were held, but that the number of registered voters in these 479 cantons represented 46 per cent of the total number of registered voters for the 1508 cantons where elections took place. This striking difference indicates that the MRP competed especially in urban cantons or in densely populated rural cantons. The opposite was true for the conservatives and radicals, whose electoral support comes from less densely populated cantons.

Map V

Departmental Elections of March, 1949
Number of M.R.P. councillors

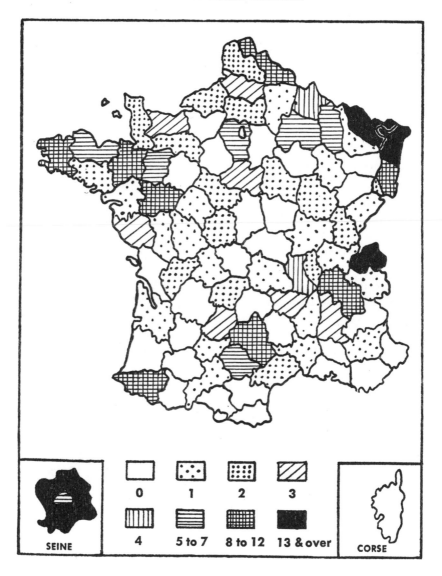

Third Republic for us to doubt that it is mainly these parties that the MRP has replaced. This does not mean that the MRP is a moderate or conservative party, but that the clientele of these to the MRP's efforts to pose political problems differently from parties rather than those of the old left has been more receptive the way they were presented during the Third Republic.

The few seats that the MRP holds in the departmental councils confirms, on the other hand, the impression given by the map of the senatorial elections: with a few exceptions, Haute-Savoie, Alsace and Lorraine, the MRP is much weaker in local elections than in legislative elections. The party organization, that it has created since 1944, obviously does not extend to the little towns and the rural cantons as efficiently as does the network of Radical Party committees and Socialist sections. It is, certainly, much more recent and this partially explains the difference. But the reluctance of bourgeois and moderate circles to participate in local electoral contests is too old and too general a phenomenon in France for us to doubt that this also handicaps the MRP. To a great extent an ideological party, the MRP is also necessarily more at home in a legislative election than in a municipal or a cantonal election.

The elections of June 17, 1951, to the National Assembly confirm the analysis of the results of the municipal and cantonal elections of 1947 and 1949. The MRP has been considerably weakened since 1946, for it has lost altogether a little more than half of its voters, but this weakening is not a disaster, and leaves the Popular Republicans in a situation slightly superior to that of the Radicals when comparing the number of votes obtained.

The MRP obtained on June 17, 1951, 2,353,544 votes or 12.3 per cent of the ballots cast. But it is interesting to note, independently of the geographic distribution indicated by Map VI, that, in the 17 most industrialized departments, that is, where the industrial workers exceed 20 per cent of the active population, it obtained a percentage equal to 13.8 per cent of the ballots cast, a little more than that of the Radicals. The Radicals obtained 11.5 per cent of the votes throughout the country, but only received 6.2 per cent in the industrial departments. This fact con-

Map VI

National Assembly Elections of June 17, 1951
M.R.P. votes (percentage of registered voters)

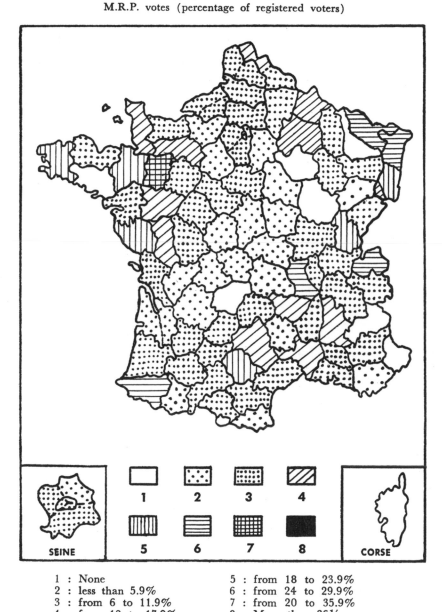

1 : None
2 : less than 5.9%
3 : from 6 to 11.9%
4 : from 12 to 17.9%

5 : from 18 to 23.9%
6 : from 24 to 29.9%
7 : from 20 to 35.9%
8 : More than 36½

firms the results of the polls taken in 1946, which were later recalled: the MRP, which stresses the solution of the social problem created by large industry, is stronger in the regions where the electoral body is aware of the existence of this problem than in those where the social structure, founded on the preponderance of the artisan and the peasant, at least partially masks the situation.

Moreover, the geographic distribution obtained by the MRP [18] indicates that, for the most part, Catholic regions were the ones to give the party an appreciable percentage of votes. The zone where it is the weakest, in the center of France, is a region where religious practice in general is rather weak. But it is by no means certain that it is exclusively as a Catholic party, favorable, in particular, to the subsidy of private schools, that the MRP has obtained votes; in each case, one or more lists presented a program on this point analogous to its own.

One has, therefore, the right to say — contrary to what happened in 1945 and 1946 — that those who voted for the MRP in 1951 were fully aware of what they were doing and intended to support a party whose doctrine and program they approved, particularly in economic and social matters. Numerically weakened, the MRP is, however, politically reinforced by the greater homogeneity of its electoral body. The election of June 17 proves that it has attained a popular and electoral base much stronger than it possessed before the second world war.

IV. *Tactical Issues*

As is natural during a period of rapid transformation of political circumstances, the tactics of the MRP from its foundation in the fall of 1944 until June 1951, have undergone marked variation. The most important of these changes concern, on the one hand, its relations with General de Gaulle and on the other, its attitude toward the Communist Party.

---

[18] In other than the departments indicated on the map, the MRP participated in coalition lists in le Morbihan, la Corrèze, la Cote-d'Or, la Meurthe-et-Moselle and les Hautes-Alpes; but the candidate heading the list was a Radical or a Moderate, and the votes of these lists were therefore not attributed to the MRP on the map.

Until January 1946, the MRP collaborated very closely *with* *de Gaulle*. It supported him against those who attacked him and, at the same time, identified itself with him before the electorate. From January 1946, when the President of the Provisional Government resigned, until the spring of 1947, when the *Rassemblement du Peuple Français* was created, the MRP participated in the government *without de Gaulle*. And, finally, since the spring of 1947, having taken a position hostile to the RPF and having forbidden its members and its office holders to participate in the RPF, the MRP has operated *against de Gaulle*.

The MRP's attitude toward the Communists from 1944 to 1950 has progressively grown more hostile. From the time of the liberation, it has struggled actively against the grasping tentacles of the Communists and has seen to it that the reestablishment of democracy was not accompanied by the measures which, in eastern Europe, permitted the Communists to use democracy for their own purposes. Nevertheless, it agreed to collaborate in the government with the Communists. Going further, it voted, with them and the Socialists, the nationalization acts of 1945 and 1946. In the political field, however, during the first half of 1946 the MRP carried on the struggle for a genuine democracy by opposing the first constitutional draft and by contributing decisively to its rejection at the referendum of May 5, 1946. At this time, a complete and final break with the Communists would have been in keeping with the MRP's position. This, however, was delayed until a time when relations between the Socialists and the Communists had become strained enough to allow the passage of the latter into the opposition without also dragging along the former. Since May 1947, the anti-communism of the MRP has been an obvious and constant fact. Still, it must be distinguished from that of the Radicals and conservatives, for the MRP is opposed to discriminatory measures, incompatible with its conception of democracy, and desires to avoid a reactionary policy in the social sphere so that the hold of the Communists on the proletariat will not be reinforced.

These are, from the point of view of its relations with Gaullism and Communism, the broad outlines of the evolution of the MRP's tactics for the last five years.

The Period of the Liberation: September 1944-October 1945

During the fourteen-month period which ran from the installation of the provisional government of General de Gaulle, a few days after the liberation of Paris, until the meeting of the first National Constituent Assembly, which was elected on October 21, 1945, the tactics of the MRP were built around the following themes: expression of complete fidelity to the person and policies of General de Gaulle; support of the government in order to re-establish the authority of the state; persevering search for an agreement with the Socialists; a desire to break with the traditions of the Third Republic; a no less clear refusal to adopt, under the pretext of "maintaining the unity of the resistance," political formulas incompatible with free and honest elections.

The MRP's fidelity to de Gaulle was at first, obviously, the product of appreciation and admiration. This sentiment included a share of careful calculation. In the France of 1944, the Communist Party occupied important political positions, due to its participation in the Liberation Committees and the existence of its own militia, the *Francs-Tireurs et Partisans*. Many of its traditional adversaries, those people in the provinces who should have been able to oppose its influence locally, did not dare or were unable to do so, either out of fear of reprisals or because they had temporarily lost their influence because they had been compromised by their support of the Vichy government. General de Gaulle's authority, the incomparable prestige which he had won because of his appeal of June 18, 1940, and the resolution with which he had organized and directed the continuation of the struggle against Nazi Germany, seemed to be the only force psychologically able to counter-balance Communist influence. It is certain that the "Gaullism" of the Popular Republicans in the fall of 1944 and in 1945 can be explained to a great extent by the desire to do nothing which might diminish the authority of the General and, at the same time, by the desire to benefit indirectly from his popularity.

It is partially for these reasons and partially because of its desire for order, something natural in men who undoubtedly wanted to make a revolution, but a "revolution by the law," that the MRP took an unequivocal stand in favor of the complete restoration of the traditional authority of the state, an authority which had been seriously weakened in two ways. First of all, there was the formation in the provinces of something similar to proconsulates, under the rule of regional Commissioners of the Republic, who were surrounded and sometimes fought by Committees of Liberation which opposed their authority to that of the central government. In addition, there was the armed militia of the resistance and especially of the Communists. In November 1944, at its first congress, the MRP vigorously opposed this disintegration of sovereignty into numerous local or partisan atoms. "The French Republic," it declared, "must have only one army." This signified approval of the provisional government's move to incorporate the militia into the regular army, to subject it to army discipline and to disarm those elements who did not enter the regular army. "The French Republic must have only one government." This meant that the role of the resistance organizations and of the Committees of Liberation that they had appointed was to disappear in favor of the local representatives of the central government.

The Popular Republicans were in agreement with the Socialists and with de Gaulle, without any mental reservations, with respect to collaboration and the restoration of the state. The Moderates and the Radicals, however, distrusted de Gaulle at least as much as they did the Communists and, accordingly, could not aid the provisional government in reestablishing the authority of the state. As to the Communists, who were the masters of most of the bodies which menaced the state, they wanted to protect their influence from any harm and to prolong their existence. The desire to seek an agreement with the Socialists came quite naturally to the Popular Republicans and they sought one with perseverance. This was the era of the negotiations over the formation of a *Union travailliste* and when a committee (whose chairman was Socialist André Philip, a Protestant professor, and whose members included Catholics and anti-clericals) sought unsuccessfully to resolve the antagonism traditionally separating the Catholics and the left on the educational problem.

At that time, the Socialist Party included a rather strong wing which favored, for theoretical reasons, unity of action, or even structural unity, with the Communists. In spite of the fact that their most influential leaders distrusted the Communists, the Socialists could not break with the Communists who, in any case, had representatives in the provisional government. It seems clear that if the MRP agreed at this time to collaborate with the Communists, it was to a great extent in order not to lose contact with the Socialists.

It is this preoccupation which also explains, at least partially, the vigor with which the MRP opposed the traditions of the Third Republic, categorically condemned by the Socialists as well. Certainly, the leaders of the MRP came, to a great extent, from Catholic circles which had always remained reserved about the Third Republic, out of distrust for politics and out of fidelity to a tradition born at the time of militant anti-clericalism. Being poorly acquainted with the real customs and political traditions of the Third Republic, these men were quite willing to condemn it beyond appeal, because they considered it responsible for the defeat of 1940 and for the abdication to Vichy to which its parliament had agreed. But when the MRP called itself "the party of the Fourth Republic" it was also referring to the social sphere. It meant to condemn the individualistic and conservative traditions of the pre-war regime and to state its desire to realize the "economic and social democracy" implied in its doctrine. Of course, the formulas which expressed this program differed in tone from Marxist dogmatism: "We are in the midst of a tide that will not be turned," said the first MRP congress, "we will not make the miners of the Nord work any longer for the *Comité des Houillères*." This was a declaration of fact, almost resignation to a fact, rather than the expression of a positive desire; but the acceptance of the principle of "structural reforms" and of the "nationalization of the great key industries" nevertheless created the prerequisite for a rapprochement with the Socialists. Politically, the reaching of this agreement, under the aegis of General de Gaulle, clearly was the essential point of the MRP's tactics in 1944

191

and 1945, and a rupture with the Third Republic was essential for its success.

A rupture with the Third Republic, but not with traditional democracy: this is the final aspect of the MRP's tactics. Under the pretext of maintaining "the unity of the resistance," the Communists advocated the fusion of the resistance organizations. This meant essentially a fusion of the *Mouvement de Libération Nationale,* which included non-Communist organizations, with the *Front National,* which was controlled by the Communists. At the end of 1944, in agreement with the Socialists, the Popular Republicans had this proposal rejected by the congress of the *Mouvement de Libération Nationale.* The maintenance of a multiplicity of resistance organizations guaranteed the maintenance of a multiplicity of political parties.

The Communists wanted single coalition lists, representing the resistance, to be presented at the municipal elections scheduled for the spring of 1945. As everyone knows, it is this system of single lists that has enabled the Communists to conquer the state in several eastern European countries. In November 1944, the MRP opposed such a suggestion. "The Fourth French Republic," it said, "must be the work of the French people. The MRP demands genuine elections. The single list system is not democratic because it actually abolishes elections."

As a whole, the tactics employed by the MRP in 1944 and 1945 were crowned with success.

Of course, the MRP did not succeed in abolishing the political tradition of the Third Republic which distinguished the parties in terms of their attitude toward the religious problem, or more concretely, the educational system. As the Vichy government had granted government subsidies to the private Catholic schools, the question of their maintenance or abolition was raised in the spring of 1945, shortly before the municipal elections. The Communists and Radicals demanded their immediate abolition, and the Socialist Party, many of whose militants were public elementary school teachers, could do nothing but join them. The MRP took the opposite position. The religious question therefore appeared as the major obstacle to a rapprochement between the Socialists and the Popular Republicans, at least as far as elections were concerned.

In the government, however, the solidarity of the Socialists and the Popular Republicans continued after the municipal elections of April and May 1945; it was especially affirmed in July and August. General de Gaulle, after some hesitation, took a stand against reestablishing the constitutional laws of 1875 in favor of the election of a constituent assembly. This clean break with the Third Republic conformed with the desires of the Socialists and the Popular Republicans. But, in order to avoid the risks involved in convoking a sovereign assembly with all political power concentrated in its hands, the MRP and the Socialists supported the General's proposal to submit to a popular referendum both the question of whether or not the laws of 1875 should be abrogated and the question of whether or not the constituent assembly should be limited to a duration of seven months and its relations with the provisional government, whose president it would elect, regulated in advance.

The Communists and the Radicals fought the latter proposal violently and asked the voters to reject it. But at the referendum of October 21, 1945, two-thirds of the voters were in favor of limiting the powers of the Constituent Assembly. This was unquestionably a victory for de Gaulle, the Socialists and the Popular Republicans. The MRP won an unexpectedly large number of seats in the Constituent Assembly, ranking just behind the Communists and a bit ahead of the Socialists.

The virtual eradication of the Radicals and the moderates, however, gave the Communists and the Socialists combined a majority in the assembly. This fact was to determine all the tactics of the MRP in the next period.

The Period of the Constituent Assemblies: November 1945-November 1946

When the first Constituent Assembly met, it seemed that the tactics of the Communists would consist in trying to solidify the existing "Marxist" majority by reinforcing it when necessary with some "secular" radical elements. The Socialist Party did not want

193

to be associated with this maneuver. The myth of "working-class unity," however, still enjoyed too much prestige among some Socialist militants for it to be able to consider consenting to the formation of a majority without the Communists. Refusing, on the other hand, too close camaraderie with the Communists, it advocated a "tripartite" solution and sought to unite around it both the MRP and the Communist Party.

The provisional government, formed by de Gaulle in 1944, rested on precisely just such a coalition, rounded out by the participation of some Moderates and Radicals. The authority and the personal prestige of the General were obviously indispensable for imposing on the parties, whose mutual hostility had just been confirmed during the electoral campaign, the concessions which the formation of this coalition required. This presented the MRP, which sought to prevent the Socialists from making an entente with the Communists, with the obligation of supporting, at all costs, the designation of General de Gaulle as President of the new Provisional Government.

In any case, this designation seemed to move ahead on its own momentum, but after the National Assembly unanimously named de Gaulle President, the Communists set certain conditions on their participation in the government. These conditions concerned the distribution of ministerial portfolios and were clearly calculated to provoke de Gaulle's refusal. Their aim was obviously to bring about the General's resignation.

It was then that the MRP loudly declared itself to be the "party of fidelity." It stated categorically that it would be party to no maneuver to eliminate de Gaulle and that it would participate in the government only if he were President. The Socialists, for their part, required the participation of the MRP and the Communists. The affair finally was settled by a compromise concerning the ministries given to the Communists. But it was plain that General de Gaulle would run into serious difficulties in his relations with the parliamentary majority. He thought he could count on the unswerving support of the MRP, but the "fidelity" of the latter was due essentially to its opposition to the formation of an extreme leftist government. If the circumstances changed, it was not going to maintain its position, at least not in its original form, of unconditional supporter of the person and policies of de Gaulle.

De Gaulle very quickly came into conflict with the Constituent Assembly. His conception of the relations between a Chief of Government and the parties which support him was hardly in harmony with the traditions of French parliamentary government. In addition, he saw with apprehension the direction that the work of the constitutional committee was taking; but the members of the government were not agreed on this subject and it was just about impossible for him to intervene in this sphere. After a conflict with the Socialists over the size of military appropriations, which nearly provoked a ministerial crisis on January 1, 1946, de Gaulle suddenly decided to resign on January 20, leaving to the parties which, in his opinion, were thwarting governmental action, the task of bearing the responsibilities of the economic, political and international position of France.

It can hardly be doubted that General de Gaulle hoped that his departure would demonstrate the impossibility of getting along without him and that he would soon return to power with increased authority. This was to disregard the parliamentary situation, which arithmetically permitted the formation of a Socialist-Communist majority. Now, the political obstacles to such a solution were weakened by the similarity between the Socialist and Communist programs in the constitutional committee, both being favorable to the establishment of a government by assembly.

Faced with such a risk, the MRP leaders decided that the maintenance of three party cooperation was preferable. Within the government they would be able to stand with the Socialists and, together, they could prevent the conquest of the whole administrative and political structure by the Communists. At the same time, they would keep alive the possibility of an eventual realization of a "labor" coalition between them and the Socialists. They therefore agreed to participate in the cabinet formed by Socialist Félix Gouin. This inaugurated the era of "pure" three party cooperation, or the collaboration of the Communists, Socialists and MRP, to the exclusion of the other groups.

This decision marks the beginning of the estrangement, which was to be ceaselessly accentuated, between the MRP and de Gaulle. De Gaulle was deeply hurt by an attitude apparently contradicting the affirmations of "fidelity" which had been lavished on him a few weeks earlier. He lost confidence in the Popular Republican leaders, who seemed to him to be imbued with a partisan spirit. The MRP was angry at de Gaulle for his resignation, which it regarded as desertion before the danger of a Communist seizure of power. It felt abandoned and without support against the attacks of the extreme left. These basic reasons for its attitude were often not understood by its militants and especially by its voters, and it knew that it was taking a great risk by adopting an attitude in favor of three-party cooperation. It seemed paradoxical to the MRP to be reproached for not having taken the easy way out and gone into the opposition, while its decision had been dictated essentially by the desire to remain in the government where resistance to the Communists could be decisive.

If the Popular Republicans had gone into the opposition, this would have created another danger for their movement: opposition would have drawn it closer to the conservatives and Radicals, causing it to lose its originality. Such a course would have posed great difficulties in working for the structural economic reforms which had been started by de Gaulle's government with the nationalization of the commercial banks, and which were to be followed by the nationalization of insurance, the coal mines and the electricity and gas industries. These reforms were regarded by the MRP as indispensable for preventing the reestablishment of a capitalistic economy identical with that of the pre-war era, which the Popular Republicans considered to be incompatible with the achievement of the economic democracy required by its doctrine. And politically speaking, if the MRP had allowed the Socialists and Communists to form a government together, it would have decisively contributed to the re-formation of right-wing and left-wing blocs, hostilely facing each other. If it had broken with the Socialists, there would have been nothing to counterbalance the operation of factors which were driving the Socialists to reestablish secularism as the major battle cry, especially as it was not impossible for the Radicals, or a fraction of them, to have participated in an extreme-left majority. The achievement of some of the major goals of the MRP would therefore have been compromised.

All this explains the position which the MRP took in January 1946. But this position could be completely justified only if, while in the government with the Communists, the MRP succeeded in checking them decisively.

The intransigent way in which the Communists and the Socialists handled the constitutional problem made things easier for the MRP. Having won concessions neither to its initial position nor to its compromise proposals, the MRP was led to vote against the draft prepared by the first Constituent Assembly and to oppose it before the electorate at the referendum of May 5, 1946.

The constitutional draft was rejected by more than a million votes; in addition to the MRP, the moderates and the Radicals opposed it. But the Popular Republicans seemed to have played a decisive role in bringing about the referendum result, which marked the beginning of the decline of Communist influence in France. At the elections of June 2, 1946, the MRP won 800,000 more votes than it had received in October. It became the largest party in the second Constituent Assembly.

When the Gouin ministry resigned, Georges Bidault became president of the new government which, like the preceding one, was composed of Communists, Socialists, and Popular Republicans, with the addition of one Radical, who participated as an individual and without committing his group. Actually, the reasons why the MRP had refused in January to join the right and the Radicals in the opposition were still valid. Thanks to the support of some overseas deputies, the Communists and the Socialists had a slight majority in the Assembly. The Popular Republicans, on the other hand, still wished to distinguish themselves from the conservative parties. Lastly, the Socialists were not yet disposed to break with the Communists.

The political situation, therefore, led the MRP to seek a compromise with the Communists and the Socialists over the constitutional problem. This compromise could consist only in harmonizing the assembly regime adopted by the first Constituent Assembly with the rules of classical parliamentary government. But, in June 1946, General de Gaulle broke the silence he had maintained since his resignation and delivered a speech at Bayeux in which he recommended a constitutional system somewhere in between the American presidential system and the parliamentary system. Such a solution had no chance of being accepted by the Socialists. The MRP would have been able to rally to it only in accord with the moderates and the Radicals, that is, by participating in a right-wing bloc whose very existence would have been enough to solidify a counterbalancing bloc of Socialists and Communists. In addition, the Popular Republicans had difficulty understanding why de Gaulle had left them almost alone to bear the burden of the fight against the first constitutional draft. In spite of some toying with the idea of reaching an understanding with the General, the MRP soon recognized that such an agreement was no longer compatible with its interpretation of the French political situation which, doctrinally and tactically, led them to persevere in the attempt to cooperate with the Socialists, even if it meant enduring, for some time, the presence of the Communists in the governmental coalition.

Amidst these circumstances the second constitutional draft was written. The MRP, though failing to secure all the concessions asked for, decided to support the draft. The grounds advanced for this were that the draft could be revised later, while the provisional French regime had to be ended. De Gaulle, on the other hand, opposed the constitution and asked the voters to reject it.

Many MRP voters heeded his appeal: at the referendum of October 13, 1946, part of them voted against the constitution and most of them abstained. The constitution was accepted by a small majority.

This result represented a warning to the MRP. The moment had come for it to stiffen its attitude toward the Communists. The risk of losing contact with the Socialists because of this was less great than it had been at the beginning of the year, for relations between the two left-wing parties were growing strained. The Socialist congress in August had decided to abolish the *comité d'entente* that the Communists and Socialists had created together in 1944 and which, in any case, had produced almost no results because of the obvious incompatibility of the Socialist and Communist conceptions of democracy.

The election of the National Assembly was to take place on

November 10. Between the referendum and the election, the MRP based its campaign on the slogan "Bidault without Thorez," that is, it advocated the dissolution of the tripartite governmental coalition and the ejection of the Communists into the opposition. On November 10 this attitude recaptured most of its June voters who had not voted for the constitution and did not create any real dissatisfaction among the Socialists. Although the MRP did not win, as it had in June, first place among the parties represented in the National Assembly, it followed closely on the heels of the Communists.

The tactics followed by the MRP in 1946 seemed to have been most successful. It had practically maintained its strength, it had inflicted a decisive defeat on the Communists in May when the first constitutional draft was rejected and it had maintained contact with the Socialists long enough to reach a period when everything indicated that a break between the Socialists and the Communists involved fewer obstacles than would have been the case right after the liberation. On the negative side of the balance sheet, one must put the MRP's break with de Gaulle. The result of the referendum of October 13 proved that a large number of the MRP's voters were receptive to the counsels of the General. But de Gaulle did not personally take part in the creation of the political organization, *l'Union Gaulliste,* which exploited his name; he seemed to want to remain aloof from party struggles. It was not inconceivable that the flow of political events would eventually permit an understanding between him and the parties which, like the MRP, disagreed with him over the constitutional problem but still respected and admired him for his activities from June 18, 1940 until the liberation.

The Break with the Communists and with de Gaulle: November 1946-October 1947

The new attitude of the MRP toward the Communists was displayed when the National Assembly first met. The issue was the designation of a new President of the Provisional Government, whose powers were to last until the constitution entered into force and a new President of the Republic was elected. The Communists proposed their leader, Maurice Thorez, as their candidate and the Socialists decided to accept him, on the pretext that the largest party in the assembly had the right to lead the government. This Socialist position was taken because they desired to arrange a deal with the Communists whereby the latter would in January support the election of a Socialist as President of the Republic and they were almost certain that Maurice Thorez would be unable to attract a majority of the assembly. This is actually what happened; the MRP, the Radicals, the moderates, and even some Socialists refused to vote for Thorez, who received only 259 votes of the 310 necessary for election. The attitude of the Popular Republicans had been decisive and seemed to mark the end of three party cooperation.

Georges Bidault was then named as a candidate, but he did not receive the necessary majority as the Communists, Socialists and Radicals refused to vote for him.

Finally, the late Léon Blum was elected. He tried to form a tripartite government, but the Communists demanded certain ministries, one of which was the Ministry of National Defense, and the MRP refused to participate in the new cabinet under these conditions. Léon Blum did not want to form a government consisting only of the Socialists and Communists, who would not have had a majority in the National Assembly. Thus, he formed an all-Socialist cabinet.

The MRP's initiative seemed to have broken three party cooperation. It reappeared, however, in somewhat altered form, in January 1947, when the first regular government of the Fourth Republic was formed. President Auriol named Socialist Paul Ramadier to form it and, after being accepted by the National Assembly, Ramadier called for the collaboration of Communists, Socialists, Popular Republicans and certain Radicals and moderates. This was no longer pure three party cooperation. The MRP, however, had to decide whether to collaborate again with the Communists in a government.

If the MRP resigned itself to do so, it was undoubtedly because it was becoming more and more obvious that this collaboration would not last long and because it did not want to break with the Socialists. To remain friendly with the Socialists meant retaining the opportunity of urging the Socialists to stay in the government, even when the Communists joined the opposition. The precariousness of the role of the Communists as a government party was due to the growing gap between their ideas and the ideas of the other parties on certain basic problems, like that of the wage-freeze and the policy of lowering prices which was started by Léon Blum or that of Indo-China. In addition, international developments were marked by increasing tension between the USSR and Britain and the United States, a situation which was obviously going to oblige France to align itself with the latter.

As was only to be expected, the collaboration of the Communists in the Ramadier government did not last long. In March, a crisis almost occurred over Indo-China. The Communist group voted against an appropriation which was necessary for the expeditionary corps, but the Communist ministers voted for it and the difficulty was postponed. A new crisis occurred at the end of April, after the failure of the Moscow conference and the definite rapprochement between the diplomatic positions of France and the United States.

On the issue of starting to freeze wages, the Communist ministers voted against the government of which they were members. The next day, a presidential decree relieved them of their duties; three party cooperation had come to an end.

The MRP strove to persuade the Socialists to stay in the government with it and with some of the Radicals. Many Socialist militants were unenthusiastic about retaining governmental responsibilities, when their party would be unable to impose its views on a majority which had to include Radicals. The prospect of being aided by the MRP in maintaining a policy favorable to the working classes and in protecting the economic and social reforms accomplished after the liberation, the nationalization of industries and the extension of social security, undoubtedly helped convince the national council of the Socialist Party to agree, but by a meager margin, to stay in the government without the Communists. This decision represented a major victory for the MRP, since it had been precisely the constant goal of all its efforts after December 1945. The events seemed to justify the tactics that it had followed, since the Communist participation in the government had not resulted in their seizure of control of the state and since, after the dissolution of three party cooperation, the Socialists had chosen to continue to collaborate with the Popular Republicans.

But the MRP was faced with new difficulties. At the very moment when the Communists left the government, General de Gaulle announced the creation of the *Rassemblement du Peuple Français*. This was a political movement, under the leadership of the General, whose objectives were revision of the constitution and the achievement, amid opinions "artificially divided by the parties," of the unity necessary for defending the higher interests of the nation.

The RPF claimed to be not on the same level as the parties but above them, and it appealed to the members of all the existing parties, with the exception of the Communist Party, to aid in achieving its objectives, while remaining members of their original groups. Actually, the reaction to de Gaulle's appeal was not the same at all points on the political horizon. At the right, among the conservatives, at the center, among the Radicals, that is, among those groups which had opposed the constitution, it was judged that participation in the RPF would enable them to overcome the discredit which had fallen on them in 1945 and 1946 and to form a coalition which would benefit from the personal prestige of General de Gaulle and which would be very profitable electorally. In addition, political discipline had never been very strong among the moderates, most of whom were "independents," and it was not much stricter among the Radicals. The groups of the right and the center did not object to their members joining the RPF.

The attitude of the Socialists was very different. The circumstances which had surrounded the creation of the RPF, especially the lack of any prior contact with trade union elements hostile to the colonization of the CGT by the Communists, and the tone of the General's attacks against the political parties created the impression that the RPF would be nothing but a conservative, if not a reactionary, organization. At the time when the Socialist Party parted company with the Communists, it was indispensable for it to do nothing to lead its voters and its militants to believe that it was going to move closer to the right. General de Gaulle had certainly underestimated the power of the traditional political sentiments of the left which was greatly disturbed by political movements directed against parties and apparently favorable to an authoritarian regime. Even before the First World War, at the time of the Boulanger episode and the Dreyfus affair, similar ideas of the right had created agitation which almost caused the downfall of the Republic. Between the wars, the anti-parliamentary leagues, more or less inspired by Fascism, had revised the hostility of the left to revisionist attempts. In spite of the past service of General de Gaulle and the gratitude which the Socialists freely bestowed upon him, the very fact that he was a professional soldier reminded them of the precedents of General Boulanger and Colonel de la Rocque, not to mention the role played by the general staff in the Dreyfus affair.

Both for reasons of principle and for especially imperative tactical reasons at the time when it entered into open hostility with the Communists, it was impossible for the Socialist Pary to authorize its members to participate in the activities of the RPF. It actually prohibited them to do so almost immediately.

This decision put the MRP in a very difficult position. The result of the referendum of October 13, 1946 showed how many of its voters were sensitive to the appeals of General de Gaulle. For the party, which less than two years before had proclaimed itself to be the "party of fidelity," to take a stand against the RPF, would undoubtedly mean offending the majority of the people who had just placed their confidence in it. It also involved the risk of allowing the RPF to become the prisoner of the conservative political groups, which were the only ones not to oppose it. Such a development would disable the MRP from influencing the orientation of the Gaullist movement. That being the case, the MRP then could not prevent the RPF from committing the errors which would surely alienate from it the many Frenchmen who remained faithful, despite its rather abstract nature, to the *mystique* of the traditional left. Finally, it would mean destroying the personal attachment that many Popular Republicans still felt to de Gaulle despite the disagreements that had arisen between them during the last few months.

On the other side of the picture, to permit "double membership" in the MRP and the RPF would mean renouncing the political autonomy of the movement and the discipline which its leaders regarded as a major source of its effectiveness. To collaborate again with de Gaulle would surely mean running into difficulties which had their source in the General's personality: his unwillingness to follow advice which differed from his own, his tendency to consider that the final word must always rest with him; characteristics which had marked the brief period when he was head of the provisional parliamentary government. Last and most important, to adopt an attitude toward the RPF different from that of the Socialists would mean destroying deliberately the results of the tactics followed by the MRP for the last eighteen months and making impossible the continuation of its accord with the Socialists.

The Popular Republicans did not share all of the General's views about the consequences of the regime of parties and they were astonished to see him consider only strictly political problems to the exclusion of those economic and social questions which they regarded as crucial, for they are convinced that political democracy cannot be achieved without also achieving social democracy.

Undoubtedly, there were few MRP members who completely shared the Socialists' sentiments toward the RPF and considered it as the successor of *boulangisme* and the *Croix de Feu*. But if most of the members of the MRP did not share these sentiments, they recognized that such sentiments did exist, they understood their meaning and they accepted them as a fact.

The MRP's leaders knew, of course, that by taking a friendly attitude to the RPF they would almost be guaranteeing the continued support of most of the voters who had voted for them on November 10. But they were afraid of renouncing at the same time that which gave their movement its originality and its *raison d'être;* if it were supported by the Radicals and the Moderates as well as the MRP, the RPF would insure the re-creation of the old right-wing bloc. It would be faced with the syndicalist and political forces of the working class; it would certainly promote a rapprochement between the Socialists and the Communists on the basis of resisting "Fascism." The death-knell would be tolled over all the hopes that had been raised during the resistance of a new, fruitful way of presenting political issues, no longer in ideological terms and elementary sentiments which ended in dividing public opinion into two abstract blocs, one conservative and the other revolutionary.

The executive committee of the MRP decided to forbid its members to join the RPF. This decision provoked several resignations from the MRP's parliamentary group. Several of its members, the best known of whom are Edmond Michelet, a former minister in de Gaulle's government, and Louis Terrenoire, the former editor-in-chief of *l'Aube* and the son-in-law of Francisque Gay, decided to regain their freedom in order to be able to participate in the RPF. Among the local party workers, however, the decision was generally understood and approved; no important schism took place on this level.

There remained the question of knowing how the MRP electorate would react to its break with de Gaulle. As could easily be predicted, the municipal elections of October 1947 showed that the great majority of them, faced with choosing between de Gaulle and the MRP, chose de Gaulle. In Paris and in the large cities, the MRP lost exactly 60 per cent of its votes in comparison with November 10, 1946.

In the National Assembly, at least, the MRP retained a sufficiently strong representation, more than one hundred and fifty deputies, to be able to continue, in combination with the Socialists and part of the Radicals, to govern against the double opposition of the Communists on the extreme left and the Gaullists on the right, the two groups with which circumstances had allowed or forced the MRP to part company during 1947.

The MRP as a Member of the Third Force:
November 1947-June 1951.

The day after the municipal elections of October 1947, which had unquestionably demonstrated that profound changes had taken place in the respective strength of the parties since the general elections of November 1946, General de Gaulle, in the name of the RPF, declared that it was essential to pass a law ending the term of the National Assembly and to hold new elections.

The really crucial decision of the MRP to oppose the RPF dates from the moment it refused to satisfy this demand and resolved, on the contrary, to persevere in applying the formula of a middle-of-the-road government operating against a dual opposition or, in other words, what has been known as the Third Force. The Socialists, who were uneasy about the risk of Fascism which, in their eyes, was what was implied by the electoral victory of the RPF, rallied unanimously in the fall of 1947 to this solution. In the previous spring they had accepted it only by a narrow majority. The Ramadier government resigned without having been reversed by parliament to allow the formation of a new cabinet, which in its program and composition would clearly symbolize the desire of the center parties to govern despite the Gaullists and the Communists. Léon Blum, who was proposed as Premier by Vincent Auriol, could not obtain a majority in the National Assembly because of the opposition of some Radicals and independents. It was Robert Schuman, one of the most moderate and one of the most respected leaders of the MRP, who became leader of the new government.

According to the Socialists and the leaders of the MRP, the justification for the Third Force lay in its resolution to carry out an imaginative economic and social policy in the interest of the working classes. But the defeat of Léon Blum showed clearly the obstacles which would impede the achievement of this program. In order to obtain a majority in the National Assembly, the Socialist Party and the MRP could not dispense with the support of about thirty Radicals or Moderates, who were adversaries of the reforms carried out since the liberation and convinced partisans of economic liberalism. The necessity for this support gave to these groups the means of almost irresistible pressure on the middle-of-the-road government. It is significant that since November 1947 the Ministry of Finance and Economic Affairs, successively entrusted to René Mayer, then for a few weeks to Paul Reynaud, and then to Maurice Petsche, has constantly been in the hands of men who had voted against the nationalization acts and who did not hide their enthusiasm for the capitalist system.

It would be tedious to trace chronologically the attitude of the MRP during 1948, 1949 and 1950, years which were punctuated by a succession of cabinets: the Schuman cabinet until July 1948, the Marie cabinet of August 1948, the Queuille cabinet from September 1948 to October 1949, the Bidault cabinet from October 1949 to June 1950, the Pleven cabinet from July 1950 to March 1951, and the Queuille cabinet since that date. What is important is not a series of separate episodes but the continual operation of certain general conditioning factors which we shall describe. It should be pointed out, however, that the impossibility of any government surviving without Radical support was confirmed at the beginning of September 1948 when a Schuman cabinet, which had been formed after the resignation of Andre Marie, with Socialist Christian Pineau at the Ministry of Finance and Economic Affairs, was overturned on its first appearance before the National Assembly.

The pressure exercised by the liberals on the majority and on the middle-of-the-road governments affected, first of all, their social policies. Preoccupations with maintaining intact the purchasing power of the workers and increasing it in proportion with progress in production were, in the opinion of the liberals, secondary to the desire to restore the classical mechanisms of capitalism, to restore freedom of activity to businessmen and to apply the profit motive. The Socialists and the Popular Republicans would have preferred to see the desire for social justice triumph over the desire for economic liberty or, at least, to see the two go hand in hand. It was not possible for them to have their views prevail, partly, perhaps, because the MRP had no strict economic doctrine and did not understand that the restoration of liberalism would inevitably sacrifice the interests of the wage earners. The Popular Republicans could not fail to respond to the growing desire for economic liberty on the part of the middle classes, who were the principal support of the MRP. The party's position, which was to a certain extent inconsistent, was cleverly exploited by the liberal members of the government and of the majority.

From a purely economic point of view, the position of the liberals was not without its dangers also. Opposed to all sorts of government control of the economy, even to government investment in industry, and blindly confident in the virtues of economic liberty, they wanted to curtail even the government measures designed to modernize the country's industrial equipment. The objective of the liberals was to lighten the tax burdens of the country and to stimulate private enterprise. In this case, the resistance of the MRP and the Socialists, supported by the technical experts and even by some liberals who were aware of France's backwardness in the area of industrial equipment, was more effective than it was in the case of protecting the purchasing power of the workers. The Monnet Plan was not abandoned; it was revised and adapted to the European economic plans prepared within the general framework of the Marshall Plan and its realization is being achieved at a satisfactory pace.

Cooperation of the MRP with the Radicals and Moderates, a measure of political necessity, prevented the party from remaining completely faithful to its social program. It was led to accept measures designed to reinforce the political influence of those groups which were diverting the party from its initial program. When the Council of the Republic was to be renewed in November 1948, a new electoral arrangement had to be prepared. The desire to reduce the parliamentary influence of the Communists and the necessity for making some concessions to the elements of the majority which wanted a gradual return to the institutions of the Third Republic, led the government to propose an electoral law based on the system used to elect the old Senate. As we have seen above,[19] it was decided to have the members of the Council of the Republic elected by the delegates of the municipal councils. But the number of these delegates was arranged in such a way as greatly to favor the countryside over the cities. It is in the country that the Radicals and independents have their greatest strength. This system was, therefore, to favor them to a great extent, to the detriment of the parties which were strongest in the cities and the industrial areas, that is, the Communists and the MRP. The Socialists are strong in certain rural areas in central France and in the southeast, so the system did not harm them very much. As for the RPF, whose electoral strength is mainly urban, it could count on the personal support of most of the Moderates from the west and the east who wanted to continue the tactics which, since the municipal elections of October 1947, had proven to be most likely to restore the political influence of the conservative parties.

The MRP was driven by the circumstances of the composition of the majority coalition to consent to an electoral system for the

---

[19] See note 12.

second chamber which not only operated to its disadvantage but which tended to shift the center of gravity of the electorate of the Council of the Republic from a real to an artificial basis. The dominant areas would be the less densely populated areas with a traditional social structure and a static, individualistic type of economy, while the real center of gravity of the French population is in the urban and industrial regions, which are densely populated, whose social structure is in flux and whose economy is collective and dynamic. The consequence of this artifice, although somewhat diluted because of the limited powers of the Council of the Republic, was to accelerate the return to the political habits of the pre-war period. One more obstacle was placed in the way of the Popular Republicans' desire to renovate the climate of political competition in France by reducing the influence of historically-rooted ideological and religious antagonisms and establishing the criteria of the demarcation between parties on the basis of genuine contemporary problems and particularly of social problems.

The persistence of the antagonism between parties because of the religious problem was also to aggravate the difficulties of the Third Force. Dissension between the Socialists and Popular Republicans enabled the Radicals further to increase their influence. Difficulties arose over the educational question in 1948. The MRP wanted subsidies to be given to the private Catholic schools. It thought it had found an indirect means to reach this result by authorizing groups of family organizations, which could themselves be subsidized by the departments and the towns, to donate certain grants to the parents of students in private schools as well as those in public schools. A decree to this effect was issued in the spring of 1948 by Mme. Poinso-Chapuis, the MRP minister of Public Health and the Family in the Schuman cabinet. But this was a violation of a fundamental principle of the laic legislation of the Third Republic, according to which public funds, even these of local communities, could not be used either directly or indirectly for the benefit of private schools. The Poinso-Chapuis decree aroused heated parliamentary debates in the course of which the Socialists opposed it. This is what really caused the fall of the Schuman ministry in July 1948, although the occasion was a debate on military appropriations. The Communists, eager to divide the majority, and the Radicals, in the hope of increasing their influence, both did their best to exacerbate the debate. Their action forced the Socialists to become intransigent, as they were obliged, in order to satisfy their electoral clientele, to be constantly vigilant in the defense of secularism.

The same thing happened, at about the same time, over the question of the secularization of the old private schools which had been owned by the nationalized coal industry. The MRP was unable to convince its allies to secularize the schools gradually, by allowing time for the Catholic miners who wanted to do so to build new schools, and this failure served to alienate the MRP from the Socialists.

The reappearance of the religious problems at the forefront of the political scene had contributed to dividing the majority group of parties which saw social problems in the same light and to increasing the influence of the Radicals and the Moderates on the government.

In addition, participation in the government and the responsibility for maintaining order and authority all during this period caused the centrist majority to appear to be moving toward the right. One of the characteristics of the French conception of democracy is that government must inevitably be reactionary. Democracy is too often regarded as the absence of government or the struggle against government rather than as a certain kind of government. This can undoubtedly be explained by the struggle the state waged against the democratic parties during most of the nineteenth century. But the MRP and the Socialists were compelled on several occasions, especially in December 1947 and in October and November 1948, to stand up against major strikes called by the Communists, to maintain order and to put down violations of the freedom to work or threats to the safety of industrial equipment. Because of this, the government automatically assumed in the public's eye a certain reactionary or conservative tinge. The same thing was true with respect to the military operations in Indo-China for the maintenance of the Bao-Dai government against the hostility of Viet Minh.

The MRP, except for its small left-wing, could be reconciled to this situation as it does not share the opinion which holds that the requirements of government are naturally reactionary. The Socialists, obliged to take into account the growing discontent of their voters, could not endure it so easily.

This explains the increasing difficulties which have confronted France's middle-of-the-road governments. In the fall of 1949, the Radicals refused to grant a wage increase which the Socialists demanded, and there was a long ministerial crisis. It ended with the formation of the Bidault government. Once again assuming the leadership of the government, the MRP was going to try to impose the economic and social policies to which it adhered. The new government granted a bonus to the most needy wage earners and decided to end government wage-fixing and return to a system of collective bargaining. It succeeded, despite the bitter opposition of the liberals and the Communists, in passing a budget which provided for receipts sufficient to cover the continuation of the plans for re-equiping industry. These plans are, also, partially financed by the counterpart funds from the Marshall Plan.

The lengthy debates over the legal framework of collective bargaining provoked the demand for a new bonus for the workers. The MRP ministers did not believe they could go as far in granting the claim as the Socialists wanted. In February 1950, the Socialists left the government for some months and this seemed to seal the failure of the Third Force. But, after several months during which the Socialists faithfully sustained the Bidault government, it was overturned in June, 1950 because of a dispute concerning the salaries of civil servants. M. Henri Queuille then attempted to constitute a government, not only without the participation, but without the support of the Socialists, also orienting his majority as much to the right as possible. The executive committee of the MRP agreed only by 10 votes against 8 with 5 abstentions to the participation of the Popular Republicans in this attempt. But, in spite of the presence in the government of 12 MRP ministers (out of 30), a third of the Popular Republican deputies voted against the cabinet or abstained, and the Queuille cabinet was overturned, by 334 votes against 221, the same day it was presented to parliament. The left wing of the MRP had contributed much to the defeat of the attempted shift of the majority to the right.

The international tension born of the events in Korea persuaded the Socialists to return to the government, and from July 1950 to July 1951 the old centrist majority was reestablished, at first under the leadership of M. Pleven, then under that of M. Queuille. The Popular Republicans were always part of it, thus continuing the tactics they had followed since 1947.

In the elections of 1951, their participation in a great number of departments in alliances ranging from the Socialists to the Moderates, has contributed greatly to the checking of the two oppositions—Communist and Gaullist.

The tactics followed by the MRP since October 1947 have not been as successful as had been expected. The MRP sacrificed everything, including its obvious electoral interests, to the attempt to prevent the re-creation in France of two hostile political blocs. "The MRP," says a document published in October 1947 by the general secretariat for its militants, "has opposed the terrible danger for France of the existence of two blocs which the RPF and the Communist Party deliberately tried to create. Each of these two forces is characterized above all by its desire to destroy the other. Each tends equally to exclude from the nation the citizens who place their confidence in the other, and lets it be understood that, if necessary, any means will be appropriate to that end. If these two blocs were to be alone and facing each other, without anything to separate them, the inexorable logic of the situation would lead to civil war: torn by hate and violence, the nation would be destroyed. Whichever side won, France, already exhausted by five years of war, of occupation, of pillage, would collapse.[20] Nevertheless, if France was not divided into two blocs at the elections of 1951, but really into three — the Gaullist and the Communist blocs, both minorities, and the majority centrist bloc — the unity of the third exists only in the field of purely political problems and risks being put to a severe test when it must confront economic, financial and social problems.

To have been completely effective, the policy of the center bloc should have been to improve not only the general economic situation but also the living conditions of the workers. Only such a

[20] *Notes d'Information Politique,* No. 26, November 5, 1947, Bulletin hebdomadaire aux dirigeants fédéraux du MRP, p. 2.

policy could have definitively weakened the hold on public opinion of the two extremist blocs and relaxed the dangerous tension created by their mutual antagonism. But the divergent views of the majority parties too often made their economic policy uncertain and hesitant, and the influence of the Moderates and Radicals prevented them from following a progressive social policy. The Third Force succeeded in weakening the RPF, but for the profit of those independents and Radicals whose influence grew to such an extent that the Socialists, for a time, thought it necessary to abandon the government: will not the same difficulty occur in the new Assembly, where independents and Radicals will balance in number Popular Republicans and Socialists?

The MRP undoubtedly saw the danger. Its inability to avert the danger was due in part to the unavoidable facts firstly of the parliamentary, and secondly of the electoral situation, which did not allow the Third Force to do without the aid of conservatives hostile to the RPF. Moreover, within the MRP parliamentary group, if not among the leaders of the movement, there has often been some sympathy for the liberal economic measures advocated by the right wing of the majority. Even when they are politically progressive, the French middle classes and peasants remain closely attached to the basic principles of economic liberalism, and the MRP, whose parliamentary personnel is largely drawn from these groups, would have been able to escape this influence only if it had had a precise and firmly held economic doctrine. Instead, the MRP holds generous but vague ideas which are founded on a general conception of society rather than on an original analysis of the facts of production and exchange.

It must be added that it is difficult to see anything else that the MRP might have done. No majority could have been formed in the first National Assembly without its support and it felt the obligations of government so keenly that it could not avoid the responsibilities which governing imposed upon it. From the moment when it rejected the RPF demand that new general elections be held in 1949, because it feared that these would only result in the exacerbation of political passions and in the election of an ungovernable assembly, the MRP had no choice but to follow the tactics of the last four years. Finally, the basic reasons for its attitude, after everything is considered, seem in harmony with the main elements of its own doctrine and of its conception of French political life.

V. The Attitude of the Other Parties Toward the MRP

One cannot completely understand the difficulties confronting the MRP without considering the attitudes adopted toward it by the other French parties. In a political system which imperatively requires coalitions, such attitudes are of great practical importance.

With respect to this problem, the essential fact is that in the eyes of almost all the other parties, the MRP appears to be a nuisance, to the very extent that it has given itself the task of changing the way in which French political problems have traditionally been presented. The force of habit is so great that even those people who, during the Third Republic, were to a great extent the victims of these traditions find it difficult to admit that there are people who want to transform them. This is, for example, the case of the conservative Catholics who for so long were singled out as untouchables. They are so accustomed to this state of affairs that it represents a permanent alibi for them and confers upon them a most convenient sort of irresponsibility. Any attempt to change this situation disconcerts them if it does not irritate them.

Nothing can better illustrate the perplexity and irritation of traditional political groups in respect to the MRP than the difficulties which arose when the houses of parliament were deciding in which part of the semicircular chambers the representatives of the MRP should sit. An old tradition requires that the parties sit from left to right, starting with the most advanced groups and ending with the most conservative. Now what were to be the respective places for the Radicals and the MRP? The latter asked to be seated next to the Socialists because of the general affinity of their economic and social program with that of the SFIO. But the Radicals could not permit newcomers to French politics, like the MRP deputies, who made no secret of their Catholic affiliation, to be inserted between them and the men who had always been their neighbors. The Moderates also shared this view to a certain extent, for they considered the Popular Republicans, like the Popular Democrats, as Catholics, to be closer to themselves than the Radicals.

The question was resolved by a compromise. The MRP was seated next to the Socialists on the lower benches of the chamber; the Radicals were seated next to the Socialists on the upper benches. But the irritating problem which Christian Democratic principles presented to the old parties was not so easily solved.

The second common feature of the attitude of the other parties toward the MRP is in the charge of hypocrisy that they levy against it. This accusation can be explained by the differences between the language used by the Popular Republicans and that used by the other parties. The language of the MRP includes constant references to moral and spiritual values and to certain sociological ideas, like the "common good," the "communities," and the "eminent dignity of the human person," which come from Catholic philosophy. To the other parties these expressions seem to be insincere and tainted with affectation. For the MRP parliamentary group really knows how to employ, whenever necessary, the rules of political tactics, and these rules are inspired by a concern for effectiveness rather than moral preoccupations. This leads some people to think that the concerns which the MRP proclaim are only facades and that, although it pretends otherwise, it is really motivated by the same interests as its competitors.

There are, however, subtle lines of distinction between the sentiments which the various parties entertain towards the MRP. These we shall try to explain.

The RPF as a whole, possibly following the example of its leader, General de Gaulle, does not forgive the "party of fidelity" for having allowed the General to leave politics in January 1946 and for having opposed him since May 1947. But, at least in parliament, the RPF was not a coherent group until July 1951 and this resentment was not felt by all its elements with the same intensity. The most conservative elements reproached the MRP especially for having cooperated in the reforms after the liberation and for its refusal to let them be reconsidered. The most authoritarian elements reproached it for its attachment to the parliamentary system, in the form of the "regime of parties" which they render responsible for all the difficulties of French politics. As to the dissidents from the MRP, the six members of the little group in the first National Assembly, the *Independent Popular Republican*

Movement, they felt a certain nostalgia for their old party and for a long time they certainly did not despair of helping to restore its old "fidelity." It is to one of them, Edmond Michelet, that General de Gaulle delegated the task of proposing to Georges Bidault, on February 7, 1950, a reconciliation of the two groups. Bidault, although he did not formally reject the proposal, has for all practical purposes disregarded it.

The antagonism of the conservatives toward the MRP seems even more general than that of the RPF. It can be explained mainly by the common religious affiliation of most of the conservatives and the MRP. The fact that the MRP appears to understand the "anti-clericals" and has accepted parts of their program, irritates and disturbs the Catholics of the right-wing groups. They object, for example, to the over-long collaboration of the MRP with the Communists, to the assault that it is ready to levy against the traditional structure of French society and its perseverance in seeking an agreement with the "Marxists" of the Socialist Party. In addition, the MRP aims in most regions at the same electoral clientele as do the conservatives, and this competition, in 1945 and 1946, resulted in the severe defeat of the conservatives. They remember this even after their relative victory in 1951 and they are not disposed to forgive the people whose demagogy they consider as the basic cause of this defeat. Despite the hostility which for a long time has separated the conservatives from the anti-clerical Radicals, it would not be going too far to say that today they prefer the latter to their Catholic colleagues of the MRP.

The bewilderment at and the incomprehension of the MRP are undoubtedly greatest among the Radicals. At times one gets the feeling that these two groups do not belong to the same political species and that no basis for agreement could ever be found for them. Anti-clerical and conservative, Radicalism obviously has no common point of reference with a Christian and imaginative movement. What the Radicals can neither understand nor allow is that "clericals" like the Popular Republicans pretend to be more "advanced" than they. In the literal sense of the word, that seems to them to be cheating, a violation of the rules of the political game.

Neither do the Radicals forgive the MRP for having played a decisive role in changing the political institutions of the Third

Republic by introducing the Fourth, for having changed the name of their old citadel, the Senate, for having amputated its power and for having opposed a return to the single-member district electoral system.

If we look at things from a different angle, however, we can find certain analogies between the Popular Republicans and the Radicals. Both groups represent the middle classes; both want, or say they want, orderly progress, reform without revolution; both, and this is undoubtedly their clearest common ground, appreciate the meaning of the state and the necessity for government. Because they, more than others, are aware of their responsibilities in this connection, in spite of their sharp rivalry, in spite of mutual criticism that is more than severe, they have nevertheless been able to cooperate with each other for four years and are even today in close contact. This may prove to be temporary but the fact remains significant.

The attitude of the Socialists toward the MRP is not the same in the higher councils of the Party as it is in the lower. The leaders of the SFIO, especially the late Léon Blum, have on several occasions expressed their sympathy for the MRP. Its creation seems to them to be one of the major political events of the postwar period and they are ready to collaborate with it without any mental reservations. "A sincerely republican party," Léon Blum wrote to the MRP shortly before his death, "as has been demonstrated by the way it has protected itself from Gaullist infiltration; sincerely social, as demonstrated by the way it protects itself from employer and capitalist penetration — allied, consequently, with socialism by the affinities between the labor unions with which we maintain the closest connections in thought and action." And the Socialist leader, after having mentioned the only "burning question," secularism, which stands between his party and the MRP, concluded: "Since it has remained extinguished for so long (from the liberation to the Poinso-Chapuis decree) it can easily remain extinguished." [21]

But the militants of the Socialist Party do not seem to regard the activity of the MRP with as much confidence and optimism as did Léon Blum.

---

[21] *Le Populaire,* February 10, 1950.

Whatever one may say in Paris, in many provincial areas the question of secularism is still burning. The essential criterion of republicanism, namely anti-clericalism, has been accepted there too long for the Socialist militants to come to an understanding with "clericals" at the risk of seeing the Communists use it as a pretext for accusing them of going over to the reactionaries. On this issue, many members of the Socialist Party do not differ from the Radicals; the attitude toward the religious problem and especially toward the educational problem appears to them to be fundamentally more important than the attitude toward capitalism. This is what recently led a Radical statesman to declare: "The Socialists will always prefer any Radical to a Popular Republican." The MRP fears that nothing could be truer; several electoral experiences have taught this lesson at a dear price. This is why they have been so violently — and successfully — opposed to the reestablishment of single-member electoral districts, which would be most advantageous to the resurrection of the anti-clerical coalitions of the Third Republic.

Since the creation of the MRP, the Communists have launched against it more virulent attacks than against any other party. It is they who, during the electoral campaign of 1945, baptized it the *Machine à Ramasser les Pétainistes*. They undoubtedly understand that because of the strength that the Church can lend it and because of its social program, which they take for obscurantism but whose effectiveness for propaganda purposes they fully recognize, the MRP can be one of the worse obstacles to their complete capture of the French proletariat. They know the share it had in their defeat in May 1946 and in their elimination from power in May 1947. One cannot expect any friendliness on their part toward the Popular Republicans.

They undoubtedly also have more respect for the MRP than they have for any other political party. They know what its members did during the resistance. They know, because they know the French workers well, that the MRP has an authentically proletarian wing. The Communists are sufficiently removed doctrinally from the MRP to feel less aversion for it than for the Socialist Party, since they cannot accuse it of treason; occasionally they feel close enough to the MRP socially to think momentarily of some impossible collaboration. This is especially clear on the trade union level where, for a limited problem, the Communist CGT more easily arrives at united action with the Christian workers of the CFTC than with the Socialists of *Force Ouvrière*.

CONCLUSION

What is, in the last analysis, the record of the political activity that the MRP has carried out in France for seven years? What prospects for the future are open before it? These are the two questions which we shall now try to answer.

One cannot claim that the MRP has achieved all the goals that it set for itself at the time of the liberation. In spite of all its efforts there is still social injustice in France in the form of flagrant inadequacy of the purchasing power of the workers, which contrasts with the considerable increase in production and with the increase of corporate profits since the end of the war. The reconciliation of the proletariat with the nation, which seemed to take place during the resistance and which the MRP proposed to make permanent after the liberation, has, on the contrary, been faced with new obstacles. This became clear when the Communist Party, in which at least one half of the industrial workers unquestionably continue to place their confidence, again assumed an attitude of violent opposition toward all the other French political currents. Thus, precisely because social injustice has not been sufficiently reduced, because there has been no real change in the condition of the workers relative to the pre-war period, it is impossible to see how, within the near future, the solidarity of the proletariat with the Communist Party can be broken.

It cannot be said that the efforts of the MRP to change the political attitude of the social groups, generally impregnated with Catholicism, who before the war had supported the conservative parties, has been crowned with success. The MRP tried to inculcate them with a larger conception of the "common good," by persuading them to accept the prospect of a sweeping reform of the traditional structure of French society. The ease with which the voters who had supported the MRP in 1945 and 1946 abandoned it in 1947, not only for the RPF (which, after all, expresses at least politically, if not socially, a desire for reform) but for conservatives, Moderates or Radicals who exploited de Gaulle's name, proves that the attitude of these people was not really changed after the liberation. They had supported the MRP for the lack of something better, because it seemed to them to be able to check Communism, but they had never really supported either the program or the doctrine of the party for which they voted.

Similarly, the MRP's attempt to shatter the simplified dialectic which for so long had reduced all French political life to two opposing blocs, by making possible a center coalition determined to follow a policy of social justice and political liberty, has had only a relative success. If the center governments have been able to survive from May 1947 to July 1951, it has been by emphasizing political liberty (and a political liberty which has occasionally been conceived of in somewhat obsolete terms) rather than social justice. The MRP's electoral decline since 1946 suggests that a large part of the French public has today returned to an economically and socially conservative attitude. The slight majority — 54 per cent of the electors — who in June 1951 remained in favor of a transformation of the capitalist system is divided by the breach between the Communists on the one hand and the Socialist democrats of the SFIO and the MRP on the other.

This certainly does not mean that the balance sheet of the MRP's activities shows only a deficit. Its objective was so considerable that success could not have been achieved in a few months. The political determination, rooted in several decades of political experience, is not so quickly swept aside. The success of the Popular Republicans in 1945, due to circumstantial and necessarily temporary causes, for a moment concealed the difficulties of the task which the party had assigned to itself. If it has not completely fulfilled it, that in no way implies that it has not started to do so.

On the contrary, the preceding pages have described the major role of the MRP in the political activities which have eliminated the risk of the complete capture of the governmental machinery by the Communists. By contributing to the preservation of political democracy based on liberty and free elections, the independent administration of justice and a diversity of opinions and parties, the MRP has definitely preserved the instrument by which its program may be achieved in the future. If, right after the liberation, France suffered no civil war between the Communists and their enemies, a possibility which was feared by many people, it is to a great extent because of the shrewdness with which some men, among them Popular Republicans, agreed to pay the price of collaboration in the government with the Communists. This relationship remained one of collaboration, not of surrender. If, when de Gaulle formed the RPF on a violently anti-Communist program, the brutal clash of two extremist blocs was again avoided, it is thanks to those men who refused to accept the simplified alternatives which were presented: the MRP was among them. If, despite the inadequacies of an economic policy handicapped by the divergent doctrines of the governmental coalition, the revival of French industry has been but insignificantly delayed by social conflicts, if the Monnet Plan has preserved future opportunities for the French economy against liberal opposition, it is again to a great extent the MRP which is responsible. If, despite the impassioned criticism of the liberals, the system of social security and family grants, which relieves some of the more crying inequalities in the distribution of income and which has contributed to increasing the birth rate and therefore to the human stock of France's future, has on the whole been conserved, it is again to the MRP that a large share of the credit must go. The MRP is responsible for that crowning development in the decline of anti-clericalism, the Socialist recognition that Catholics can be both republicans and interested in social justice. It would, therefore, be inexact to say that because its task has not been completely accomplished, the record of the MRP is one of failure. The results are not all that it had hoped or desired; they are, nevertheless, results. It is clear that the existence and the activity of the MRP have played a decisive role in the evolution of French political life for the last seven years. Only the partisan prejudice or the blindness of the doctrinaire could lead one to think that this evolution has had only disastrous aspects. If one believes, on the contrary, that its good aspects surpass the bad, one must acknowledge that it has largely, though not exclusively, been the work of the MRP.

Will the MRP be able to carry on its work? This raises the whole question of the prospects which lie before it. Will it be able to remain faithful to itself? Will it find the support in public opinion which is so indispensable?

The results of the election of June 17, 1951, permit us to say that with an eighth of the electoral body behind it, with 85 deputies in a National Assembly of 624, the MRP remains, in spite of numerical weakening, a party sufficiently strong to leave its mark on the future political evolution of France. We have the right to say that it has successfully affirmed in the political sphere the ideals of a democracy of Christian inspiration. The resistance that it has offered to the attraction of Gaullism suggests that, if Gaullism should ever be weakened or dislocated, a sizeable number of the electors who supported the RPF in 1951 would return to the MRP.

But in the new National Assembly, can it succeed in remaining faithful to itself, that is to say, not to sacrifice social justice to political liberty nor political liberty to social justice? The 380 centrist deputies are divided almost evenly between partisans of laissez-faire capitalism (94 Radicals, 98 Moderates) and defenders of a policy of control of economic activity by the state and of systematic support of the interests of the wage-earners (104 Socialists, 85 MRP). It is hardly probable that the 103 Communist deputies could exercise any attraction whatsoever upon the Socialists; but it is not impossible that a fraction of the Moderates might be tempted to make common cause with the 120 deputies of the RPF.

The central position of the MRP gives its decisions particular importance: let it break with the Socialists, and a majority of the right, comprising all or part of the RPF, becomes theoretically possible: let it refuse to take that step and the assembly can become ungovernable. Its interest evidently will be to propose compromises acceptable at the same time to its neighbors on the left — the Socialists — and to those on the right — the Radicals and the Moderates. For that it will be necessary to exercise, notably in the economic and social fields, a creative imagination more pronounced than that which it has displayed up to now, plus remarkable tactical abilities. One can, on this last point, rely on Georges Bidault; on the first point, unhappily there is less certainty that the MRP economic experts — for example, Robert Buron, under-secretary for economic affairs since October 1949 — will succeed in convincing all his colleagues of the Popular Republican group in the National Assembly.

It is in any case certain that the MRP cannot accept any injury to the principles of the social and economic reforms of the liberation (nationalizations, social security, family allotments) without breaking with Socialism and opening the way to a reconstitution of the old right-wing bloc. But, it is not also sure that it will succeed at the same time in making the Socialists accept certain technical measures for the necessary improvement of these reforms, and in assuring the Radicals and Moderates that it has not gone too far.

In the religious sphere, it is a task of the same kind that the MRP must undertake: to the measures that the assembly certainly wishes to take in favor of free schools, it must impart just such a stamp as not to force the Socialists, passionate defenders of secularism, into an irreconcilable opposition. It will not be an easy task.

The MRP appears as a typical center party, a party which cannot break completely with the right nor with the left. This is a difficult situation, but one which is decisive in maintaining political stability. Nothing indicates that the MRP will not in the years to come be equal to the tasks which thus devolve upon it as a result of the political composition of the National Assembly and its own marginal position. But, also, nothing indicates that it will be able to overcome all the difficulties which are involved in the complete realization of its aims.

The only thing certain is that it remains, by its numerical force, as well as by the originality of its doctrine and of its program, one of the essential elements of French political life.

SELECTED BIBLIOGRAPHY

GENERAL WORKS ON FRENCH POLITICAL PARTIES

Jacques Fauvet. *Les partis politiques dans la France actuelle.* Paris, 1947.
———. *Les forces politiques en France.* Paris, 1951.
François Goguel. "Les partis politiques en France," in *l'Encyclopédie Politique de la France et du Monde.* Vol. I, 2nd ed., Paris, 1950.
———. *La vie politique dans la société française contemporaine* (multigraphed course given at the *Institut d'Etudes Politiques de Paris*). 3 vols., Paris, 1949.
Paul Marabuto. *Partis politiques et mouvements sociaux sous la Quatrième République.* Paris, 1947.

REVIEW ARTICLES

Etienne Gilson. "Le système et l'esprit," *Politique,* October 1947.
Georges Hourdin. "Devant la crise française: pour une République Populaire," *Politique,* December 1947.
Joseph Hours. "Les chrétiens et la politique," *La Vie Intellectuelle,* May 1948.
Albert Gortais. "Signification politique du congrès de Toulouse," *Politique,* July 1948.
François Goguel. "Destin du M.R.P.", *Terre humaine,* June 1951.

DOCUMENTS PUBLISHED BY THE MRP

Le MRP, parti de la IV° République, 1945.
Albert Gortais. *Démocratie et Libération.* Paris, 1947.
Vers une démocratie nouvelle. Paris, 1947.
d'Aujoulat. *La Vie et l'avenir de l'Union Française.* Paris, 1947.
Léo Hamon. *Vers une réforme municipale.* Paris, 1947.
Pierre Pflimlin. *Perspectives sur notre économie.* Paris, 1947.
Charles Viatte. *La sécurité sociale.* Paris, 1947.
Etienne Gilson. *Notre Démocratie.* Paris, 1948.
André Colin. *Le courage au service de l'espérance française.* Paris, 1948.
Georges Coudray. *Loger les Français.* Paris, 1948.
Paul Coste-Floret and A. Le Guenedal. *Construire l'Union Française.* Paris, 1948.
Albert Gortais, Marc Scherer and Jacques Madaule. *L'homme nouveau sera-t-il marxiste ou spiritualiste?* Paris, 1948.
En marche vers l'avenir. Travaux du 5ème congrès national du MRP. Paris, 1949.

INDEX